edition

EFFECTIVE CRISIS COMMUNICATION

3 edition

EFFECTIVE CRISIS COMMUNICATION

Moving From Crisis to Opportunity

Robert R. Ulmer
University of Arkansas at Little Rock

Timothy L. Sellnow
University of Kentucky

Matthew W. Seeger
Wayne State University

Los Angeles | London | New Delhi
Singapore | Washington DC

Los Angeles | London | New Delhi
Singapore | Washington DC

FOR INFORMATION:

SAGE Publications, Inc.
2455 Teller Road
Thousand Oaks, California 91320
E-mail: order@sagepub.com

SAGE Publications Ltd.
1 Oliver's Yard
55 City Road
London EC1Y 1SP
United Kingdom

SAGE Publications India Pvt. Ltd.
B 1/I 1 Mohan Cooperative Industrial Area
Mathura Road, New Delhi 110 044
India

SAGE Publications Asia-Pacific Pte. Ltd.
3 Church Street
#10-04 Samsung Hub
Singapore 049483

Copyright © 2015 by SAGE Publications, Inc.

Printed in the United States of America

Library of Congress Cataloging-in-Publication Data

Ulmer, Robert R., 1969–

Effective crisis communication : moving from crisis to opportunity / Robert R. Ulmer, University of Arkansas, Little Rock, Timothy L. Sellnow, University of Kentucky, Matthew W. Seeger, Wayne State University. — 3rd edition.

pages cm
Includes bibliographical references and index.

ISBN 978-1-4522-5751-8 (pbk.)

1. Crisis management. 2. Emergency management. 3. Communication in management. 4. Communication in organizations. I. Sellnow, Timothy L. (Timothy Lester), 1960– II. Seeger, Matthew W. (Matthew Wayne), 1957– III. Title.

HD49.U44 2015
658.4'77—dc23   2013032048

This book is printed on acid-free paper.

Acquisitions Editor: Matthew Byrnie
Editorial Assistant: Gabrielle Piccininni
Production Editor: Jane Haenel
Copy Editor: Deanna Noga
Typesetter: C&M Digitals (P) Ltd.
Proofreader: Rae-Ann Goodwin
Indexer: Terri Corry
Cover Designer: Edgar Abarca
Marketing Manager: Liz Thorton

MIX
Paper from
responsible sources
FSC
www.fsc.org
FSC® C014174

14 15 16 17 18 10 9 8 7 6 5 4 3 2 1

BRIEF CONTENTS

DETAILED CONTENTS

The third edition of *Effective Crisis Communication: Moving From Crisis to Opportunity* supports the central thesis that crisis communication is not solely about managing crisis-induced threat but also about creating the potential for opportunity, renewal, and growth through effective crisis communication. From a communication focus, crises are most often described as destructive, threatening, and negative events without any redeeming value. Consequently, communication following a crisis is often defensive and negative. Organizations deny responsibility for the crisis, look for scapegoats to attribute responsibility to, minimize the extent or impact of the damage, take a rigid legalistic approach, or say nothing at all. These types of responses have resulted in a declining confidence in our public and private institutions. Much of the current crisis communication theory has effectively categorized strategies that organizations employ to preserve their images and reputations.

The approach to crisis communication described in this book is different in that it provides the reader with more options for responding to a crisis beyond managing the organization's image or reputation. This is certainly a mind-set shift. All crises carry a level of threat. However, we suggest that an organization experiencing a crisis also take the opportunity to learn from the event, communicate honestly and ethically, work to minimize harm to those most directly impacted by the crisis, and develop a prospective vision with which the organization can move forward. This approach suggests that organizations should enact strong and positive ethical core values and effective crisis communication principles to guide their crisis responses. If this approach seems radical and unconventional, it is. However, as you will see in this book, we have tested this approach through many different case studies, crisis types, and contexts, including international applications.

As you read the third edition of this book, you will notice that it is reorganized from previous editions. The book is still comprised of three sections. The first section of the book, Chapters 1 and 2, provide the conceptual foundation for the book. Chapter 1 defines crisis communication, and Chapter 2 examines current crisis communication theory. The second section of the book, Chapters 5–8, is comprised of lessons for managing crises, followed immediately by practical applications. For instance, Chapter 3 discusses lessons on effective communication practices during a crisis. Chapter 4 follows up with several cases for applying those lessons to a wide variety of crisis types. Chapter 5 delineates lessons on managing crisis uncertainty effectively. Chapter 6 examines many cases to test the reader's ability to apply the lessons on managing uncertainty across crisis contexts. Chapter 7 describes lessons on effective crisis leadership. Chapter 8 provides several case examples to consider each of the lessons and how they function during a crisis. Taking time with the lessons and the cases will help the crisis communication researcher and practitioner analyze, consider, and evaluate theory and practice in these crisis communication contexts. The reader who spends some time answering the questions at the end of the cases will build a strong foundation for developing effective crisis communication skills.

The last section of the book, the opportunities, examines the role of organizational learning, risk communication, and ethical communication in creating opportunities following a crisis. These chapters provide suggestions for the reader to resist a threat bias in crisis communication and consider more mindfully the opportunities the crisis may produce. The last chapter of the book introduces our theory, the Discourse of Renewal, as an approach to effectively manage crises. Researchers can use this approach to test the viability of the theory across contexts and to assess the strengths and weaknesses of particular instances of crisis communication. Researchers and practitioners will be able to use the Discourse of Renewal to develop crisis messages and more fully consider risk and crisis communication policy decisions.

Theories help us understand and view the world around us in different ways. We view theory as a lens to help better understand the world around us. This book provides lessons and new perspectives for examining crises of all types. We hope that our suggestions for effective crisis communication help the reader expand and reconsider the way he or she views and communicates about crises. We also hope that the cases we describe in the upcoming chapters provoke thoughtful debate and discussion about how people perceive and communicate about these events. Finally, we hope this book provides the impetus for an expanded understanding about research, practice, and policy in crisis communication.

ACKNOWLEDGMENTS

We have many people to thank who have helped us develop these ideas. The following colleagues have provided helpful feedback: Andrew Pyle, Alesia Ferguson, Shari Veil, Steven Venette, Jeffrey Brand, Julie Novak, Joel Iverson, Kimberly Cowden. We also have many students at each of our universities who have pushed our thinking about effective crisis communication and the Discourse of Renewal. We would particularly like to thank Kathryn Anthony, Curtis Liska, Patty Mossett, Alyssa Millner, Elizabeth Petrun, Kathleen Vidoloff, Kelly Wolf, Carina Cremeen, Fan Ku, Reagen McGee, Rhonda Troillett, Ashley Bocarossa, Jennifer Medley, Mary Busby, Jessica Smith-Ellis, and Mark Friedlander.

We would like to thank the following reviewers for their valuable feedback on the third edition:

Jeffrey D. Brand, Millikin University

Michael A. Caudill, Western Carolina University

Arlene MacGregor, Massachusetts Maritime Academy

JJ McIntyre, University of Central Arkansas

Patric R. Spence, University of Kentucky

R. Tyler Spradley, Stephen F. Austin State University

Jerry Thomas, Lindsey Wilson College

We would also like to thank the following reviewers for the first and second editions of this book:

Second Edition

John R. Fisher, Northwest Missouri State University

Carol M. Madere, Southeastern Louisiana University

Joseph Eric Massey, National University

Melinda Bond Shreve, University of Detroit Mercy

R. Tyler Spradley, Stephen F. Austin State University

Shari R. Veil, University of Oklahoma

First Edition

Jeffrey Brand, Millikin University

Elise Dallimore, Northeastern University

Roberta Doggett, University of North Florida

Vicki Freimuth, University of Georgia

Keith Hearit, Western Michigan University

David Ritchey, University of Akron

The Conceptual Foundation

Defining Crisis Communication

We live in a society continually affected by natural disasters, such as hurricanes, tsunamis, and forest fires, and by organizational crises, such as food-borne illnesses, corporate malfeasance, and terrorism. Regardless of where you live or the kind of work you do, many different types of crises have the potential to significantly disrupt your personal and work life. No community and no organization, public or private, is immune from crises.

At the writing of the third edition of this book, the need for understanding effective crisis communication practices and building those skills are in more demand than ever. In 2 short years since the last edition, fast food company Chick-fil-A experienced a crisis over its charitable giving; Netflix experienced a crisis after it changed its customer billing practices; the BBC experienced a crisis after shelving and erroneously reporting sexual abuse; the LiveStrong Foundation experienced a crisis after Lance Armstrong, the foundation's founder, admitted to using performance enhancing drugs to win his seven consecutive tours de France; and finally, Penn State University experienced a crisis after it covered up sexual abuse on its campus for years. This is not an exhaustive list but rather highlights, or lowlights, by organizations that experienced devastating crises recently. Beyond organizational crises, communities experienced natural disasters like the recent tornadoes in Moore, Oklahoma, Superstorm Sandy that hit the East Coast of the United States, and the tsunami and nuclear meltdown in Japan at Fukashima to name a few. Check out www.disaster-report.com for an update on the current status of natural disasters around the world. We continue to experience devastating crises of all types and, as a result, the current need for effective crisis communication understanding and skills continues to grow.

Because of the prevalence of crises, organizations like the Department of Homeland Security (DHS), the Federal Emergency Management Agency (FEMA), the Centers for Disease Control and Prevention (CDC), local and state emergency management departments, and public health departments along with government agencies, public relations firms, and corporations across industries, need professionals who have sound crisis communication skills. In short, crisis communication skills and knowledge are useful in any industry. However, due to the prevalence of crises, crisis communication skills are some of the most sought after by employers. Regardless of the type of work that you do, the knowledge and skills discussed in this book will enable you to communicate more effectively during a crisis.

Some might ask, "Who would want to work in a depressing field studying negative crises?" We answer by saying crises are not intrinsically negative forces in society. In fact, our proposition is that crises can actually lead to positive outcomes. We see crises as opportunities for learning and improvement, viewing them as they are perceived in Chinese culture, where the symbol for crisis in the Mandarin language is interpreted as *dangerous opportunity* (see Figure 1.1). By their nature, crises are dangerous moments or turning points in an organization's life cycle; nevertheless, crises provide opportunities with the potential to leave the organization stronger in some ways than it was before the crisis.

If we do not study crisis communication, organizations and the many people associated with them are likely to be stunned, frightened, and depressed when enveloped by a crisis. In fact, some organizations communicate so poorly in the wake of a crisis that they are forever

| Figure 1.1 | The Chinese symbol for crisis |

weakened, having lost the confidence of both their own members and the public.

This book presents strategies accumulated over many years of research, as well as our experience as organizational consultants, emphasizing the opportunities in a crisis rather than the calamities of these events. The chapters illustrate key communication lessons to create renewal, growth, and opportunity following a crisis. At the crux of our argument is the contention that effective communication skills are essential to creating positive, renewing opportunities at these turning points.

The new edition of this book is organized into three parts designed to increase the reader's understanding and skills in crisis communication. Part I contains two chapters that develop the conceptual understanding of effective crisis communication. Chapter 1 directs the reader to consider expanded definitions of crisis communication and explains the many types of crises that one may experience. Chapter 2 introduces the reader to key research and theories in crisis communication. This chapter serves as a tool for building the reader's vocabulary for describing, explaining, and understanding crisis communication. Part II moves from the conceptual to the practical. In this section, the reader is presented with practical lessons, based on empirical research, for communicating effectively, managing uncertainty, and leading during a crisis. After each chapter of lessons, the reader is presented with an opportunity to apply those lessons to crisis case studies in the next chapter. For instance, Chapter 3 focuses on effective crisis communication. This chapter contains 10 lessons for effectively communicating during a crisis. Chapter 4 is comprised of six current cases to be assessed for their effective crisis communication practices. In this chapter, the reader is able to build his/her skills by applying the lessons of effective crisis communication to each case. Chapter 5 contains 10 lessons for managing uncertainty during a crisis. Every crisis carries with it some level of uncertainty. Chapter 5 explains how to communicate effectively under crisis-induced uncertainty. Chapter 6 introduces six cases that the reader can use to test their skills at communicating under high levels of uncertainty. Chapter 7 delineates 10 leadership lessons for effective crisis communication. Chapter 8 consists of six cases designed to test the reader's ability to assess the effectiveness or ineffectiveness of the leader's crisis communication. In each of the case chapters, the reader is asked to make the call regarding the effectiveness of the crisis response.

Parts I and II thus provide the conceptual understanding and skill development for effective crisis communication practices. Part III contains chapters on learning through failure, risk communication, communication ethics, and a final chapter on inspiring renewal following a crisis. This third part of the book describes several content areas that every crisis communicator should consider as opportunities in crisis communication. In Chapter 9, we explain how organizations can improve their crisis preparation and response capacity by learning through their failures. In Chapter 10, we demonstrate how effective risk communication provides crisis communicators opportunities to prevent future crises. Chapter 11 examines the ethical implications of crisis and the opportunities provided by strong ethical stances and communication. Chapter 12 proposes a theory of effective crisis communication we call the *Discourse of Renewal*. We provide a description of this theory along with its applications to crisis communication. Throughout the book, we turn to a small group of landmark cases to illustrate the various aspects being discussed.

A DEFINITION OF CRISIS COMMUNICATION

Initially, we need to clarify what we mean by *crisis*. In daily conversation, the word is used quite casually. As a simple experiment, listen to the people around you for a day or two. Most likely, you will hear friends, fellow employees, or fellow students describe routine problems they are facing—fender benders, forgotten appointments, disgruntled mothers-in-law, bad hair days, or losing records of favorite university football teams—as crises. All are bad experiences; however, they are not, by our definition, crises. Similarly, with some degree of regularity, organizations face events, such as unexpectedly low sales or the defection of key employees. Again, these are difficult times for organizations, but they are not necessarily crises. *Crises are unique moments in the history of organizations.*

In a classic study, Hermann (1963) identified three characteristics separating crises from other unpleasant occurrences:

1. Surprise

2. Threat

3. Short response time

A troubling event cannot reach the level of crisis without coming as a surprise, posing a serious level of threat, and forcing a short response time. Let's take a moment to define Hermann's characteristics of crisis.

SURPRISE

Even naturally occurring events, such as floods, earthquakes, and forest fires, do not escalate to the level of crisis unless they come at a time or a level of intensity beyond the expectations of government officials and residents. For example, weather conditions combined in such a way that the 2013 tornadoes that hit Moore Oklahoma introducing a high degree of surprise to the situation. Hundreds of homes were lost, 24 people died, and the city was declared a disaster area.

Similarly, in 2011, a FedEx customer posted a YouTube video (see http://www.youtube.com/watch?v=cpVFC7bMtY0 or search FedEx delivery goes terribly wrong) of the carrier throwing his computer monitor over a high gate and into his yard. The video was viewed millions of times. At the time, this event was certainly a surprise and a crisis for FedEx. FedEx quickly responded to the surprise of the crisis (see http://www.youtube .com/watch?v=4ESU_PcqI38 or search FedEx response to customer video) by communicating with its customers and the general public about the crisis. Ultimately, this crisis threatened the long-standing values of FedEx and the viability of its service for customers.

THREAT

All crises create threatening circumstances that reach beyond the typical problems organizations face. The threat of a crisis can affect the organization's financial security, its customers, residents living near a production facility, and others. For example, when a BP oil rig exploded in the Gulf of Mexico in 2010 and spilled millions of gallons of oil into the Gulf, the crisis threat was widespread. The considerable amount of oil on the water's surface was devastating to the fishing industry in the area. Birds and other sea animals were also impacted by the spill, thereby adding levels of threat to the ecosystem of the region. To begin to learn about the effects of the oil spill, BP initially contributed $500 million through a Gulf of Mexico Research Initiative to study the short- and long-term effects of the oil spill on the environment and marine life. One would expect the response and recovery efforts, along with a complete understanding of the effects of the oil spill on the Gulf of Mexico, to continue for many years.

Oil spills occur with some regularity worldwide. They are usually contained quickly, causing little long-term damage. Oil spills seldom reach the crisis level. In BP's case, however, the amount of oil spilled created a heightened threat level. Ultimately, the crisis became the largest environmental disaster in U.S. history.

SHORT RESPONSE TIME

The threatening nature of crises means that they must be addressed quickly. BP was criticized initially for not communicating and responding more quickly to the crisis. In addition, the company was criticized for not having clear risk and crisis communication provisions in place for a disaster of this magnitude. As a result, after the explosion, the crisis appeared to be beyond BP's control as oil rapidly gushed into the water. Tony Hayward, the CEO of BP at the time of the crisis, was widely criticized for several communication missteps including minimizing the scope and intensity of the crisis and for lacking compassion and empathy in his initial postcrisis responses. Organizations must provide effective communication immediately following the crisis. This can be difficult due to the inherent uncertainty of crisis events and because little is often known about the cause of the crisis. However, organizations have a short window to take control of the crisis and set the tone for the response and recovery efforts.

As you can see from these examples, one of the most frustrating and distressing aspects of crisis is the persistent urgency of the situation. This urgency is compounded by the fact that a crisis comes as a surprise and introduces extreme threat into a situation.

EXPANDING THE TRADITIONAL DEFINITION OF CRISIS

In this book, we discuss organizational crises of many types, ranging from those caused by industrial accidents to natural disasters. To account for all these types, we offer the following description as a working definition of organizational crisis:

> An organizational crisis is a specific, *unexpected*, and *nonroutine* event or series of events that create high levels of *uncertainty* and simultaneously present an organization with both *opportunities* for and *threats* to its *high-priority goals*.

As we have established, much of the intensity of a crisis comes with some degree of surprise. Even in cases where there are clear warning signs, most people are still surprised when a crisis actually occurs. Thus, crises are almost always unexpected events. Because they exceed any planning expectations, they cannot be managed with routine procedures. Once an organization abandons its routine procedures, its leadership is faced with managing this uncertainty by emphasizing either opportunities for growth or renewal or threat to the organization's image or reputation in their crisis communication. See Table 1.1 for a description of each component in our working definition.

Table 1.1	Key Components of a Working Definition of Organizational Crisis
Unexpected	An event comes as a surprise. This surprise may be something for which the organization could not have anticipated or planned. It could also result from conditions that exceed even the most aggressive crisis management plans.
Nonroutine	Problems occur daily in nearly all organizations. To account for these problems, organizations engage in routine procedures. Crises are events that cannot be managed by routine procedures. Instead, crises require unique and often extreme measures.
Produces uncertainty	Because they are unexpected and beyond the routine actions of organizations, crises produce tremendous uncertainty. Organizations cannot be aware of all causes and ultimate effects of crises without some degree of investigation. Efforts to reduce uncertainty may continue for months or even years after a crisis.
Creates opportunities	Crises create opportunities that may not be available during normal business opportunities. Crises create opportunities to learn, make strategic changes, grow, or develop new competitive advantages.
Threat to image, reputation, or high-priority goals	Crises can produce an intense level of threat to the organization and its affiliates. This threat is often described as damage to the image or reputation of an organization. However, crises can also be threatening enough to permanently destroy an organization.

DISASTERS, EMERGENCIES, CRISIS, AND RISK

The term *crisis* most often relates to organizations experiencing high consequence events. However, communities often experience disasters like tornadoes and hurricanes. Similarly, on a much smaller scale compared to crises and disasters, organizations or communities might experience an emergency, which is a small-scale crisis that is more contained and controlled than crises or disasters. For the purposes of our discussions in this book, an evacuation of a building due to a gas leak is an emergency. Now, there are important communication protocols for handling emergencies; however, they are outside the scope of this book. Conversely, a gas explosion at an organization is a crisis. The type of response necessary to deal with this type of crisis is directly within the scope of this book. Similarly, as you will see in the case chapters, the ideas discussed in this book are useful for understanding organizational and community responses to a wide range of disasters like terrorism, natural disasters, and environmental disasters.

Furthermore, note that the foregoing definition does not mention risk. We separate crisis and risk because we believe that, while risk is a natural part of life, crisis can often be avoided. Naturally, some people live with more risk in their lives than others. For example, some people choose to live next to oil refineries, on hurricane-prone coasts, or in areas susceptible to mudslides or forest fires. Please understand, however, that crisis and risk are closely connected, as poor risk communication can cause a crisis. In Chapter 10, we talk more about the opportunities associated with effective risk communication. What follows is a discussion of various crisis types.

TYPES OF CRISES

Now, with that definition of organizational crisis in mind, think about some of the events that would qualify as a crisis. Have you been in a crisis situation either directly or indirectly? You may not have faced a Fortune 500 company bankruptcy, but you may have witnessed a flood, an organizational leader's dishonesty, a food-borne illness outbreak at a national restaurant chain, a catastrophic industrial fire, or the wide-reaching impacts of a terrorist event. All these incidents can be described as crisis situations.

Crisis communication researchers develop classification systems of crisis types to assist them in their crisis planning and, in so doing, reduce the uncertainty when crises occur. The simplest and possibly the most useful distinction to make in crisis types is to divide them into two categories: intentionally caused crises and crises caused by natural, uncontrollable factors. When crisis planners attempt to think the unthinkable regarding all the potential crises they could face, the list is not only endless, but it is also unique to the organization. We do not pretend to list every possible type of crisis that could be caused by intentional or unintentional acts. Rather, we provide a list of categories into which most crises fall.

INTENTIONAL CRISES

We identify seven general categories for crises that are initiated by intentional acts designed to harm an organization:

1. Terrorism

2. Sabotage

3. Workplace Violence

4. Poor Employee Relationships

5. Poor Risk Management

6. Hostile Takeovers

7. Unethical Leadership

Since the distressing events that occurred on September 11, 2001, *terrorism* tops the list of the most urgent intentional causes of crisis. Organizations of all types must now be aware of their vulnerability to terrorist acts that can disrupt both the organization and the nation as a whole.

Organizations are also vulnerable to *sabotage*, which involves the intentional damaging of a product or the working capacity of the organization by someone inside the organization. Typically, sabotage is done for revenge or for some benefit, such as economic gain. Similarly, *workplace violence* has become all too common in the United States. Distressed over their perceived mistreatment by an organization, employees or former employees undertake violent acts. Sadly, this form of violence has become more frequent even on college campuses. The result is often multiple injuries, deaths, and disruption of the organization and its workforce.

Wide-scale crises can also result from *poor employee relationships*. If an organization cannot develop positive relationships between management and its workers, trouble is likely to occur. For example, an organization could develop a reputation of having poor working conditions. If these conditions persist, the organization is likely to have difficulty both retaining and recruiting employees. Without enough qualified employees, an organization cannot continue to function.

Another possibility is that, when unionized employees become very frustrated with their working conditions, they may choose to take some action, such as striking. In most cases, employee strikes adversely affect an organization's financial stability. We realize that poor employee relationships are not responsible for all strikes or employee turnover problems. We are convinced, however, that when turnover and strikes lead to crisis situations, the relationships between management and employees are often controversial.

If organizations are guilty of *poor risk management*, the outcomes can be disastrous for consumers, employees, or both. For example, a beef processing plant in a Midwestern city failed to adequately maintain its sewer system, creating a dangerous public health hazard. The sewer system overflowed, sending foul-smelling cattle waste and remnants from the slaughter process directly into a river flowing through the community of nearly 100,000 people. The ultimate consequence of this poor risk management was heavy fines that forced the plant to close.

Hostile takeovers are still a major threat to organizations. Simply put, hostile takeovers occur when the majority of an organization's stock is purchased by a rival organization. The result can be an overthrow of the current leadership and the dismantling of the organization. Hundreds or thousands of employees can find themselves unemployed due to actions that have taken place completely outside their workplace. Federal regulations address some of the issues related to hostile take-overs, but such aggressive assaults on organizations still exist.

The broadest and most inclusive subcategory of intentional crises is *unethical leadership*. An extensive review of more than 6,000 newsworthy organizational crisis events reported annually by the Institute for Crisis Management found that management was in some way responsible for the majority of them. Worse, many of these crises were caused by criminal acts of managers (Millar & Irvine, 1996). We dedicate Chapter 11 of this book to ethics. At this point, we want to emphasize that unethical behavior can and often is the ultimate cause of a crisis situation. When an organization's leadership knowingly puts its workers, consumers, investors, or the surrounding community at risk without being honest about that risk, two events are likely to occur. First, a breakdown in the system occurs, which often results in a crisis. Second, when the public learns of the organizational leadership's dishonesty, it is likely to be unforgiving. Thus, the road to recovery is likely to be much longer for dishonest leaders than it is for honest leaders.

UNINTENTIONAL CRISES

Clearly, not all crises are caused by the intentional acts of individuals with questionable motives. Rather, many are simply unforeseeable or unavoidable. In this section, we describe five types of unintentional crises:

1. Natural Disasters
2. Disease Outbreaks
3. Unforeseeable Technical Interactions
4. Product Failure
5. Downturns in the Economy

Like us all, organizations are vulnerable to *natural disasters*. Tornadoes, hurricanes, floods, wildfires, and earthquakes have the potential to destroy organizations' and industries' physical plants and entire communities. Although these events are largely unpredictable, some steps can be taken to reduce their impact on an organization. For example, building a nuclear reactor on or near an existing earthquake fault line would be unwise. Similarly, locating an organization in an area that is uncommonly susceptible to floods or tropical storms is indefensible. The earthquake in Haiti was much more damaging due to poor building practices. In short, organizations must take into account possible threats of natural disasters before they invest in their facilities. A natural disaster can be made much worse due to decisions made by organizations. Despite this caution, natural disasters are unavoidable as potential crises.

Disease outbreaks are an inevitable form of crisis. Some of these occur naturally. For example, the H1N1 virus caused worldwide alarm in 2009. Other crises, such as food-borne illness, occur due to organizational failure. For example, Schwan's Sales Enterprises discovered that its ice cream, distributed nationally, was contaminated with salmonella. Thousands of consumers became ill. Schwan's successful crisis recovery was based largely on the fact that the company responded quickly with a recall in an effort to limit the number of illnesses caused by the tainted product. Product failures at some level are nearly impossible to prevent. The severity and frequency of these failures, however, can be reduced significantly with good crisis planning.

Many of the malfunctions that lead to crises are the result of *unforeseeable technical interactions.* In his classic text, *Normal Accidents,* Charles Perrow (1999) describes dozens of examples of organizations whose monitoring and safety equipment became inaccurate and inoperable because of a series of seemingly unrelated errors or equipment failures. For example, he describes how a commercial aircraft was forced to crash-land after a coffeemaker shorted out, causing an electrical fire in a series of wires and disabling other safety equipment and vital control systems. In this case, the pilots and maintenance crew were following all the prescribed procedures. The coffeemaker was wired appropriately. The crisis resulted from an almost unimaginable sequence of events piling on top of one another.

Product recalls are rather commonplace. Organizations discover unintended risks or flaws in a product, issue a recall, repair or replace the product or refund the purchase price, and move forward. Americans are so used to recalls based on *product failure* that many consumers weigh the inconvenience of having a product repaired or replaced against the risk posed by a flawed product. In many cases, consumers do not even respond to the recall. Some, however, reach crisis level. Organizations like Safe Kids Worldwide (http://www.safekids.org) monitor and list product recalls of all types for parents. By checking websites like this, one can see the varied and numerous product recalls that affect organizations and children across the world. For this reason, product recalls are one of the more frequent crisis types.

Last, organizations of nearly every kind are subject to crises caused by *downturns in the economy.* Even organizations that are ethical, thoughtful in their planning, and strict in their maintenance of safety regulations can be victims of economic crises. If consumers cannot afford an organization's products, there is little opportunity to resolve the situation with better communication. Downsizing and plant closings are often the result of economic downturns. From 2008 through 2010, the United States experienced one of the worst financial downturns in the economy since the Great Depression. The crisis, caused by increased risk taking by the banking industry and the collapse of the housing market, led to a complete collapse of our financial system. Businesses large and small had no access to credit, and as a result, several large banks, such as Lehman Brothers, Merrill Lynch & Co., Washington Mutual, and Wachovia Corporation, went bankrupt or were taken over by other companies. In addition, companies like General Motors (GM) and Chrysler also declared bankruptcy because of a lack of access to credit and the downturn in the economy. Economic downturns can create unexpected crises that have consequences that are far-reaching beyond the organizations that are responsible for creating the problems.

THE SIGNIFICANCE OF CRISIS IN A GLOBAL ENVIRONMENT

Organizational crises are a consistent part of our existence. We cannot prevent them and, as consumers, we cannot avoid them. Worse, crises are becoming more prevalent. Perrow (1999) explains that, as technology continues to advance and as our population continues to grow, we are increasingly exposed to and affected by crises that we could not have imagined 20 or 30 years ago.

As consumers, we are also dependent on more organizations than ever before. Twenty-five years ago, the Internet was a concept, cable television was considered a luxury, satellite television was in its infancy, and cell phones were nearly the size of chainsaws. Now, these technologies and the organizations that support them are central features in our daily lives. As we become more and more dependent on the services of an increasing number of organizations and technologies, our exposure to potential crises naturally increases.

In addition, as we move closer to a truly global society, the incidents on one continent can create a crisis an ocean away. Think of the impact that the most recent economic downturn had on the global economy. Excessive risk taking in one economy can create a global recession. Another example of our global society is our food system. As we mentioned earlier, the 2008 crisis that began in China had severe effects for many infants and young children across the world who drank imported milk products tainted with artificially inflated levels of the protein supplement melamine. This crisis resulted in many countries banning, recalling, or creating more elaborate testing measures for any milk products produced in China. As our world becomes more complex, interconnected, centralized, and efficient, the frequency and forms of crises will steadily increase. Understanding how to effectively engage in crisis communication, then, is a skill ever increasing in value. To be effective, one must be able to recognize and resist the varied misconceptions associated with effective crisis communication.

UNDERSTANDING THE MISCONCEPTIONS ASSOCIATED WITH CRISES AND CRISIS COMMUNICATION

Before we move on to presenting key theories in crisis communication, we want the reader to consider 10 misconceptions that people have about crises and crisis communication. Our misconceptions relate not only to how we define and understand crisis but also how we should communicate during a crisis. For this reason, this understanding is an important transition to our next chapter that addresses theories of crisis communication. More important, our misconceptions about defining crisis and crisis communication practice often leads to ineffective and maladaptive crisis communication in practice. To be an effective crisis communicator means to resist these misconceptions. The preponderance of miscues and ineffective responses to crisis communication suggest that leaders and crisis communicators have some misconceptions about communication and crisis. What follows are 10 common misconceptions of crisis and crisis communication and descriptions of how correcting those misconceptions can lead to more productive and effective crisis responses (see Table 1.2).

Table 1.2	Misconceptions of Crisis Communication

1. Crises build character.
2. Crises do not have any positive value.
3. Crisis communication is about determining responsibility and blame.
4. Crisis communication is solely about getting information out to stakeholders.
5. Crisis communication involves taking a rigid and defensive stance.
6. Crisis communication is about enacting elaborate prefabricated crisis plans.
7. Crisis communication is about overreassuring the public about the impact of the crisis to avoid panic.
8. Crisis communication is about communicating only when new information is available.
9. Crisis communication is primarily about managing the image or reputation of an organization.
10. Crisis communication involves spinning the facts surrounding the crisis.

First, a common misconception is that going through a crisis helps an organization build its character. We believe that crises do not build character but expose the established character and values of organizations through their communication. In fact, a crisis is one of the only times an organization's stakeholders can view the values of an organization in action. For instance, it was not until the now famous crisis at Enron that stakeholders were able to see firsthand the greed and unethical business practices inherent to the organization's culture, even though these practices had been going on for some time. Similarly, Aaron Feuerstein's crisis communication following his plant fire in 1995 illustrated the care and value he had established over time for his workers and the community in which he operated. Both cases are discussed extensively throughout the book and suggest that crises serve as an opportunity to expose the current values inherent to an organization.

A second misconception about crises is that they are inherently negative events. As this book suggests, crises can present both threat and opportunity if viewed mindfully. Although threat often becomes the most salient feature of crisis events, we contend that crises should be viewed mindfully as dangerous opportunities, as discussed in our first chapter. For instance the Greensburg, Kansas, case, discussed in Chapter 4 illustrates that crisis ultimately created an opportunity to save a town that was slowly in decline already. The food-borne illness crises for Schwan's and Odwalla, discussed in Chapters 4 and 8, allowed the companies to update their pasteurization processes and create safer food processing systems.

The third misconception about crisis is that resolution to a crisis solely involves retrospectively determining fault, assigning blame, and investigating what happened. Crisis leadership and effective crisis communication involves creating a vision for moving beyond the crisis, learning, and creating meaning. As you read the case chapter of this book, pay special attention to how the most effective leaders are able to develop a prospective vision during a crisis. Effective crisis communicators should not get mired in the investigation processes of a crisis. Pay special attention to the industrial fires of Cole Hardwood and Malden Mills, discussed in Chapters 4 and 8, as excellent examples of how leaders can resist the misconception that crisis communication is about determining blame and responsibility. In both cases, insurance companies and other agencies determined the causes of those fires. However, the leaders of both companies, Milt Cole and Aaron Feuerstein, focused on setting a vision for moving their companies beyond the crises.

A fourth misconception about crisis communication is that it is inherently about providing scripted messages designed in advance. We find that crisis communicators would do well to devote more attention to listening to and adapting messages for their stakeholders. Recognizing and responding to stakeholder concerns is far more important than producing prefabricated messages based on what the organization feels its stakeholders need to hear. Clearly, organizations can work with stakeholders to consider risks before a crisis and develop a crisis needs assessment of types of messages and preferred channels to be most effective. However, crises are dynamic and, by definition, a surprise to most or all the people impacted by the event. Consider the 2008 collapse of the United States' financial institutions. Even with strong economic models and countless organizations in the financial industry, almost no one predicted the collapse of the housing market and subsequent credit crisis. This example reveals that effective crisis communicators listen to the unique needs of those impacted by these surprising events to comprise their messages. The best crisis messages in this book come from leaders who responded to a crisis authentically based on laudable values and what they believed was in the best interests of their stakeholders. In each case, they met regularly with stakeholders to hear their concerns.

Our fifth misconception is that organizations and social systems need to become more rule-based and rigid in their organizational structure following a crisis. We believe that the more flexible and agile an organization or system is, the more it is able to respond to the uncertain, complex, and ever-changing demands of the crisis. Effective crisis communicators need to change accordingly and follow the dynamic nature of a crisis. Organizations would do well to take some action during a crisis to make sense of the situation. More often than not, organizations freeze and fail to act, often making the crisis worse. Organizations that embrace the situation and the uncertainty, and take action to reduce uncertainty, are more effective crisis communicators. Rudy Giuliani was effective for many reasons following 9/11; he was very agile with his response following the terrorist attack. He left his office and went to the street where he could assess the situation himself. Further, he frequently held media briefings for the people of New York and around the world. He did not have all the answers, but he was engaged, agile, and effective in his response to the crisis.

Misconception six is that having a crisis plan in place is the best preparation for a crisis. Although crisis plans can be helpful in preparing for a crisis, the best predictor of effective crisis management is strong, positive stakeholder relationships. As you read the cases in this book pay special attention to how many effective organizations relied on stakeholders to support them during a crisis. For this reason, organizations looking to prepare for crises should work with their stakeholders to establish strong, positive relationships with them. We recommend that organizations work through problems and concerns before a crisis happens. Organizations that spend time establishing these relationships are better able to respond to the needs of these groups following a crisis.

Overreassuring stakeholder safety regarding the impact of a crisis is the seventh common misconception of effective crisis communicators. Effective crisis communicators do not overreassure their publics but provide information to their stakeholders to help protect themselves. In Chapter 5, we discuss this type of communication as self-efficacy. The more you can do as a crisis communicator to help protect your stakeholders, the better. Overreassuring stakeholders about the outcome of a crisis is sure to kill the credibility of any spokesperson.

The eighth misconception about crisis communication is to say *no comment* or to stonewall. Effective crisis communicators meet regularly with their stakeholders and the media to answer questions, remain open and accessible, and keep everyone updated with information about the crisis. Organizations are typically caught so off guard following a crisis that they do not know what to say. In this case, we suggest that they tell people what they know, tell them what they do not know, and tell them what they are going to do to collect information about the crisis.

Misconception nine is to focus more on the organization's image and less on solutions to the crisis. Ineffective crisis communicators try to control their images, scapegoat other parties, and absolve themselves from blame. Once a crisis occurs, there is not much that can be done to save or repair an image. Rather, effective crisis communicators focus on finding solutions to the crisis and lessen the impact on those most impacted by the crisis. We contend that it is impossible to control the image or reputation of a company. Multiple events and perspectives by many different stakeholders comprise the overall image or reputation of a company. Ultimately, we argue that organizations should control what they can, which is correcting the problem and learning from the crisis.

The final misconception is that spin is a viable option in effective crisis communication. Spin only makes the crisis worse and makes the crisis communicator look unethical and irresponsible once the truth comes out. Be wary of any advice to use spin as a strategy in crisis communication. Organizations should be wary of those who suggest trying to spin the information surrounding a crisis to obscure responsibility. Organizations that resist this strategy are going to be more effective in their crisis communication.

SUMMARY

This chapter provided an expanded definition of crisis, explained different crisis types, and delineated key misconceptions associated with the understanding and practice of crisis communication. The next part of this book examines key theories of crisis communication. These theories provide both a vocabulary for understanding crisis communication along with ways to describe, explain, and prescribe the practice of crisis communication. Let's now examine how different theories help us understand and practice crisis communication.

REFERENCES

Hermann, C. F. (1963). Some consequences of crisis which limit the viability of organizations. *Administrative Science Quarterly, 8,* 61–82.

Millar, D. P., & Irvine, R. B. (1996). *Exposing the errors: An examination of the nature of organizational crises.* Paper presented at the Annual Conference of the National Communication Association, San Diego, CA.

Perrow, C. (1999). *Normal accidents.* New York, NY: Basic Books.

Understanding Crisis Communication Theory and Practice

To define and better understand crises of all types, researchers have developed theories to understand and manage these events. Crises are studied by a wide variety of disciplines including psychology (Morgan, Fischhoff, Bostrom, & Atman, 2002; Slovic, 1987), sociology (Chess, 2001; Clarke & Chess, 2008; Mileti & Peek, 2000; Mileti & Sorensen, 1990; Quarantelli, 1988), business (Mitroff, 2005; Mitroff & Anagnos, 2001; Weick, 1988; Weick & Sutcliffe, 2007), mathematics and physics (Bak, 1996; Lorenz, 1993; Mandelbrot, 1977), and political science (Birkland, 2006; Comfort, Sungu, Johnson, & Dunn, 2001; Ramo, 2009) among others. In addition, there are a number of practitioners who have written books about crisis communication (Reynolds, 2002; Witt & Morgan, 2002). James Lee Witt, former director of FEMA from 1993 to 2001, provides clear advice about effective crisis communication through his experiences managing major natural disasters. Barbara Reynolds provides a guide for crisis and emergency risk communication based on her considerable experience communicating about public health outbreaks around the world. Each of these disciplines and practitioners has contributed greatly to defining and better understanding how to manage crises.

Psychology, for instance, provides the theoretical background on mental model approaches to crisis communication and the social amplification of risk and crisis communication. These theories help us better understand how people cognitively perceive and ultimately respond to risk and crisis situations. Sociology provides theories on how to conduct community evacuations during all types of disasters and how communities respond to these disasters. The field of business examines sensemaking processes of leadership before, during, and after a crisis; the role

Table 2.1	Academic Disciplines Contributing to Understanding of Risk and Crisis Communication

Discipline	Theory Contribution
Psychology	Mental models approach to risk and crisis communication
	Social amplification of risk and crisis perceptions
Sociology	Disaster evacuation theory
	Social response to disasters
	Social and institutional networks during disasters
Business	Organizational sensemaking theory
	Organizational learning theory
	High reliability organizational theory
Mathematics and Physics	Chaos theory
	Complexity Theory
	Sandpile/Self-organized criticality theory
Political Science	Policy change theory and catastrophic disasters
	Deep security theory

of organizational learning in response to crisis; as well as organizational structures that exemplify a crisis-prepared or crisis-prone organization. Mathematics and physics produced chaos and complexity theories that have been used widely in the communication discipline as metaphors for the disruption and self-organization produced by crisis events (Gilpin & Murphy, 2008; Murphy, 1996; Sellnow, Seeger, & Ulmer, 2002). Political science provides theories, such as Ramo's (2009) deep security theory, that build on complexity and network theories for policymakers to prepare and respond to crises such as terrorism. For full discussions of the interdisciplinary approach to crisis communication and the theoretical approaches associated with them, take a look at one of the recent handbooks on risk and crisis communication (Coombs & Holladay, 2010; Heath & O'Hair, 2009; Pearson, Roux-Dufort, & Clair, 2007). You will find that many of the lessons described in the upcoming chapters are grounded in the interdisciplinary research described above. However, the communication discipline has produced considerable research on crisis communication. What follows is a discussion of the several important theories of crisis communication. The first section examines the important role media theories provide for contributing to the understanding of crisis communication.

MEDIA THEORIES AND CRISIS COMMUNICATION

Considerable theory building in crisis communication has focused on the role of media in the life cycle of a crisis. In some cases, media coverage can amplify the public's fear beyond what is reasonable (Pidgeon, Kasperson, and Slovic, 2003). Conversely, the media often moves beyond "environmental surveillance" to the point of "community building" to assist with crisis recovery period (Wilkins, 1989, p. 33). In either case, the media is a prominent player, making a substantial impact during crises. For this reason, Seeger (2006) prioritizes forming partnerships with the media as a best practice of crisis communication. In this section, we review three theories that have been adapted through considerable research to explain the role the media play during crises. These theoretical perspectives include news framing, focusing events, and crisis news diffusion.

NEWS FRAMING THEORY

At the heart of news framing theory is the fact that "reporters and editors routinely choose among various approaches to the presentation of news stories" (Hook & Pu, 2006, p. 169). The approach selected results in a pattern of coverage that can frame a topic positively or negatively. The controversy

Table 2.2	Media Theories Contributing to the Understanding of Crisis Communication

Theory	Characteristics
News Framing	Emphasizes the degree to which the crisis is framed positively or negatively
	Focuses on news reporting
	Features messages by both the media and organizations (often contrasting) designed to frame the crisis
Focusing Events	Emphasizes policy decisions made in response to crisis events
	Focuses on policy debates that are played out publicly
	Features determining blame, likelihood of similar crises in the future, and lessons learned
News Diffusion	Emphasizes the distribution of information in response to crises
	Focuses on the speed and accuracy of messages shared
	Features the diverse means through which people receive information and the resilience of those sources during crises

inherent in many crises often intensifies and polarizes the framing process. For example, an organization may seek to frame a crisis as an aberration or as unavoidable. Conversely, the media may frame the same crisis as having manifested from a lack of responsible caution on the part of the organization. This type of polarity in framing crises is not unusual.

The news framing process can have a profound impact on how readers and viewers perceive a crisis. For this reason, Holladay (2010) argues, "it is imperative that organizations participate in this framing process" (p. 161). If organizations remain passive in the framing process they make themselves completely vulnerable to their adversaries who will likely strive to tip the media coverage of the crisis negatively. For example, a metropolitan hospital recently responded to a budget shortfall by laying off a large number of nurses. Area media reported on the layoffs, framing the budget issues as having been caused by administrative mismanagement. Worse, the stories often featured laid off nurses with young children in tears over their impending financial hardship. Meanwhile, another hospital in the community offered to hire some of the nurses at comparable wages. The financially struggling hospital remained silent throughout the crisis. The hospital never fully recovered from the crisis and was eventually sold to another health management company. Had the hospital offered a competing explanation or frame for needing to lay off employees, the outcome might have been very different.

As the hospital example reveals, the framing process influences the public's perception of the organizations afflicted with the crisis. If the crisis is framed in a way that reflects negatively on an organization, that organization's ability to recover from the crisis is impaired or delayed. Hence, news framing theory advocates that organizations take an active role in the framing process.

Occasionally, news stories that would not normally top the media's agenda do so when they are reported in a way that *exemplifies* the story. Exemplars are elements of a news story that are made memorable by their "visually vivid and emotionally strong" content (Aust & Zillmann, 1996, p. 788). Stories that are graphic in nature or that include a particularly disturbing visual element can capture audience attention and cause them to exaggerate the seriousness of the issue or event (Westerman, Spence, & Lachlan, 2009). This exaggeration is intensified when the viewers believe they are directly exposed or vulnerable to the risk that is exemplified (Westerman, Spence, & Lachlan, 2012). For example, when ABC News portrayed Lean Finely Textured Beef as "pink slime" in a series of news stories, the network, in essence, created an exemplar that, due to public outrage, rose on the media's agenda and created a crisis for the product's primary producer, Beef

Products Incorporated. The power of exemplars to shift the media's attention warrants caution on the part of reporters. Zillmann, Gibson, Sundar, and Perkins (1996) urge reporters to comprehend the influence of exemplars as well as the challenges for correcting or countering them once they are introduced to the public.

FOCUSING EVENTS

Focusing event theory is an extension of agenda setting theory. *Agenda setting* refers to the way the media determines the importance of various news stories or political issues. The higher a story ranks on the media's agenda, the more attention or coverage it receives. Crises become focusing events when they are high on the media's agenda and the discussion moves from reporting on the cause and impact of the crisis to the reconsideration of existing policies or the consideration of new polices for preventing similar crises in the future.

Wood (2006) explains that focusing events include four consistent attributes. First, like all crises, they occur suddenly. Second, they are rare. Third, they garner large-scale attention. Finally, both the public and policy makers simultaneously prioritize them. Fishman (1999) argues that the combination of "a dramatic news event, and the media's coverage of that event creates an urgency to take action" (p. 353). That action takes the form of policy debates and recommendations for revising current policies or developing new policies. For example, the tragic shooting at Sandy Hook Elementary School in the village of Sandy Hook in Newtown, Connecticut inspired considerable debate over gun laws. Although no meaningful change occurred on the national level, many communities revised existing policies regarding firearms and schools after the Sandy Hook crisis.

Policy debates stemming from focusing events are typically based on three topics: blame, normalcy, and learning. Questions of blame ask whether or not the crisis was caused by human or mechanical failures that could be addressed with policy changes. Questions focusing on normalcy address the extent to which the crisis is a manifestation of routine procedures. In Chapter 1, we discussed various types of recurring crises. A normal crisis would fit within this typology. Sadly, mass shootings, as discussed above, are repeated with enough frequency that they are considered normal and warrant policy debates. By contrast, novel crisis types are highly unusual and difficult to address through policy changes. For example, Ebola outbreaks occur rarely in parts of Africa. The virus causes grotesque bleeding and is almost always fatal. The occurrence of these outbreaks, however, has always been contained quickly. Finally, learning is central to policy debates.

The changes in policy that occur in response to focusing events are, in essence, a manifestation of lessons learned from the crisis.

As we mentioned in Chapter 1, crises often lead to new opportunities for organizations and communities. Focusing events can provide the practical means for formalizing such opportunities into formal policies. Thus, focusing events inspire crisis communication that is dedicated to seizing the opportunity to improve public safety in the aftermath of a crisis.

CRISIS NEWS DIFFUSION

The shock and impact of crises create intense public interest. The media play a central role in diffusing or spreading that information. As crises emerge, curious and concerned publics often view television or Internet coverage continuously for extended periods of time. As McIntyre, Spence, and Lachlan (2011) explain, "media exposure is a popular method of coping with crises" (p. 303). Theories of crisis news diffusion seek to understand how and when people receive information about crises. News diffusion includes all channels of communication ranging from television and the Internet to newspapers, radio, and face-to-face interpersonal communication as well as all forms of social media.

The surprise and uncertainty during crises pose challenges for reporters. These trials are further intensified by the high demand for information. Those who study news diffusion are interested in the accuracy as well as the expediency of coverage. Social media resources such as Twitter address the void of information during crises. Recent crises such as the tornadoes in Joplin Missouri and Hurricane Sandy reveal that many people experiencing and observing crises build networks and access information regularly via social media. Interestingly, Brian Stelter, a *New York Times* reporter, happened to be near Joplin, Missouri, when the town was destroyed by a massive tornado. The reporter had no access to traditional forms of media coverage. Using his smart phone, he was able to post photos and brief statements using Instagram and Twitter. These posts were viewed by thousands of people wanting information about the devastation in Joplin.

The resilience displayed by the *New York Times* reporter in Joplin is a central feature of news diffusion research. For example, Spence, Lachlan and Westerman (2009) studied the preparation by local radio stations to continue broadcasting in the wake of a serious crisis such as a tornado or flood. They found that the majority of stations surveyed had plans for remaining resilient and continuing to broadcast during natural disasters.

Two classic studies in crisis news diffusion occurred when President John F. Kennedy was assassinated in 1963 and when President Ronald

Reagan was wounded in an assassination attempt in 1981. Nine out of 10 people surveyed knew President Kennedy was shot within an hour of the crisis (Greenberg, 1964). Nearly two decades later, the results were similar. Those surveyed after the Reagan attack were aware as quickly and mentioned interpersonal communication, television, and radio as their means of first learning about the crisis (Bantz, Petronio, & Rarick, 1983). Today, the speed of crisis news diffusion is much faster. We can receive news alerts on our smart phones within minutes of a story having been confirmed by a news source. We can also share the information much more quickly and efficiently through social media. Thus, new media channels have revitalized the study of crisis news diffusion. Beyond the role of the media in framing, understanding, and diffusing information during organizational crises, organizations must also respond and communicate during the crisis. What follows are several prominent theories of crisis communication.

ORGANIZATIONAL THEORIES OF CRISIS COMMUNICATION

For the past 20 years, communication researchers have developed theoretical approaches for responding to organizational crises (see Table 2.3). This research includes Corporate Apologia (Hearit, 2006), Image Repair Theory (Benoit, 1995), Situational Crisis Communication Theory (Coombs & Holladay, 2002), and Organizational Renewal (Ulmer, Sellnow, & Seeger, 2009). Corporate Apologia, Image Repair Theory, and Situational Crisis Communication Theory identify strategies an organization can use to repair its image and reputation after a crisis. Organizational Renewal focuses on learning from the crisis, communicating ethically, considering both the threat and the opportunities associated with the crisis, and creating a prospective vision. We briefly examine each of these research traditions.

CORPORATE APOLOGIA

Research on Corporate Apologia was initially conceptualized as the speech of self-defense (Ware & Linkugel, 1973). Hearit (2001) defines an *apologia* as not exactly an apology but rather "a response to criticism that seeks to present a compelling competing account of organizational accusations" (p. 502). In this case, crises are created by an accusation of wrongdoing. Hearit and Courtright (2004) explain that apologetic crises "are the result of charges leveled by corporate actors (e.g., media or public interest groups) who contend that an organization is guilty of wrongdoing" (p. 210). Corporate Apologia provides a list of communication

Table 2.3	Theories of Crisis Communication

Theory	Characteristics
Corporate Apologia	<u>Emphasizes</u> managing the threat created by a persuasive attack against an organization <u>Focuses</u> on an apology for wrongdoing <u>Features</u> communication strategies for the apology
Image Repair Theory	<u>Emphasizes</u> repairing the threat to the image of the accused <u>Focuses</u> on accounting for organizational actions that caused the crisis <u>Features</u> communication strategies for managing the account
Situational Crisis Communication Theory	<u>Emphasizes</u> lowering crisis attributions of responsibility for the crisis <u>Focuses</u> on determining communication based on the type of crisis and the organization's reputational assets <u>Features</u> flow-chart decision-making process for using crisis response strategies to influence stakeholder perceptions or attributions of responsibility
Organizational Renewal Theory	<u>Emphasizes</u> opportunities to learn and grow from the crisis <u>Focuses</u> on creating opportunities inherent to crisis events <u>Features</u> broad leadership and organizational communication guidelines, emphasizing strong positive values, an optimistic forward-looking perspective, and learning to overcome the crisis

strategies that the organization can use to respond to these accusations. These communication strategies include "denial, counterattack, differentiation, apology, and legal" (Hearit, 2006, p. 15). These strategies are primarily defensive and are designed principally for an organization to account for its actions after a crisis.

IMAGE REPAIR THEORY

Benoit (1995) developed a comprehensive theory of image repair. *Image* refers to how the organization is perceived by its stakeholders and publics. Similar to Corporate Apologia, Benoit (1997) explains that "the key to understanding image repair strategies is to consider the nature of attacks or complaints that prompt such responses" (p. 178). He suggests that two components of the attack are essential. First, the organization must be "held responsible for an action" (Benoit, 1997, p. 178). Second, "that [action must be] considered offensive" (Benoit, 1997, p. 178). Benoit's (1995) theory contains a list of 14 impression management strategies. Five major strategies include denial, evasion of responsibility, reducing the offensiveness of the event, corrective action, and mortification. Each strategy can be used individually or in combination (Sellnow & Ulmer, 1995; Sellnow, Ulmer, & Snider, 1998). Consistent with Corporate Apologia, Benoit's image repair strategies focus on how organizations respond to accusations or account for their actions after being accused of a transgression. An effective response is designed to repair the organization's damaged image or reputation.

SITUATIONAL CRISIS COMMUNICATION THEORY

A third prominent theory on crisis communication is Situational Crisis Communication Theory. Coombs developed this theory by linking attribution theory and crisis response strategies (Coombs, 2012; Coombs & Halladay, 2002). His theory "evaluates the reputational threat posed by the crisis situation and then recommends crisis response strategies based upon the reputational threat level" (p. 138). The crisis response strategies in this approach are a synthesis of work on Corporate Apologia, Impression Management, and Image Repair Theory. He developed the list by selecting "those [strategies] that appeared on two or more lists developed by crisis experts" (p. 139). He describes four major communication approaches, including denial, diminishment, rebuilding, and bolstering. In all, he delineates 10 crisis response strategies. The crisis communication strategies are then used according to the threat to the organization's reputation based on "crisis type, crisis history, and prior reputation" (Coombs, 2012, p. 141).

Coombs (2012) explains that crisis type can be defined by three categories: "victim crisis cluster, accidental crisis cluster, and preventable crisis cluster" (p. 142). The victim cluster involves crises such as natural disasters, rumors, workplace violence, and malevolence. Accidental crises involve challenges, technical error accidents, and technical error product harm. Preventable crises include human error, accidents, human error product harm, and organizational misdeeds. Beyond crisis type, crisis response strategies should also be selected according to the organization's crisis history and prior reputation.

Crisis history and prior reputation are important because organizations that have recurring crises or poor reputations are not likely to have their messages accepted by stakeholders. Coombs's (2012) theory is based on the idea that, after a crisis, stakeholders "assign responsibility for negative unexpected events" (p. 138). Depending on the crisis type, crisis history, and prior reputation, Coombs provides crisis response recommendations to address the attributions of responsibility toward the organization.

DISCOURSE OF RENEWAL THEORY

As you have seen in the previous three theories, much of the research on crisis communication focuses on managing the threat to the image or reputation of the organization during a crisis. We argue there is also potential for positive discourse following a crisis that emphasizes the opportunities inherent to crises. Reputation and image are important organizational concepts, but they do not always play a central role in resolving organizational crises. The upcoming cases in this book provide many examples in which rebuilding, learning, and opportunity are more important than reputation or image. For this reason, we argue that crises also carry the potential for opportunity. To illustrate this idea, we developed a theory we call the *Discourse of Renewal* that emphasizes learning growth and opportunity following crises of all types. We see four theoretical objectives central to the Discourse of Renewal: organizational learning, ethical communication, a prospective rather than retrospective vision, and sound organizational rhetoric. We discuss this theory in much more depth in the final chapter of the book. However, what follows is a brief description of each of the theoretical components of our theory.

Organizational Learning

We believe that an organization that emerges successfully from a crisis must learn from the event. Chapter 9 provides an in-depth understanding of how organizations and communities can learn through failures, including crises. It is also important that the organization illustrates to stakeholders how its learning will help ensure that it will not experience a similar crisis in the future.

Ethical Communication

A second key factor in creating a renewing response is communicating ethically before, during, and after the crisis. Organizations that have not prepared adequately for crisis or are unethical in their business practices are going to have to account for those actions at some time. In fact, unethical actions are often the cause of a crisis. One of the key factors of a crisis is that it reveals the ethical values of the organization. Crises do not build character; they expose the character of the organization. If an organization is unethical before a crisis, those values are likely to be identified during the crisis. Organizations that institute strong, positive value positions, such as openness, honesty, responsibility, accountability, and trustworthiness, with key organizational stakeholders before a crisis happens are best able to create renewal following the crisis. Chapter 11 provides an in-depth examination of the importance of ethical communication and the opportunities associated with this crisis communication.

Prospective Versus Retrospective Vision

A third feature of a renewing response is communication focused on the future rather than the past. Theories that emphasize image or reputation emphasize a retrospective vision focused on who is responsible. Organizations that want to create a renewing response are more prospective and emphasize focusing on the future, not on the past. They learn from their mistakes, infuse their communication with bold optimism, and stress rebuilding rather than issues of blame or fault. Chapter 12 provides a detailed examination of Organizational Renewal Theory and the importance of developing a prospective vision to communicate about crisis.

Effective Organizational Rhetoric

Managing a crisis most often involves communicating with stakeholders to construct and maintain perceptions of reality. Establishing renewal involves leaders motivating stakeholders to stay with the organization through the crisis, as well as rebuilding the organization better than it was before. We advocate that leaders who hope to inspire others to embrace their views of crisis as an opportunity must establish themselves as models of optimism in and commitment to communicating ethically and responsibly. Effective organizational rhetoric then involves leadership with vision and a strong, positive reputation to effectively frame the crisis for stakeholders and persuade them to move beyond the event. The final chapter of this book examines communication strategies for developing sound organizational rhetoric during a crisis.

CRISIS COMMUNICATION THEORIES THAT DESCRIBE, EXPLAIN, AND PRESCRIBE

As you can see, there is considerable research from a communication perspective on how to manage and communicate about crises and disasters. In general, theories can describe communication, explain the effectiveness or ineffectiveness of communication, and prescribe how we should communicate. The media theories described in this chapter serve to describe and explain the role of media in framing, focusing, and setting the agenda in crisis communication. The communication theories of Corporate Apologia and Image Repair Theory describe common responses to organizational crises and can be used to explain the effectiveness or ineffectiveness of those responses. The Situational Crisis Communication Theory describes, explains, and prescribes communication strategies to protect the reputation of organizations managing crises. Consistent with Situational Crisis Communication Theory, the Discourse of Renewal describes, explains, and prescribes effective responses to crisis. However, a central difference is the diminished role of threat to the reputation of the organization in the Discourse of Renewal. In many examples of renewal, issues of blame, culpability, image, or reputation never arise as dominant narratives following these types of crisis responses. What makes renewal responses so effective is they mobilize the support of stakeholders and give these groups a vision to follow to overcome the crisis. A crisis response that emphasizes threat to the reputation of an organization typically lacks these qualities and often has the potential to extend the life cycle of the crisis. These organizations often suffer from what we call a *threat bias* in crisis communication.

UNDERSTANDING AND DEFINING THE THREAT BIAS IN CRISIS COMMUNICATION

We believe that an organization that is willing to view a crisis from a balanced perspective including both threat and opportunity has a much greater potential for recovering from a crisis. Despite this potential, we observe a persistent bias toward viewing crises solely from the perspective of threat in both theory and practice. As we mentioned at the outset of this chapter, threat is an important part of defining and understanding a crisis. However, we believe that researchers and practitioners often overemphasize and concentrate too much on the threat to an organization's reputation or image to respond effectively. What follows is a discussion of threat bias in defining effective crisis communication.

To avoid the threat bias exemplified in current crisis communication research, we suggest that crisis communicators mindfully define and examine crisis events from a more inclusive perspective. Nathan (2000a) explains the inclusive perspective we recommend:

> [I]n crisis the threat dimensions are usually seen most quickly and are then acted upon, while the potential for opportunity lies dormant. When a crisis is anticipated or when it occurs, the manager should be able to see both threat *and* opportunity features before deciding how to proceed. (p. 4)

Nathan (2000b) goes on to explain that our understanding of crisis and our crisis communication choices are inextricably linked. In fact, he suggests that focusing solely on the role of threat in crisis "promotes threat response that may, in turn, magnify and even intensify the state of [the] crisis" (Nathan, 2000b, p. 12). We argue that full consideration of both the potential threat and opportunity associated with crisis is a more appropriate and effective way to think about and communicate about crises. For this reason, we argue for mindfully reconsidering our definitions of crisis to include the perceived threat as well as the potential for opportunity emerging from the crisis.

Crises, by their nature, are threats to the survival of organizations. Certainly, no organization should hope for a crisis simply to experience the opportunities described by the theory of renewal. Rather, crises are inherent and inevitable elements of the organizational experience. Those organizations that see crises solely as threats to their public images are likely to respond in defensive and potentially manipulative manners. This defensive posture, at best, offers one benefit—survival. We contend that a combined emphasis on the threat and opportunity of crises fosters the simultaneous benefits of survival and growth. This growth manifests itself in the organization's willingness to respond with rhetorical sensitivity, make ethical decisions, learn from the crisis, and focus on the future. As we have argued throughout this chapter, these elements exemplify a balanced approach to crisis. Applying these elements can produce an opportunity for renewal that far exceeds basic survival.

SUMMARY

In this book, we hope to convince you that effective crisis management is a natural and essential part of the organizing process. We believe that effective crisis planning and communication can enable organizational leaders to better cope with the surprise, threat, and short response time that are a part of all crises. Although there are many types of intentional and unintentional organizational crises, there are consistent strategies that can help an organization turn a crisis situation into an opportunity for improvement. All crises involve effective communication. Resisting the threat bias and understanding the skills needed to communicate effectively is the focus of the next section of this book. Understand that the lessons described in the upcoming chapters are based on well-established research and practice in the multidisciplinary field of research in crisis communication. Furthermore, the next section takes us from conceptually understanding crises and crisis communication theory and moves us toward improving our crisis communication skills. Good luck with this next section of the book.

REFERENCES

Aust, C. F., & Zillmann, D. (1996). Effects of victim exemplification in television news on viewer perception of social issues. *Journalism & Mass Communication Quarterly, 73*, 787–803.

Bak, P. (1996). *How nature works: The science of self-organized criticality.* New York: Copernicus.

Bantz, C. R., Petronio, S. G., & Rarick, D. L. (1983). News diffusion after the Reagan shooting. *Quarterly Journal of Speech, 69*, 317–327.

Benoit, W. L. (1995). *Accounts, excuses and apologies.* Albany: State University of New York Press.

Benoit, W. L. (1997). Image repair discourse and crisis communication. *Public Relations Review, 23*, 177–186.

Birkland, T. A. (2006). *Lessons of disaster: Policy change after catastrophic events.* Washington, DC: Georgetown University Press.

Chess, C. (2001). Organizational theory and stages of risk communication. *Risk Analysis, 21*, 179–188.

Clarke, L., & Chess, C. (2008). Elites and panic: More to fear than fear itself. *Social Forces, 87*(2), 993–1014.

Comfort, L. K., Sungu, Y., Johnson, D., & Dunn, M. (2001). Complex systems in crisis: Anticipation and resilience in dynamic environments. *Journal of Contingencies and Crisis Management, 9*, 144–158.

Coombs, W. T. (2012). *Ongoing crisis communication: Planning, managing, and responding.* Thousand Oaks, CA: Sage.

Coombs, W. T., & Holladay, S. J. (2002). Helping crisis managers protect reputational assets: Initial tests of the situational crisis communication theory. *Management Communication Quarterly, 16*, 165–186.

Coombs, W. T., & Holladay, S. J. (Eds.). (2010). *The handbook of crisis communication.* Hoboken, NJ: Wiley.

Fishman, D. A. (1999). ValuJet flight 592: Crisis communication theory blended and extended. *Communication Quarterly, 47*(4), 345–375.

Gilpin, D. R., & Murphy, P. J. (2008). *Crisis management in a complex world.* New York: Oxford University Press.

Greenberg, B. S. (1964). Diffusion of News of the Kennedy Assassination. *Public Opinion Quarterly, 2*(22), 225–232.

Hearit, K. M. (2001). Corporate apologia: When an organization speaks in defense of itself. In R. L. Heath (Ed.), *Handbook of public relations* (pp. 595–605). Thousand Oaks: Sage.

Hearit, K. M. (2006). *Crisis management by apology: Corporate response to allegations of wrongdoing.* Mahwah, NJ: Lawrence Erlbaum.

Hearit, K. M., & Courtright, J. L. (2004). A symbolic approach to crisis management: Sears' defense of its auto repair policies. In D. P. Millar & R. L. Heath (Eds.), *Responding to crisis: A rhetorical approach to crisis communication* (pp. 201–212). Mahwah, NJ: Lawrence Erlbaum.

Heath, R. L., & O'Hair, D. H. (Eds.). (2009). *Handbook of risk and crisis communication.* New York: Routledge.

Holladay, S. J. (2010). Are they practicing what we are preaching? An investigation of crisis communication strategies in the media coverage of chemical accidents. In W. T. Coombs & S. J. Holladay (Eds.), *The handbook of crisis communication* (pp. 159–180). Chichester, United Kingdom: Wiley-Blackwell.

Hook, S. W., & Pu. X. (2006). Framing Sino-American relations under stress: A reexamination of news coverage of the 2001 spy plane crisis. *Asian Affairs: An American Review, 33*(3), 167–183.

Lorenz, E. N. (1993). *The essence of chaos.* Seattle: University of Washington Press.

Mandelbrot, B. B. (1977). *Fractals: Form, chance, and dimensions.* San Francisco: W. H. Freeman.

McIntyre, J. J., Spence, P. R., Lachlan, K. A. (2011). Media use and gender differences in negative psychological responses to a shooting on a university campus. *Journal of School Violence, 10,* 299–213. doi: 10.1080/15388220.2011.578555

Mileti, D., & Peek, L. (2000). The social psychology of public response to warnings of a nuclear power plant accident. *Journal of Hazardous Materials, 75,* 181–194.

Mileti, D., & Sorensen, J. H. (1990). *Communication of emergency public warnings.* Washington, DC: Federal Emergency Management Association.

Mitroff, I. I. (2005). *Why some companies emerge stronger and better from a crisis: 7 essential lessons for surviving disaster.* New York: AMACOM.

Mitroff, I. I., & Anagnos, G. (2001). *Managing crises before they happen: What every executive and manager needs to know about crisis management.* New York: AMACOM.

Morgan, M. G., Fischhoff, B., Bostrom, A., & Atman, C. J. (2002). *Risk communication: A mental models approach.* Cambridge, UK: Cambridge University Press.

Murphy, P. (1996). Chaos theory as a model for managing issues and crises. *Public Relations Review, 22,* 95–113.

Nathan, M. (2000a). From the editor: Crisis learning—Lessons from Sisyphus and others. *Review of Business, 21,* 3–5.

Nathan, M. (2000b). The paradoxical nature of crisis. *Review of Business, 21,* 12–16.

Pearson, C. M., Roux-Dufort, C., & Clair, J. A. (Eds.). (2007). *International handbook of organizational crisis management.* Thousand Oaks, CA: Sage.

Pidgeon, N., Kasperson, R. E., Slovik, P. (2003). *The social amplification of risk.* New York: Cambridge University Press.

Quarantelli, E. I. (1988). Disaster crisis management: A summary of research findings. *Journal of Management Studies, 25,* 273–385.

Ramo, J. C. (2009). *The age of the unthinkable: Why the new world disorder constantly surprises us and what we can do about it.* New York: Little, Brown and Company.

Reynolds, B. (2002). *Crisis and emergency risk communication.* Atlanta, GA: Centers for Disease Control and Prevention.

Seeger, M. W. (2006). Best practices in crisis communication: An expert panel process. *Journal of Applied Communication Research, 34,* 232–244. doi: 10.1080/00909880600769944

Sellnow, T. L., & Ulmer, R. R. (1995). Ambiguous argument as advocacy in organizational crisis communication. *Argumentation and Advocacy, 31,* 138–150.

Sellnow, T. L., Seeger, M. W., & Ulmer, R. R. (2002). Chaos theory, informational needs, and natural disasters. *Journal of Applied Communication Research, 30,* 269–292.

Sellnow, T. L., Ulmer, R. R., & Snider, M. (1998). The compatibility of corrective action in organizational crisis communication. *Communication Quarterly, 46,* 60–74.

Slovic, P. (1987). Perception of risk. *Science, 236,* 280–286.

Spence, P. R., Lachlan, K. A., & Westerman, D. (2009). Presence, sex, and bad news: Exploring the responses of men and women to tragic news stories in varying media. *Journal of Applied Communication Research, 37*(3), 239–256. doi: 10.1080/00909880903025929

Ulmer, R. R., Sellnow, T. L., & Seeger, M. W. (2009). Post-crisis communication and renewal: Understanding the potential for positive outcomes in crisis communication. In R. L. Heath & D. H. O'Hair (Eds.), *Handbook of risk and crisis communication.* New York: Routledge.

Ware, B. L., & Linkugel, W. A. (1973). They spoke in defense of themselves: On the generic criticism of apologia. *Quarterly Journal of Speech, 59,* 273–283.

Weick, K. E. (1988). Enacted sensemaking in crisis situations. *Journal of Management Studies, 25,* 305–317.

Weick, K. E., & Sutcliffe, K. M. (2007). *Managing the unexpected: Assuring high performance in an age of complexity* (2nd ed.). San Francisco: Jossey-Bass.

Westerman, E., Spence, P. R., & Lachlan, K. A. (2009). Telepresence and exemplification effects of disaster news. *Communication Studies, 60,* 542–557. doi: 10.1080/10510970903260376

Westerman, E., Spence, P. R., & Lachlan, K. A. (2012). Telepresence and Exemplification: Does spatial presence impact sleeper effects? *Communication*

The Lessons and Practical Application

Lessons on Effective Crisis Communication

I n the first two chapters, we defined crisis communication and discussed the key theories of crisis communication. This chapter builds on these ideas by discussing how to effectively communicate during a crisis. Over the past 20 years, a considerable amount of crisis communication research has been conducted. Some of the more recent research focuses on strategies to help organizations effectively respond to a crisis. This chapter defines key approaches to producing effective crisis communication. We believe that an effective response to a crisis can turn what could be a disaster for an organization into an opportunity to move beyond the event and to grow, prosper, and renew.

This chapter contains 10 lessons for effective crisis communication. These lessons should give any crisis communicator the key elements of an effective crisis response. The lessons, culled from numerous case studies and research on crisis communication, address a multitude of issues. Some of the lessons—such as determining your goals, for example—can be accomplished quite quickly and easily. Other lessons, such as managing stakeholder relationships, can be much more complex and time-consuming. You may even be surprised by some of the advice we provide in this chapter. For instance, we discuss seriously considering the use of clear and accurate communication in your initial crisis response. In addition, we provide some advice about overassuring stakeholders. These lessons may appear somewhat counterintuitive. Nevertheless, research has consistently revealed these strategies to be effective means for managing crises.

DETERMINING YOUR GOALS

One of the first things a crisis communicator needs to determine following a crisis is the goal of the crisis response. Goals are often broad value statements that can help guide decision making for the organization. One goal of crisis communication can be to reduce the impact of the crisis on those affected. Another goal of a crisis communicator may be to keep the organization's image intact or maintain the customer base. The CDC recently adopted the goals of "be first, be right, be credible" for their crisis communication (Reynolds, 2002). These broad goals provide clear objectives for how the CDC would like to communicate during a crisis. In essence, the CDC's objective during a crisis is to establish contact with stakeholders quickly and credibly. Determining goals is a key step in preparing for and responding to crisis. This strategy can also reduce uncertainty for the organization because, once goals are defined, the organization is better able to consciously think about what strategies it can use to accomplish its objectives.

Some of an organization's crisis communication goals may actually contradict one another. For instance, public health departments typically have a key goal of informing the public about health crises. However, at times, they are not able to meet this goal due to individual right-to-privacy laws that prohibit such communication. Determining, ranking, and identifying potential obstacles to goals of crisis communication before a crisis is a key step in effective crisis communication. We hope that when organizations prepare for crises, they consider their crisis communication goals. In addition, we believe that they should collaborate with other groups, work out potential goal conflicts, and establish partnerships.

LESSON 1

Determine your goals for crisis communication.

PARTNERING WITH CRISIS AUDIENCES

We believe that, once goals for a crisis response are established, the second essential part for crisis communicators is developing a mind-set about the role of stakeholders in crisis communication. A critical part of effective crisis communication is determined by the relationships organizations have with their stakeholders. Organizations should work before a crisis to cultivate strong partnerships with stakeholders.

We define *partnerships* as follows:

> Partnerships are equal communication relationships with groups or organizations that have an impact on an organization. Partnerships are established through honest and open dialogue about important issues for each group or organization. Partners may be advocates for the organization or they may be groups that are antagonistic toward the organization.

We believe that effective crisis communication starts long before a crisis hits and should be part of every organization's business and strategic plans. Establishing and maintaining equal relationships and partnerships with groups and organizations is critical to effective crisis communication. We do not advocate manipulating stakeholders in a way that gets them to do what you want. Rather, we believe organizations should create a dialogue with stakeholders about important issues and work out equitable

> ### LESSON 2
>
> Before a crisis, develop true, equal partnerships with organizations and groups that are important to the organization.

solutions. This can be a time-consuming process, but it is essential to crisis preparedness and, eventually, your crisis response.

We advise organizations, such as public health departments, to partner with local media when preparing for public health crises. As we mentioned earlier, public health departments are charged with providing important health information to the communities they serve. The media are often the outlet for this communication. However, individual right-to-privacy laws often preclude public health departments from being completely transparent in their communication. This limitation can lead to frustration on the part of the media. Through open and honest discussions, public health departments can explain their positions on privacy laws, and the media can express expectations for public access to information. Our experience suggests that, through these discussions, expectations can be set and uncertainty reduced about how public health departments will communicate about important health issues and how the media prefer to receive that information.

Research suggests that the public or an organization's stakeholders can even help an organization move beyond a crisis. For instance, during a 3-week period in October 2002, 10 people were shot and three others were critically injured by gunfire in public places, like restaurants and gas stations, in Washington, DC, and Maryland. The media dubbed the killer or killers as the "beltway sniper" or "DC sniper." In response, the Montgomery County police chief Charles Moose actively used both the local media and the public to look for and identify the snipers. This collaboration among the different stakeholders enabled the police to widen the search for the snipers and also gave the public a role in the search. By including the media and the public as partners in the crisis, the police were able to capture the snipers after receiving two separate tips based on reported sightings of a suspect's vehicle. In this case, the media and a vigilant public were treated as partners by law enforcement in ending the

> ### LESSON 3
>
> Acknowledge your stakeholders, including the media, as partners when managing a crisis.

terror in Washington, DC, and Maryland. (For more information about this situation and its resolution, see "Beltway sniper," n.d.)

UNDERSTANDING THE DIVERSITY OF YOUR AUDIENCES

Effective crisis communicators tend to consider the diversity of the audiences they will be in contact with after a crisis rather than viewing them as one large, homogenous public. In Chapter 2, we defined stakeholders as internal or external groups that can have an impact on the organization. A list of possible stakeholders can provide a map of communication partners, for instance:

▶ Employees

▶ Competitors

▶ Creditors

▶ Consumers

▶ Government Agencies

▶ The Community

▶ The Environment

▶ Stockholders

▶ The Media

This list could be even larger, depending on the organization and its interests. To better manage a crisis and our time in preparing for a crisis, we must determine which stakeholders the organization considers primary and secondary.

PRIMARY AND SECONDARY STAKEHOLDERS DEFINED

When considering the diverse nature of a single organization's stakeholders, an understanding of primary and secondary stakeholders is essential. Heath (1997) explains that this identification of stakeholders must include both "allies-supporters and opponents" (p. 28).

Primary stakeholders are those groups defined by an organization as most important to its success.

Secondary stakeholders are key groups that do not play an active role in the day-to-day activities of the organization but are still important to its overall success.

When using the stakeholders to define organizational audiences, we then ask the following questions:

▸ How often do you communicate with these stakeholders?

▸ What groups or organizations view you as a stakeholder?

▸ How often do these groups communicate with you?

▸ Are you aware of and do you listen to the concerns of these groups?

▸ On which issues of importance to both primary and secondary stakeholder groups do you agree and disagree?

We find that many organizations are aware of their stakeholders but do not communicate with them, or if they do, they converse only on rare occasions. When organizations need to communicate following a crisis, they are often communicating with groups they do not know very well. This lack of familiarity exists because the organization has not established any prior relationships and has no base for the communication. If an organization does not have a partnership with stakeholders prior to a crisis, the communication following one can be quite awkward and often ineffective. Effective crisis communicators listen to their stakeholders and treat their concerns as legitimate. Hence, effective crisis communicators know the expectations of their stakeholders and their information needs following a crisis.

What is worse than not knowing your stakeholders is having a negative relationship with them. One of the most important concerns for organizations is establishing strong, positive stakeholder relationships. At times, every organization is going to have stakeholders that are antagonistic and maybe even aggressive. That being true, organizations need to follow the classic advice: Keep your friends close and your enemies closer.

Organizations need to work with stakeholders to narrow gaps between stakeholder and organizational expectations. Every organization will need help during a crisis, and generating goodwill with stakeholders prior to a crisis will lessen stakeholder communication demands during and after the crisis. Typically, organizations do not readily address stakeholders who are adversaries. We believe that negotiating with antagonistic stakeholders over time and listening to their concerns is the key to better understanding their communication needs in the event of a crisis.

To communicate more effectively, organizations must determine the types of communication relationships or partnerships they currently have with primary stakeholders (see Table 3.1). *Positive stakeholder relationships*

Table 3.1 Possible Primary and Secondary Stakeholder Relationships or Partnerships

Stakeholder Relationship	Example
Positive	Symmetrical relationship in which both organization and stakeholder understand, acknowledge, communicate, and listen effectively to one another
Negative	An antagonistic relationship between organization and stakeholder; organization is not open to communicating with or listening to the stakeholder group
Ambivalent	No true partnership; organization and stakeholder each work to engineer consent with the other group, but neither group listens to the other
Nonexistent	Organization not aware of stakeholder and does not communicate with or acknowledge the stakeholder group

Lesson 4

Organizations need to develop strong, positive primary and secondary stakeholder relationships.

are defined as both the organization and the stakeholder viewing each other as partners. Neither party may agree on every issue, but both listen to one another and work to create agreements on issues over which they disagree. *Negative stakeholder relationships* develop because of poor communication between the organization and its stakeholders. The organization and the stakeholders in these groups are antagonistic toward one another. *Ambivalent stakeholder relationships* are defined as the organization and stakeholders engineering consent with one another. The relationship illustrates a lack of interest in one another and suggests that one group is trying to control the other. *Nonexistent stakeholder relationships* are defined by a lack of awareness or acknowledgment of a particular stakeholder group. In this case, the organization and its stakeholders are not even aware that they impact one another.

COMMUNICATING WITH UNDERREPRESENTED POPULATIONS DURING CRISES

Organizations must also consider the diversity and communication needs of diverse groups of stakeholders in crisis communication. Particular audiences may have specific communication needs or desires. Current research suggests there are three options in developing crisis messages for underrepresented populations (Dutta, 2007). These options include the following:

A culture-neutral approach

A culturally sensitive approach

A culture-centered approach

A culture-neutral approach takes the position that all stakeholder groups act on and access crisis communication information in similar manners. Crisis communication during Hurricane Katrina illustrates a culture-neutral approach to crisis communication. Crisis communication messages during the hurricane were constructed and presented without thought or concern for the socioeconomic background or crisis communication needs of African American and other underrepresented populations in New Orleans. As a result, these groups were either not reached or were neglected during the hurricane.

The culturally sensitive approach to communicating with underrepresented populations suggests that crisis communication messages should be adapted by cataloguing cultural characteristics of underrepresented groups to meet their crisis communication needs. For instance, some groups may want crisis information provided by members of their own cultural group. Others may want information provided at certain locations, such as churches or community gathering places. Still other groups may want crisis messages to contain certain terms or be written at a particular literacy level. The characteristics of each population can vary considerably; however, the goal of the culturally sensitive crisis communicator is to determine the characteristics of the population and develop messages to meet the needs of each group.

The final approach, and one we most prefer, is the culture-centered approach. The culture-centered approach takes the culturally sensitive approach one step further by actually including underrepresented populations in preparing for and communicating about crises. In this case, crisis communicators would involve underrepresented stakeholders in determining who would present their crisis messages and in what manner. The culture-centered approach involves including underrepresented populations in determining the appropriate crisis messages, the most effective channels for information dissemination, and the most trusted people to deliver crisis messages. This approach suggests developing partnerships with underrepresented stakeholders prior to a crisis to ensure effective communication with these groups following an event. To be successful in their crisis communications, every organization should develop relationships with underrepresented populations in their communities and make them part of their crisis communication planning. What follows is a discussion about listening, which is a key part of developing relationships with stakeholders.

A WORD ON PARTNERSHIPS AND LISTENING

Listening is critical to effective crisis communication. One of a crisis communicator's most common mistakes is attempting to engineer consent from the public by emphasizing only the organization's side of the story. This strategy, known as *spin*, often leaves the public feeling it does not have the full story, which creates resentment toward the organization. At worst, the organization does not even address the public's key concerns. When this happens, the public may be frustrated because important questions are not answered.

Listening to stakeholders is also a crucial aspect of postcrisis communication. Effective communication is not a one-way process. We advocate that, after a crisis, organizations not only provide information to stakeholders but also schedule time to listen to their concerns and to answer their questions. Listening in the form of public information sessions where stakeholders have the opportunity to voice their concerns is critical to postcrisis response and recovery efforts. Public information sessions include opportunities for stakeholders to interact with key organizational representatives, examine posters about the crisis and response and recovery efforts, and collect additional information in the form of fact or Q & A sheets if desired. Public information sessions are designed to provide stakeholders with opportunities to voice any concerns they may have about the crisis. In addition, the organization can hear stakeholder concerns firsthand. Once concerns are voiced, the organization can work to narrow the gap between what it is doing and what the public or stakeholders expect.

For some reason, listening sessions are one of the processes organizations have the most difficulty adopting. In training sessions, we often explain that organizations should keep their friendly stakeholders close and their discontented stakeholders closer. However, many organizations feel compelled to distance aggravated stakeholders and communicate with and listen to only stakeholders with whom they are in agreement. This, in our opinion, is an ineffective business practice. We have found that organizations are better able to prepare and respond to crises when they have coordinated with all stakeholder groups before and after the crisis. When dealing with aggravated or discontented stakeholders, every effort should be made to address the issues as quickly as possible. Organizations should make this exercise a part of their crisis planning.

Once you have determined that listening is a key factor in effective crisis communication, the next step is to focus on determining which audiences you should listen to and how to answer their questions.

WHAT INFORMATION DO STAKEHOLDERS NEED FOLLOWING A CRISIS?

We offer four broad suggestions for communicating effectively following a crisis: communicating early and often with stakeholders about the crisis, identifying the cause, contacting everyone affected, and communicating about current and future risks.

COMMUNICATE EARLY AND OFTEN WITH BOTH INTERNAL AND EXTERNAL STAKEHOLDERS

One of the fundamentals that crisis communicators should know is that they must make immediate contact with stakeholders and communicate about the crisis. Although the severity of the problem may not be known, stakeholders still need early and consistent communication about how the organization is moving forward. One of the things Rudy Giuliani did very well following 9/11 was to provide consistent reports to New York residents and the world about what was happening and how the cleanup was taking place. He did this even when there was no fresh news or when he had no information to provide. When holding a press conference on TV and asked to estimate the number of casualties, he acknowledged uncertainty by explaining, "The number of casualties is more than any of us can bear" (Pooley, 2001, para. 6).

Many organizations fail in communicating because they do not make themselves available to stakeholders. Our advice to crisis communication students and practitioners is to consistently provide information to stakeholders following a crisis. When information is not available, just listening to stakeholders and fielding questions is much more valuable than stonewalling or being perceived as inaccessible.

IDENTIFYING THE CAUSE OF THE CRISIS

A critical factor in resolving any crisis is determining the cause. Once the cause has been identified, some of the uncertainty is cleared up, and corrective action can be taken. The primary problem here, however, is that identifying the cause of the crisis often takes a great deal of time, as we mentioned earlier. Many different independent and governmental groups may work to identify the cause of a crisis, and they may often disagree with or question the veracity of the other groups' evidence. In addition, immediately after a crisis, accurate and appropriate information may not be available. During this time, the media and various other stakeholders often speculate about who is responsible and how the organization will recover from the crisis. Organizations can become defensive and closed to outside agencies as they try to spin the story positively or to the organization's favor, which negatively affects their credibility.

CONTACTING EVERYONE AFFECTED BY THE CRISIS

At the onset of a crisis, organizations must be able to contact each individual or group affected. When communicating with stakeholders following a crisis, make sure to communicate with compassion, concern, and empathy. This does not mean that the spokesperson should not be professional. However, due to the dramatic nature of crisis and the impact that these events have on people's lives, it is important to make sure that people are addressed with compassion for what they are going through, concern for their welfare, and empathy. James Lee Witt (Witt & Morgan, 2002), former director of FEMA, explains that communication skills are critical after a crisis:

> You can empathize with their pain and embarrassment at being helpless. You can make adjustments to the recovery process based on their need for dignity. You can make sure they have shelter and a hot meal. You can listen to their stories and acknowledge their concerns. You can hug them and let them cry on your shoulder. You can say to them as I do, we can't bring back your memories, but we can help you build new ones. (p. 147)

As you can see, compassion, concern, and empathy are key communication strategies in moving beyond the crisis and generating opportunities for renewal and optimism.

DETERMINING CURRENT AND FUTURE RISKS

To manage uncertainty, organizations must be aware of the current risks they face and potential future risks. Organizations that are able to consider potential risks in their environments are then able to prepare for and reduce uncertainty about these events, should they occur. Stakeholders will want to know whether they are at risk for similar crises in the future. In effective crisis communication cases, the organization is able to explain its corrective action to stakeholders so that these groups feel confident that the organization has made adequate corrections.

Within these four broad strategies for effective crisis communication, there are also some important communication approaches that need to be addressed. The first concentrates on the role of certainty in crisis communication. For some time, certain and clear communication has been the hallmark of effective crisis communication. Although clear and certain communication can be effective, we believe it can also get an organization into more trouble, can complicate the overall response for the organization, and can even be irresponsible.

LESSON 6

Communicate early about the crisis, acknowledge uncertainty, and assure the public that you will maintain contact with them about current and future risk.

IS CERTAIN COMMUNICATION ALWAYS THE BEST APPROACH?

Much of the initial crisis communication research suggests that organizations should provide clear and consistent messages to stakeholders as quickly as possible after crises (Marconi, 1992; Schuetz, 1990; Seeger, 1986). Although this can be good advice, we now know that when responding to some types of crises this recommendation is not always practical or even advisable. Organizations that communicate too quickly with too much certainty often must later retract their public comments. Public statements recorded by the media and noted by stakeholders can subsequently be used against an organization. We believe that, in their initial public statements, organizations can interject some level of ambiguity or uncertainty that will enable them to both communicate with their public and emphasize the level of uncertainty they are experiencing at the time—in effect, a more accurate reflection of the situation.

Peter Sandman (2004), a risk and crisis communication consultant, examined some successful and unsuccessful responses to the 2004 outbreak of avian flu in Asia, which was a devastating crisis for poultry farmers. During the crisis, various government and public health organizations were asked to comment on whether the avian flu could mutate into and become as infectious as ordinary human flu. Sandman explains that Bob Dietz, a WHO spokesperson, communicated effectively by acknowledging the uncertainty of the crisis when he confirmed that a Vietnamese woman's bird flu virus contained no human influenza genes. Dietz explained, "The results are encouraging, but unfortunately, they are still not the conclusive proof we need to fully discount the possibility of human-to-human transmission of

LESSON 7

Avoid certain or absolute answers to the public and media, until sufficient information is available.

the virus" (p. 46). Conversely, when asked if the bird flu had spread to Thailand, Thai Prime Minister Thaksin Shinawatra responded, "It's not a big deal. If it's bird flu, it's bird flu. We can handle it. . . . We have been working very hard. . . . Please trust the government. It did not make an announcement in the very beginning because it did not want the public to panic" (p. 46). Sandman argues that the language in the second example is too certain and borders on overreassuring the public that there will not be a problem. Organizations must be able to communicate what they know at the time. As a result, there will be times when they must say, "We do not know anything yet; however, this is what we are doing regarding our crisis investigation." At times, because accurate information is not always available, it is justifiable to say, "We do not know."

BE CAREFUL OF OVERREASSURING YOUR STAKEHOLDERS

Making sure the organization does not overreassure audiences about the risk or impact of a crisis is consistent with discussions about communicating uncertainty and certainty about a crisis. A common misconception about crisis communication is that when a crisis hits, the public will panic and respond with mass hysteria. Research on crisis, at this point, suggests that this is generally not the case (e.g., Quarantelli, 1988). In fact, the opposite is often true. Most of the examples in the literature suggest that people behave extremely well during crisis. No doubt, people will take protective actions for themselves, but for the most part, they act in a rational manner. Barbara Reynolds (2002), CDC spokesperson, explains that "the condition most conducive to panic isn't bad news; it is conflicting messages from those in authority" (p. 24). In this case, when the public believes that they cannot trust those in authority or that information is being hidden from them, the level of perceived threat is likely to increase substantially.

LESSON 8

Do not overreassure stakeholders about the impact the crisis will have on them.

TELL YOUR STAKEHOLDERS HOW TO PROTECT THEMSELVES

The public most often looks for statements that will give it something to ensure its safety. That being the case, organizations should not overreassure; rather, they should focus on self-efficacy—showing people how to protect themselves from the effects of the crisis.

Information communicated to stakeholders about how to protect themselves—self-efficacy—should be useful and practical and should suit their divergent needs. Barbara Reynolds (2002) suggests that crisis communicators should give minimum, middle, and maximum responses. For example, to protect oneself from impure drinking water, she suggests, "(1) Use chlorine drops if safety is uncertain, (2) boil water for 2 minutes, or (3) buy bottled water. We recommend boiling water" (p. 24). In this case, people are given information and alternatives about how to protect themselves.

> **LESSON 9**
>
> The public needs useful and practical statements of self-efficacy during a crisis.

We believe that self-efficacy messages should be valid, useful, and instructive in actually protecting stakeholders from potential risk. Instructions provided to the public by the DHS on using plastic and duct tape to seal windows and doors for protection during a terrorist attack were not very effective. However, in cases like the 1997 North Dakota floods, when the public was actively involved in sandbagging dikes to keep homes in the Red River Valley safe, including the public in a crisis response was not only necessary but proved to be an effective and renewing approach for many citizens of Fargo and Grand Forks, North Dakota, and Moorhead and East Grand Forks, Minnesota (see Chapter 6 and Sellnow, Seeger, & Ulmer, 2002).

We suggest a counterintuitive approach to crisis communication: Rather than immediately responding to questions concerning a crisis with certainty to prevent the public from panicking, we advocate that, due to the uncertainty of crisis, an organization's communication should carry with it a level of ambiguity or uncertainty. In this case, we advocate against using absolute answers or overreassuring the public until adequate information is available. In addition, once an organization communicates statements of self-efficacy after a crisis, it is one step closer to using stakeholders as a resource. However, even statements of self-efficacy should include levels of ambiguity that represent the low, moderate, and high levels of concern of organizational stakeholders.

REDUCING AND INTENSIFYING UNCERTAINTY BEFORE, DURING, AND AFTER ORGANIZATIONAL CRISES

A SUMMARY OF RESEARCH AND PRACTICE IN CRISIS COMMUNICATION AND GENERATING RENEWAL

Through extensive case study analysis and research, we have developed some ways that organizations may intensify or reduce crisis ambiguity and uncertainty. The communication strategies discussed in this chapter suggest a communication process approach to preparing for and communicating during and after a crisis. Effective precrisis communication practices include establishing strong positive leadership virtues and core values from which to make crisis decisions. Exhibiting open and honest communication with stakeholders before a crisis develops goodwill among these groups, which can serve to reduce uncertainty at the onset of a crisis. Finally, organizations that set forth a crisis plan, and in particular illustrate commitment to developing a reservoir of goodwill and commitment to their stakeholders, are more able to communicate effectively during a crisis. In this case, precrisis effective communication strategies include the following:

Strong positive leadership values and goals

Open and honest communication with stakeholders

A commitment to stakeholders and developing a reservoir of goodwill

Conversely, before a crisis, organizations can take part in activities that we predict will actually intensify the levels of ambiguity and uncertainty at the onset of a crisis. First, if there are poor communication relationships with stakeholders within or outside the organization, ambiguity and uncertainty are likely to be intensified after a crisis. Organizations should pay particular attention to superior–subordinate communication and the relationships with external stakeholders as well. Second, organizations that distance aggravated stakeholders and their needs are more likely to experience heightened ambiguity and uncertainty following a crisis. Third, organizations that communicate to engineer consent from their internal or external stakeholders rather than listening to the needs of their stakeholders are likely to experience heightened ambiguity or uncertainty during a crisis. Finally, organizations that do not take part in any simulations or crisis planning are more likely to communicate ineffectively during a crisis. In this case, predictors of ineffective precrisis communication include:

Poor communication relationships with stakeholders

Distance from aggravated stakeholders

Failure to listen to stakeholder needs

Failure to plan for a crisis

During a crisis, there are key communication strategies that are recognized as being useful to reducing the affects of crisis-induced uncertainty and ambiguity. For instance, having a mission statement and core values to inform your crisis decision making is instrumental to reducing uncertainty. Having established positive stakeholder relationships to lean on during a crisis can help reduce uncertainty and improve communication as well. Organizations that have conducted risk assessments and taken provisions to manage those risks are less likely to experience crisis uncertainty. James Lee Witt (Witt & Morgan, 2002) explains "communication when it's working can help you know when a crisis is coming sometimes early enough to prevent it" (p. 46). Organizations that provide continual and consistent updates on the crisis recovery process are able to reduce uncertainty and ambiguity for their key stakeholders. Finally, organizations that communicate openly and honestly have a better ability to reduce crisis-induced uncertainty more effectively. Crisis communication strategies that create effective communication practices include the following:

Using core values and crisis communication goals developed precrisis to guide your response

Providing consistent updates on the recovery process

Communicating openly and honestly

Organizations that stonewall or say "no comment" are likely to intensify ambiguity or uncertainty during a crisis. Not having a crisis plan or strong value positions in place is also likely to increase uncertainty. Not knowing who to call or what to say is central to increased uncertainty and ambiguity during a crisis. Communication that serves to minimize the crisis or overreassure stakeholders that the impact of the crisis will be small often serves instead to augment crisis uncertainty. Finally, communication with certainty about complex issues surrounding a crisis has the ability to create more uncertainty during a crisis. Crisis communication strategies that minimize crisis communication effectiveness following a crisis include:

Saying "no comment"

Not knowing whom to call or having established values to base your response on

Overreassuring about the impact of the crisis

Communicating with certainty about the crisis

Finally, postcrisis communication is not effective when an organization tries to spin the crisis in its favor to reduce responsibility. In this case, an organization may try to obscure blame, diminish its role in the crisis, or complicate the evidence surrounding responsibility for the crisis. Beyond being unethical, these communication tactics are unwise, heighten crisis uncertainty, and delay crisis recovery. In this case, ineffective postcrisis communication involves:

Spinning responsibility for the crisis

Obscuring blame

Conversely, organizations that emphasize learning from the crisis and ethical communication through freedom of access to information and open and honest communication and that provide a prospective vision for recovery are more likely to be able to reduce uncertainty postcrisis and generate a more effective renewing response. Postcrisis communication designed to reduce uncertainty and ambiguity involves the following:

Learning from the crisis

Communicating ethically and openly about responsibility

Providing a prospective vision for recovery

This section suggests effective and ineffective communication strategies before, during, and after a crisis. The decisions an organization's leadership makes will have a profound impact on the effectiveness of the crisis response and the amount of uncertainty stakeholders experience. Making good choices about how to prepare for, manage, and resolve a crisis can do much to help an organization recover from a crisis and create opportunities for future growth. What follows is a discussion about the potential opportunities associated with crises.

SOCIAL MEDIA AND EFFECTIVE CRISIS COMMUNICATION

Social media, such as Twitter, Facebook, YouTube, instant messaging, and blogging, are essential tools for effective crisis communication. Sherman (2010) explains that monitoring and using social media can be beneficial to crisis communicators. She explains how social media can be used:

Monitor what is being said about your company

Anticipate potential crises

Communicate to stakeholders during a crisis

Organizations can use Internet tools to track tweets and discussions of their organization's names through free sites like Google Trends, TweetBeep, and Social Mention. In Chapter 4, we examine the case of Domino's Pizza, which emphasizes the important role of using Internet tools to anticipate crises. In this case, two employees had made a prank YouTube video that depicted unsanitary food handling practices. Domino's Pizza was unaware of the crisis because they were not monitoring social media. Organizations are also able to see problems brewing long in advance if they monitor this media and take action to correct problems when they see negative comments or complaints before they become larger problems. Organizations that monitor social media are better prepared to anticipate potential crises and are better able to stay connected with stakeholders that prefer this mode of communication.

Sherman (2010) suggests the following advice for preventing small issues from becoming crises:

Acknowledge the issue, and apologize for the mistake

Publicly explain that the issue will be fixed immediately and that everyone will be notified when the issue is resolved

Privately message people who had tweeted about the problem, and assure them that the problem is being resolved

Publicly address those who cannot be reached privately by referencing them with the @ sign and their Twitter name with a personal explanation

Not every instance may demand a response such as this. In addition, we do not recommend admitting fault when you have not made an error. However, in those times that you have made a mistake, it is best to solve the problem as quickly as possible and notify the frustrated stakeholders when the problem is resolved. In this case, social media provide useful channels to address potential issues before they become problems. However, without close monitoring of these channels, organizations are likely to miss the opportunity to address potential problems in advance.

During a crisis, social media can be used to provide consistent updates and information to crisis stakeholders. Blogs, tweets, instant messages, and Facebook pages can be used to keep people up to date about the crisis and can also be used to collect information about solutions that may rectify the crisis. In the previously discussed Domino's case, the company initially responded to the hoax with traditional media releases that did not reduce the intensity or impact of the crisis. It was not until Domino's responded to the hoax via YouTube and created a Twitter account to communicate about the crisis that the crisis moved toward resolution. This example again illustrates the necessity for organizations to take social media seriously in their crisis communications.

Social media should be considered as part of any crisis communication response. However, sound crisis communication theory should be used to focus the content of the messages being delivered through social media. In other words, incorporate the lessons previously described in this chapter and the theories discussed in Chapter 2. For instance, Stracener (2012) interviewed six leading experts in social media and crisis response from public and private industries. His research findings found that these experts were not yet using theory to develop the content of their social media messages. Rather, they were emphasizing getting hits on their websites and retweets over the content of the messages being used on social media. If social media is going to be effective in crisis communication, there needs to be a closer connection between the theory and practice of crisis communication. Doing so can create unexpected opportunities for effective crisis communication. Sherman (2010) explains "every criticism now has the potential to become an opportunity to connect more closely with customers. . . . When a crisis does occur, social media can offer monitoring and communication solutions to disseminate information at a more rapid rate than most traditional media" (para. 27). Clearly, social media combined with strategies for effective crisis communication have the potential to lessen the impact or even prevent a crisis from happening. What follows are some additional positive results that can be achieved from effective crisis communication.

THE POWER OF POSITIVE THINKING

Knowing how to frame events is one of the most important strategies an organization can employ to move beyond a crisis. We have found that when an organization is able to think about the positive potential rather than the negative aspects of a crisis, it is better able to move beyond the event. Crises do offer opportunities for renewal and future growth. Many organizations frame crises in terms of alleviating responsibility and shifting the blame to other organizations. They also frame a crisis in terms of it being a terrible tragedy for the organization and its members. Organizations that are able to frame crises in more optimistic terms are better able to move beyond them. Thinking about the potential positive aspects of a crisis focuses an organization on moving beyond the event and provides a positive direction toward which organizational members can work. Meyers and Holusha (1986) discuss seven potential positive results that can come from a crisis:

1. Heroes are born.

2. Change is accelerated.

3. Latent problems are faced.

4. People are changed.

5. New strategies evolve.

6. Early warning systems develop.

7. New competitive advantages appear.

Meyers and Holusha (1986) suggest that leaders who manage crises effectively can be viewed as heroes. Clearly, Rudolph Giuliani, New York City mayor during the September 11, 2001, terrorist attacks, was viewed as a hero because of his effective response to the crisis. Change can be accelerated following a crisis, because money is typically made available, and people can clearly see the need for change. Latent problems are faced because these are typically the ones that created the crisis in the first place. People can be changed, because they now see the impact their faulty belief structures had on the organization and its effectiveness. New strategies evolve, because the organization must develop new approaches to doing business in order to move beyond the crisis. Early warning systems develop so that the organization will be better able to foresee and manage a potential future crisis. Last, new competitive advantages can appear after a crisis, because the entire nature of business may change. For instance, after 9/11, the airline industry became much different. Where large airlines dominated the market before 9/11, small niche market airlines, such as Southwest Airlines, Jet Blue, and Song, are now having the greatest success. Only time will tell how long this competitive advantage will remain. Effective crisis communication, then, involves being positive and thinking about the potential positive aspects of crisis while dealing with the event. When thinking positively, organizations have the ability to frame the event in a positive way for stakeholders.

LESSON 10

Effective crisis communicators acknowledge that positive factors can arise from organizational crises.

SUMMARY

This chapter examined effective crisis communication based on best practices in the field of crisis communication. We examined the role of listening in effective crisis communication, the need to understand the variety of audiences that an organization will face in a crisis and what these audiences want to hear, the role of certainty in crisis communication, and the power of positive thinking and its effect on moving beyond a crisis.

The next chapter illustrates how leaders can enact and employ the lessons from this chapter. Good luck with the case studies in the next chapter.

Lessons on Communicating Effectively in Crisis Situations

Lesson 1:   Determine your goals for crisis communication.

Lesson 2:   Before a crisis, develop true equal partnerships with organizations and groups that are important to the organization.

Lesson 3:   Acknowledge your stakeholders, including the media, as partners when managing a crisis.

Lesson 4:   Organizations need to develop strong, positive primary and secondary stakeholder relationships.

Lesson 5:   Effective crisis communication involves listening to your stakeholders.

Lesson 6:   Communicate early about the crisis, acknowledge uncertainty, and assure the public that you will maintain contact with them about current and future risk.

Lesson 7:   Avoid certain or absolute answers to the public and media until sufficient information is available.

Lesson 8:   Do not overreassure stakeholders about the impact the crisis will have on them.

Lesson 9:   The public needs useful and practical statements of self-efficacy during a crisis.

Lesson 10: Effective crisis communicators acknowledge that positive factors can arise from organizational crises.

REFERENCES

Beltway sniper attacks. (n.d.). Retrieved from http://www.answers.com

Dutta, M. J. (2007). Communicating about culture and health: Theorizing culture-centered and cultural sensitivity approaches. *Communication Theory, 17,* 304–328.

Heath, R. L. (1997). *Strategic issues management: Organizations and public policy challenges.* Thousand Oaks, CA: Sage.

Marconi, J. (1992). *Crisis marketing: When bad things happen to good companies.* Chicago, IL: Probus.

Meyers, G. C., & Holusha, J. (1986). *When it hits the fan: Managing the nine crises of business.* Boston, MA: Houghton Mifflin.

Pooley, E. (2001). Rudy Giuliani. *Time.* Retrieved from http://www.time.com/time/subscriber/personoftheyear/archive/stories/2001.html

Quarantelli, E. I. (1988). Disaster crisis management: A summary of research findings. *Journal of Management Studies, 25,* 273–385.

Reynolds, B. (2002). *Crisis and emergency risk communication.* Atlanta, GA: Centers for Disease Control and Prevention.

Sandman, P. (2004). *Crisis communication: Avian flu exercise: What are they doing?* Retrieved from http://www.psandman.com

Schuetz, J. (1990). Corporate advocacy as argumentation. In R. Trapp & J. Schuetz (Eds.), *Perspectives on argumentation* (pp. 272–284). Prospect Heights, IL: Waveland.

Seeger, M. W. (1986). The Challenger tragedy and search for legitimacy. *Central States Speech Journal, 37,* 147–157.

Sellnow, T. L., Seeger, M. W., & Ulmer, R. R. (2002). Chaos theory, informational needs, and natural disasters. *Journal of Applied Communication Research, 30,* 269–292.

Sherman, A. (2010). *Using social media for crisis communication.* Retrieved from http://www.iabc.com/cwb/archive/2010/0210/Sherman.htm

Stracener, M. (2012). *Social media and public health: Are we using theory to guide practice?* Doctoral Dissertation, University of Arkansas Medical Sciences, Little Rock.

Witt, J. L., & Morgan, G. (2002). *Stronger in broken places: Nine lessons for turning crisis into triumph.* New York, NY: Times Books.

Applying the Lessons to Produce Effective Crisis Communication

fter examining the 10 lessons for effective crisis communication, it is time to work on building your effective crisis communication skills. The following cases are designed to help the reader identify and discuss each of the key lessons described and discussed in the previous chapter. Following each case the reader is asked to make a determination about whether the crisis communicators were effective or ineffective. This chapter contains seven real-life cases that examine lessons on effective crisis communication. The first case provides a detailed account of BP and the United States Coast Guard's communication following BP's 2010 oil spill in the Gulf of Mexico. The second case, examines Aaron Feuerstein's crisis communication following a 1995 fire at his textile manufacturing plant in Methuen, Massachusetts. The third case, discusses a food-borne illness outbreak at Odwalla Inc., a beverage company known for its health conscious products. The fourth case describes the communication following the terrorist attack at Oklahoma City. The fifth case examines Greensburg Kansas' response to when a tornado destroyed their town in 2007. The sixth case examines a crisis that played out of social media when Domino's Pizza was blindsided by a hoax online by two of its employees. Good luck with working through these cases while developing your crisis communication skills and experience at the same time!

EXAMPLE 4.1. THE LARGEST ENVIRONMENTAL CRISIS IN UNITED STATES HISTORY: BP AND THE UNITED STATES COAST GUARD RESPOND

On April 20, 2010, at approximately 10:00 PM CDT there was an explosion on the mobile offshore drilling unit Deepwater Horizon located in the Gulf of Mexico. The semisubmersible oil rig was leased and operated by BP Exploration and Production. The explosion caused a fire on the oil rig. Shortly after the initial fire, a second explosion capsized the oil rig. The Deepwater Horizon settled 1500 feet northwest of the well site. The explosion resulted in the deaths of 11 crewmembers; 115 workers were safely rescued. The Deepwater Horizon was severely damaged from the explosions, fire, and resulting collapse into the Gulf of Mexico. Oil began to immediately gush into the gulf. Three weeks after the explosion the National Oceanic and Atmospheric Administration (NOAA) estimated 210,000 to 2,520,000 gallons of oil was released into the gulf every day. Several weeks after the crisis began, CNN put a video camera at the bottom of the gulf to show the amount of oil entering the water and televised it 24 hours a day. Ultimately it would take 87 days to cap the oil rig.

The response to the environmental crisis was complex due to the scope of the crisis, the coordination necessary among stakeholders and regulatory agencies, the difficulties and complexities associated in capping the oil rig, and the global attention that the environmental crisis attracted. The crisis communication was coordinated when the United States Coast Guard, the regulatory authority, and the Bureau of Energy Management formed a partnership with BP, the responsible party to respond to the crisis. The United States Coast Guard and BP were supported by 15 federal agencies including the Department of Homeland Security, the Department of the Interior, the Fish and Wildlife Service, the National Institute for Occupational Safety and Health, and the U.S. Department of Agriculture to name a few. A Unified Area Command (UAC) managed the entire response. The UAC was comprised of four sectors. Each sector reported to the UAC. A critical part of the unified command structure is Public Information Officers (PIOs). PIOs are charged with gathering and disseminating information to stakeholders during a crisis. They respond to media requests, craft messages for stakeholders, and coordinate communication among various agencies in the unified command structure. It is a complex communication job that is essential to an effective response and recovery operation during any type of crisis. Effective crisis communication skills are necessary for any public information officer.

United States Coast Guard fire boats battle fire on Deepwater Horizon oil rig

SOURCE: U.S. Coast Guard photo.

Pyle (2011) interviewed several PIOs from the United States Coast Guard and BP involved in the response and recovery operations during the Deepwater Horizon crisis. The PIOs had keen insight into the communication that took place during the crisis. The PIOs reported that they wished they had developed a unified communication plan or approach before the crisis or very early on during the event. However, the PIOs reported many goals or objectives in their crisis communication. Some PIOs explained that their goal was to get information out quickly, others tried to correct misinformation, while others suggested their goal was transparency. Other PIOs considered staying out in front of the crisis their primary goal.

Although many of the PIOs were brought into the crisis from many parts of the country and the world to support the massive communication needs during the crisis, they reported establishing relationships with stakeholders as critical to their response. They explained that working on functioning and developing collaboration within the ICS was critical to the unified command (Pyle, 2011). PIOs explained that the media, local communities, elected officials, the seafood industry, and frontline responders were all critical stakeholders during the crisis. To engage these stakeholders, they held open houses, created opportunities for stakeholders to come to the incident command center for tours and to meet with subject matter experts to discuss wide-ranging topics related to the crisis.

A primary stakeholder for the PIOs was the media. The global media attention for this crisis was intense. PIOs suggested that the media was important to their crisis communication because they were the primary way to get messages out to their stakeholders. However, they also discussed challenges in meeting the constant onslaught of media requests, the often aggressive questioning and demands for access, along with the divergent types of information requests they needed to respond to. They reported doing their absolute best to meet the needs of the media during the crisis. Although not perfect, PIOs provided unprecedented access to the crisis site and to key decision makers in the crisis. They reported being as accessible as possible, transparent, and did their best to correct misinformation in the media. However, the waves of media requests, the dynamic nature of the crisis, and the considerable amount of media made perfection difficult.

The PIOs reported providing as much information as possible to media and stakeholders about the crisis. In cases when they did not know the answer, they explained that they did not know. Some went further by working to try to find out the answer at a later time. However, the amount of questions and requests and changing nature of the crisis complicated the communication process. Several PIOs expressed that they should have countered media accounts that they felt were incorrect or were sensational. A large portion felt that their listening skills were essential to the crisis communication process. They explained that rather than speculating what information people needed they tried to listen and respond to the actual informational needs of their stakeholders. At times, this meant providing the information they had on hand at the time rather than speculating in their response. This was particularly true when discussing with response and recovery workers about any concerns they had about their health and safety during the crisis. The PIOs reported doing their best to meet the needs of their stakeholders by having Subject Matter Experts (SME) and health professionals answer questions for stakeholders in a clear and informative manner. This information was mostly conducted face-to-face. Other information about the crisis was most often provided in media releases, interviews, and through the website, http://restorethegulf.gov. The PIOs explained that they wanted to be more proactive in their communication. By being proactive they could have provided more information about the cleanup process and discussed in more depth the engineering feats that were ultimately developed to cap the oil rig.

YOU MAKE THE CALL

After examining this case, it is time to determine how the PIOs involved in the BP oil spill communicated in the wake of the plant fire. First, take a moment to refresh in your mind the lessons established on effective crisis communication in Chapter 3. Second, note that these lessons serve as touchstones and discussion points for what we believe are key aspects of any crisis response. As you answer the questions that follow, consider whether the PIOs were effective or ineffective in their crisis communication. We have rephrased the lessons into questions so that you are better able to address the key issues in the case.

Lessons on Producing Effective Crisis Communication

Lesson 1:   Determine your goals for crisis communication.

▶ What were the reported primary goals for PIOs in their crisis communication?

Lesson 2:   Before a crisis, develop true equal partnerships with organizations and groups that are important to the organization.

▶ Had the PIOs developed partnerships with stakeholders prior to or during the crisis?

(Continued)

(Continued)

Lesson 3: Acknowledge your stakeholders, including the media, as partners when managing a crisis.

▶ Did the PIOs acknowledge stakeholders as partners in managing the crisis?

Lesson 4: Organizations need to develop strong, positive primary and secondary stakeholder relationships.

▶ Did the PIOs work toward positive relationships with primary and secondary stakeholders during the oil spill?

Lesson 5: Effective crisis communication involves listening to your stakeholders.

▶ Did the PIOs listen to or understand the needs of their stakeholders?

Lesson 6: Communicate early about the crisis, acknowledge uncertainty, and assure the public that you will maintain contact with them about current and future risk.

▶ Did the PIOs communicate regularly with stakeholders about the crisis?

Lesson 7: Avoid certain or absolute answers to the public and media until sufficient information is available.

▶ Did the PIOs communicate certain or absolute answers about the crisis?

Lesson 8: Do not overreassure stakeholders about the impact the crisis will have on them.

▶ Did the PIOs overreassure stakeholders about the impact of the crisis?

Lesson 9: The public needs useful and practical statements of self-efficacy during a crisis.

▶ Did the PIOs provide statements of self-efficacy following the crisis?

Lesson 10: Effective crisis communicators acknowledge that positive factors can arise from organizational crises.

▶ Did the PIOs acknowledge positive factors that resulted during the crisis?

SUMMARY

The BP oil spill was the largest response and recovery operation to an environmental disaster in United States history. The United States Coast Guard and BP coordinated the crisis communication for the event. This unusual and unprecedented relationship created a unique response and recovery operation that necessitated effective communication and coordination throughout the crisis. The PIOs who responded to the crisis experienced high demands for information, an often hostile and demanding communication context, and answers that were highly scientific and uncertain. The PIOs reported high levels of exhaustion during the crisis and expressed that future PIOs should monitor their rest and stress levels when engaging in crisis communication over an extended period of time.

EXAMPLE 4.2. A PLANT FIRE AT MALDEN MILLS

Malden Mills is a textile manufacturing plant located in Methuen, Massachusetts. The company has operated in the Merrimack Valley for over a century and is one of the few textile mills still located in New England, because many of the other mills have left the area because of high wages and unions. However, Malden Mills has remained steadfast in its commitment to the community and pays some of the highest wages in the industry, providing much of the economic base for the area because it employs roughly 3,000 people. At the time of the fire, the company was privately owned by Aaron Feuerstein and had previously been owned by his father and his grandfather before that. The organization had been in the Feuerstein family for close to 100 years.

Aaron Feuerstein in front of Malden Mills

SOURCE: © Rick Friedman/Corbis.

CRISIS PREPARATION AND PLANNING

The Feuerstein family had focused on developing strong relationships with their employees and customers. Feuerstein describes his leadership values as "sensitivity to the human equation" (Ulmer, 2001, p. 599). Paul Coorey, president of the local union, described Feuerstein as "fair and compassionate" and explained that he felt Feuerstein believed "that if you pay people a fair amount of money, and give them good benefits to take care of their families, they will produce for you" (Ulmer, 2001, p. 599).

Feuerstein illustrated his belief in treating workers fairly during the 1980s, when the company filed for bankruptcy. At the time, Malden Mills was selling fur and in the process of developing Polartec. Feuerstein went to the union to request layoffs until the company could return to profitability. In addition, Feuerstein promised that he would rehire those he laid off when the company returned to profitability. Many employees took that promise seriously and did not even look for other work. Feuerstein kept his promises and hired back all the workers whom he laid off during the bankruptcy.

Beyond the workforce, Feuerstein also contributed to the community in which he operated. He sponsored job training programs, English-as-a-second-language programs, and generous lines of credit to local businesses. One owner of a local company explained Feuerstein's character by saying, "That's the kind of guy Aaron is. . . . If he's got half a loaf of bread, he is going to share it around" (Ulmer, 2001, p. 598). When a local synagogue caught fire, Feuerstein and his brother stepped forward and contributed $2 million to the rebuilding efforts. Over the years, Feuerstein consistently worked to establish strong relationships with his workers and the community.

COURAGEOUS COMMUNICATION IN THE WAKE OF A DISASTER

On December 11, 1995, the evening of Feuerstein's 70th birthday, his plant erupted into flames, burning for several days. Feuerstein immediately notified workers that he was going to rebuild the plant and keep it in Methuen and that he would pay workers full salaries and health benefits for 30 days while the plant was being rebuilt. He extended this benefit in total for 60 days and extended health benefits for 90 days or until the plant was rebuilt.

Within a day, the *Boston Globe* announced that "with one of his buildings still burning behind him, the 69-year-old owner of Malden Mills . . . spoke the words everyone in the Merrimack Valley wanted to hear" (Milne & Aucoin, 1995, p. B1). Feuerstein declared that "we are going to continue to contribute in Lawrence. . . . We had the opportunity to run to the south many years ago. We didn't do it then and we're not going to do it now" (Milne & Aucoin, 1995, p. B1).

Three days after the fire, Feuerstein held a meeting at a local high school. At this time, he declared that "at least for the next 30 days—the time might be longer—all hourly employees will be paid their full salaries" (Milne, 1995, p. B50). One month after the crisis, Feuerstein met with workers again. At this time he announced,

> I am happy to announce to you that we will once again—for at least 30 days more—pay all of our employees. And why am I doing it? I consider the employees standing in front of me here the most valuable asset that Malden Mills has. I don't consider them as some companies do as an expense that can be cut. What I am doing today will come back tenfold and it will make Malden Mills the best company in the industry. (Calo, 1996)

Over the remainder of the crisis, Feuerstein consistently met with workers and paid salaries and benefits. Two months after the crisis, 70% of workers were back on the job. At that time, Feuerstein agreed to pay salaries and benefits for the remaining 800 workers for another 30 days. At the end of this time, he paid health insurance for an additional 90 days for those still not back at the company and promised jobs for those unemployed, similar to his actions in the 1980s.

YOU MAKE THE CALL

After examining this case, it is time to determine how Aaron Feuerstein communicated in the wake of the plant fire. First, take a moment to refresh in your mind the lessons established on effective crisis communication in Chapter 3. Second, note that these lessons serve as touchstones and discussion points for what we believe are key aspects of any crisis response. As you answer the questions that follow, consider whether Aaron Feuerstein was effective or ineffective in his crisis communication. We have rephrased the lessons into questions so that you are better able to address the key issues in the case.

Lessons on Producing Effective Crisis Communication

Lesson 1:   Determine your goals for crisis communication.

▶ What were Aaron Feuerstein's primary goals in his crisis communication?

Lesson 2:   Before a crisis, develop true equal partnerships with organizations and groups that are important to the organization.

▶ How did Aaron Feuerstein develop partnerships with stakeholders prior to the crisis?

Lesson 3:   Acknowledge your stakeholders, including the media, as partners when managing a crisis.

▶ In what ways did Aaron Feuerstein acknowledge his stakeholders as partners in managing the crisis?

Lesson 4:   Organizations need to develop strong, positive primary and secondary stakeholder relationships.

▶ In what ways did Aaron Feuerstein work toward positive relationships with primary and secondary stakeholders following the fire?

Lesson 5:   Effective crisis communication involves listening to your stakeholders.

▶ What evidence is there that Aaron Feuerstein listened to or understood the needs of his stakeholders?

Lesson 6:   Communicate early about the crisis, acknowledge uncertainty, and assure the public that you will maintain contact with them about current and future risk.

▶ How and how often did Aaron Feuerstein communicate to stakeholders about the crisis?

Lesson 7:   Avoid certain or absolute answers to the public and media until sufficient information is available.

▶ Did Aaron Feuerstein communicate certain or absolute answers about the cause of the crisis?

Lesson 8:   Do not overreassure stakeholders about the impact the crisis will have on them.

▶ Is there evidence that Aaron Feuerstein overreassured stakeholders about the impact of the crisis?

Lesson 9:   The public needs useful and practical statements of self-efficacy during a crisis.

▶ How did Aaron Feuerstein provide statements of self-efficacy following the crisis?

Lesson 10:   Effective crisis communicators acknowledge that positive factors can arise from organizational crises.

▶ In what ways did Aaron Feuerstein acknowledge positive factors that could arise as a result of the plant fire?

SUMMARY

Aaron Feuerstein was universally praised for his compassionate response to the 1995 plant fire at Malden Mills. President Clinton commended Mr. Feuerstein's crisis communication in his State of the Union Address. In addition, Malden Mills received donations from around the world for several years after the fire. At the time of the crisis, Aaron Feuerstein appeared to be less concerned about the cause of the crisis or responsibility and more concerned with those most impacted by the crisis: his employees and the community. After the fire, Feuerstein communicated immediately and worked to move beyond the crisis. He gave his workers and the community hope and faith that the company would overcome this crisis. In addition, he was able to solidify and further develop the stakeholder relationships he had worked so hard to establish before the fire.

EXAMPLE 4.3. LONG-TERM COMPLEXITIES IN THE TAINTED ODWALLA APPLE JUICE CRISIS

Odwalla, a producer of juice and other products intended for health-conscious consumers, began a long and complicated process of crisis recovery on October 30, 1996. On that date, the company was notified of a link between its unpasteurized apple juice and an outbreak of *E. coli*. Odwalla voluntarily began a recall immediately on learning of the problem and willingly expanded its recall to include 12 other juices. Sadly, despite these efforts, the outbreak eventually took the life of a 16-month-old girl and seriously sickened 60 other children. In response to the crisis, Odwalla made substantial changes, pledging to make consumer safety foremost in its production processes. Many observers lauded this immediate response. In fact, Odwalla retained 80% of its accounts in the wake of the crisis ("Odwalla, Inc.," 1997).

CHALLENGES FOR MULTIPLE STAKEHOLDERS

Odwalla's crisis response, which we detail below, had a profound impact on a variety of stakeholders (Reierson, Sellnow, & Ulmer, 2009). Prior to the crisis, producers assumed that the acid in juice products would naturally destroy bacteria such as *E. coli* without pasteurization. The Odwalla outbreak inspired major changes in this way of thinking. New pasteurization techniques requiring additional equipment became the norm in the industry. Not all producers could afford such equipment. Odwalla's investors also shared in the loss mightily during the company's long and costly recovery. In addition, the recall and subsequent investigation led to layoffs—causing financial hardship for many employees. Keep these stakeholders in mind as you read the following description of Odwalla's response to its *E. coli* crisis.

ODWALLA'S CRISIS RESPONSE

From the start, Odwalla displayed a clear and impressive commitment to its customers. In addition to voluntarily recalling products and shutting down operations, Odwalla opened new lines of communication with its customers. The company launched a website dedicated to the crisis within 24 hours and created two 1-800 telephone numbers for customers and suppliers to call. Odwalla's message to consumers was clear, consistent, and compassionate. The company shared its regret for the incident and offered refunds to those who had recently purchased its products. Odwalla also offered to pay medical costs for illnesses resulting from their contaminated juice (Martinelli & Briggs, 1998). Odwalla's chairperson at the time of the crisis, Greg Steltenpohl, visited family members of sickened children and publicly acknowledged the pain and suffering the crisis had caused (Thomsen & Rawson, 1998). When the lone death caused by the crisis occurred, the company issued a press release offering condolences to her family.

The new pasteurization process at Odwalla

SOURCE: Photo courtesy of The Creamery at Pineland Farms.

Within 2 months of the crisis, Odwalla announced a revolutionary change in the production of fresh juice products. The company introduced flash pasteurization as a technique it insisted would destroy *E. coli* bacteria while maintaining much of the flavor and nutritional value that was present in its unpasteurized products (Martinelli & Briggs, 1998). Odwalla has not experienced another major recall since adopting flash pasteurization in 1996.

IMPACT ON STAKEHOLDERS

As mentioned at the outset of this case study, Odwalla was able to maintain the majority of its accounts after the crisis. The *Wall Street Journal* quoted one public relations and crisis specialist who proclaimed that Odwalla's "core principles have brought them back to probably one of the quickest recoveries in history" (Moore, 1998, para. 15). This recovery was not without cost for some of Odwalla's stakeholders. Small operators in the juice industry, investors, and some Odwalla employees all suffered during and after Odwalla's crisis response.

At the time of the crisis, Odwalla was a relatively large producer in the fresh juice industry. Consequently, the company had the financial wherewithal to retool its facility with flash pasteurization equipment. Not all producers could afford this advancement. Once Odwalla announced it was using flash pasteurization, some grocery store chains such as Safeway were no longer willing to accept juice from others unless they too adopted flash pasteurization (Martinelli & Briggs, 1998). Small operators who did undertake flash pasteurization were forced to raise their prices, thereby diminishing their competitiveness (De Lisser, 1998).

Odwalla's investors were also hurt by the crisis. Odwalla spent money aggressively during its recovery despite plummeting profits. In addition, Odwalla was fined more than a million dollars for the crisis ("Odwalla pleads," 1998). As Reierson et al. (2009) observe, "although Odwalla's actions might have been good business practice in the long run, immediately following the crisis investors were left with little to show for their original investment" (p. 122).

Odwalla's employees also suffered during the crisis. Sixty Odwalla employees were laid off in the aftermath. Although consumers were compensated as a result of the crisis, little was done to support Odwalla's employees during the crisis recovery. Several members of Odwalla's board of directors were also replaced after the crisis.

Odwalla's crisis response was decisive and effective in returning the company to profitability in the long run. This response, however, was not without cost to at least three sets of stakeholders: small operators, investors, and employees.

YOU MAKE THE CALL

After examining this case, it is time to determine whether Odwalla communicated effectively with the stakeholders involved in the crisis. First, take a moment to refresh in your mind the lessons established in Chapter 3 for communicating effectively and ineffectively during crises. These lessons should guide you in evaluating the strengths and weaknesses of Odwalla's crisis response. As you contemplate the questions that follow, consider whether Odwalla was effective or ineffective in coping with the long-term complexities of the crisis.

Lessons on Producing Effective Crisis Communication

Lesson 1:   Determine your goals for crisis communication.

▶ Did Odwalla exemplify clear goals in its crisis communication?

Lesson 2:   Before a crisis, develop true equal partnerships with organizations and groups that are important to the organization.

▶ In what ways did Odwalla develop partnerships with stakeholders?

Lesson 3:   Acknowledge your stakeholders, including the media, as partners when managing a crisis.

▶ How did Odwalla acknowledge its stakeholders following the crisis?

Lesson 4:   Organizations need to develop strong, positive primary and secondary stakeholder relationships.

▶ Is there evidence that Odwalla established relationships with its stakeholders?

Lesson 5:   Effective crisis communication involves listening to your stakeholders.

▶ Is there evidence that Odwalla listened to its stakeholders?

Lesson 6:   Communicate early about the crisis, acknowledge uncertainty, and assure the public that you will maintain contact with them about current and future risk.

▶ In what ways did Odwalla maintain contact with the public?

Lesson 7:   Avoid certain or absolute answers to the public and media until sufficient information is available.

▶ Did Odwalla provide certain or absolute answers about the cause of the crisis?

Lesson 8:   Do not overreassure stakeholders about the impact the crisis will have on them.

▶ Did Odwalla overreassure about the impact of the crisis?

Lesson 9:   The public needs useful and practical statements of self-efficacy during a crisis.

▶ In what way did Odwalla provide statements of self-efficacy following the crisis?

Lesson 10:   Effective crisis communicators acknowledge that positive factors can arise from organizational crises.

▶ Was there evidence that positive factors could arise from this crisis?

SUMMARY

Odwalla's recovery from its *E. coli* crisis was celebrated as an exemplar of excellence in crisis communication. Indeed, Odwalla communicated early and often with its consumers, showing remorse for the crisis and offering financial compensation. A closer look at the crisis, however, reveals lingering harm to small producers in the industry. Investors unable to stay with Odwalla for the long term also suffered significant financial losses. Similarly, some employees lost their jobs, at least temporarily, causing financial stress. This case provides clear evidence of the need for organizations to consider all stakeholders for the long term when developing a crisis response.

EXAMPLE 4.4. THE OKLAHOMA CITY BOMBING

The Oklahoma City bombing, the first major terrorist event in a generation and one of the largest ever to take place on U.S. soil, was a shocking crisis for a number of reasons. It happened in the heartland, in a community many saw as isolated from any large-scale threats. The bombing was devastating to the community, severely damaging many downtown buildings and creating widespread harm. Eventually, the bombing was found to have claimed 168 lives, including several children attending day care in the Murrah Building. Timothy McVeigh and Terry Nichols were convicted of planning the bombing as a way to avenge a government siege and subsequent fire at the Branch Davidian complex in Waco, Texas.

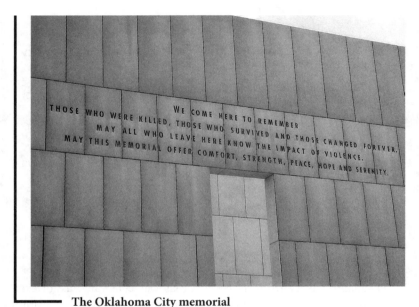

The Oklahoma City memorial

SOURCE: Photo courtesy of Paula Stout-Burke.

One of the key players in managing the response to the Oklahoma City bombing was Oklahoma Governor Frank Keating. Governor Keating, a former Federal Bureau of Investigation (FBI) agent, was first elected in 1994. After the April 19, 1995, bombing, Keating personally led the state-wide response. He was widely recognized for the effective way he handled the crisis and for his communication activities. Keating later described the event in specific terms:

> You will recall that [the] massive terror bomb was detonated at 9:02 a.m. on April 19, 1995, in front of the Alfred P. Murrah Federal Office Building in the heart of our community. It killed 168 people, injured hundreds more, and severely damaged many dozens of buildings. The rescue and recovery efforts that followed,

along with the criminal investigation, were the most massive of their kind in American history. These efforts threw together, literally overnight, more separate agencies from the local, state, and federal governments than had ever worked cooperatively on a single task. The outcome could have been chaotic—it has been before when far fewer agencies tried to coordinate their efforts on much more discrete and manageable tasks. But the outcome in Oklahoma City was not chaos. Later, observers would coin the label "The Oklahoma Standard" to refer to the way our city, state, and nation came together in response to this despicable act. (Keating, 2001, n.p.)

Keating has used the Oklahoma City bombing as an example to help generate lessons for effective crisis management. Specifically, he has described four strategies he recommends to other government leaders (Keating, 2001):

1. Train and equip your first responders, because they are the front line in meeting the terrorist threat.

2. Search for ways to support teamwork *before* an incident and emphasize that teamwork after.

3. Trust the experts to do what they know best.

4. Tell the truth, and be candid with the people we are working to protect and serve.

Regarding training first responders, Keating and many other observers point out that local first responders will be the first on the scene. It will be some time, perhaps days, before federal or other state agencies can provide significant support. Effective crisis response requires that these local first responders have the necessary skills and resources. In addition, teamwork is essential. Cooperative relationships among team members should be established long before any crisis event occurs. This includes drawing on experts who have the technical expertise to help manage an event. Team members should know one another's expertise, and there should be established procedures for coordinating and communicating. As a former FBI official, Keating's background in law enforcement helped him comprehend the situation and communicate effectively. He had personal experience dealing with many of the first-responder groups and was able to facilitate their cooperation. Last, and most important for our purposes, Keating

(2001) emphasized that the Oklahoma City bombings included many complex communication demands.

> Because the Murrah Building was located in downtown Oklahoma City for all to see, we immediately stumbled into the right answer to the eternal question, "How much do we tell the public?" That answer is simple—we tell them everything that does not need to be safeguarded for valid reasons of security. (n.p.)

Keating (2001) described his response as follows:

> Steady, 24-hour broadcasts and news dispatches came from Oklahoma City in the first days after the 1995 bombing. Our policy was to conduct regular media briefings on everything from body counts to alerts involving the composite drawings of the principal suspects in the bombing, and the results were in virtually all cases positive. Certainly many aspects of the criminal investigation were not disclosed in those early days. The Oklahoma City Fire Department and the Office of the Chief Medical Examiner carefully controlled release of information concerning the dead to ensure that families were fully notified before victim identities were made public. We did not allow open media access to the interior site itself for reasons of safety and efficiency. But in almost every other instance, our decision was in favor of openness and candor, and the results are very clear. I continue to receive letters, more than six years later, from Americans who have a permanently positive impression of how the bombing was handled. (n.p.)

Keating's open and accessible approach to the public helped ensure public cooperation and support and helped reduce the anxiety people were feeling. Through press conferences and public meetings, Keating created the impression that he was open, accessible, concerned, and shared the loss that people were feeling. He also helped convey the impression that authorities were in charge of the situation and that order was being reestablished. As he demonstrated, when leaders communicate empathy and concern, they help the community deal with the emotional aspect of the crisis. Their presence helps create a sense of order.

Governor Keating also had to address a complex set of primary and secondary stakeholders. Primary stakeholders included first-responder groups, families and friends of victims, and the immediate Oklahoma

City community. Secondary stakeholders included the entire country. Oklahoma City is a very close community, and almost everyone knew someone affected by the bombing. Paradoxically, while the closeness of the community made the crisis worse, it also gave the community additional strength to weather the crisis.

Keating worked hard to make sure first responders and other emergency workers had the necessary resources to deal with the crisis. This included cutting through bureaucratic red tape and making personal appeals to agencies for help. He even stepped in and took responsibilities from some individuals who were clearly overwhelmed by the events. His leadership was both instrumental—taking steps to help make response and recovery more efficient and effective—and symbolic, helping influence public perceptions in constructive ways.

YOU MAKE THE CALL

After examining this case, it is time to determine whether Governor Keating communicated effectively with the many stakeholders involved in the crisis. First, take a moment to refresh in your mind the lessons established in Chapter 3 on communicating effectively and ineffectively during crises. These lessons should guide you in evaluating the strengths and weaknesses of Governor Keating's crisis response. As you contemplate the questions that follow, consider whether Governor Keating was effective or ineffective in coping with the added constraints he faced during his crisis response.

Lessons on Producing Effective Crisis Communication

Lesson 1:   Determine your goals for crisis communication.
- What were the primary goals Governor Keating pursued in his communication?

Lesson 2:   Before a crisis, develop true equal partnerships with organizations and groups that are important to the organization.
- What kinds of partnerships were important to a successful response to the Oklahoma City bombings?

(Continued)

(Continued)

Lesson 3: Acknowledge your stakeholders, including the media, as partners when managing a crisis.

▶ Did Governor Keating use the media in partnership? If so, how?

Lesson 4: Organizations need to develop strong, positive primary and secondary stakeholder relationships.

▶ Who were the primary and secondary stakeholders that Governor Keating needed to address?

Lesson 5: Effective crisis communication involves listening to your stakeholders.

▶ How did Keating collect information about the crisis?

Lesson 6: Communicate early about the crisis, acknowledge uncertainty, and assure the public that you will maintain contact with them about current and future risk.

▶ What did Governor Keating do to reduce the uncertainty about the bombing?

Lesson 7: Avoid certain or absolute answers to the public and media until sufficient information is available.

▶ The Oklahoma City bombing was a very confusing and surprising situation. What were some of the unanswered questions?

Lesson 8: Do not overreassure stakeholders about the impact the crisis will have them.

▶ Did Keating overreassure about the crisis?

Lesson 9: The public needs useful and practical statements of self-efficacy during a crisis.

▶ What kind of advice could Governor Keating have offered to the public?

Lesson 10: Effective crisis communicators acknowledge that positive factors can arise from organizational crises.

▶ What kinds of positive outcomes came out of these bombings, and how could these be used to help reduce the harm?

SUMMARY

The Oklahoma City bombing was a devastating crisis for Oklahoma City and the United States. Governor Frank Keating's communication helped reduce and contain the harm caused by the crisis by facilitating coordination and cooperation among first responders. Throughout the uncertainty and stress of the crisis, Governor Keating utilized many of the best practices discussed in Chapter 3. He practiced open and honest communication with stakeholders, and his leadership and expressions of empathy and concern also helped reduce the psychological impact of the disaster.

EXAMPLE 4.5. RURAL RENEWAL AFTER A TORNADO IN GREENSBURG, KANSAS

On May 4, 2007, the roughly 1,500 residents of Greensburg, Kansas, were struck by an EF5 tornado, which killed 11 people and demolished 95% of the buildings in the city. Greensburg is located roughly 100 miles south of Wichita in south-central Kansas. The tornado was one of the largest and most violent ever recorded. Estimates suggest the tornado was 1.7 miles wide and produced winds of over 200 miles per hour. Survivors were left without

A view of the devastation in Greensburg, Kansas, following the tornado

SOURCE: Greg Henshall/FEMA/Wikimedia.

housing, running water, or electricity. The tornado literally swept away the homes, schools, and churches in Greensburg. Before the tornado, the city was known for its strong sense of community and for housing the largest hand-dug well, which served as a tourist attraction for those passing through the town. However, like many rural towns, Greensburg was slowly losing population because locals left for larger cities and children went to college never to come back. After the devastating tornado, residents of Greensburg were beginning to consider a new identity for their resilient Midwestern town.

INITIAL FRAMING OF THE CRISIS

Following the devastating tornado, there was a real sense of loss. Citizens were stunned by the impact of the tornado and were uncertain about what would happen to their community. However, almost immediately, key leaders in the community saw the potential to frame the disaster positively for its citizens. For instance, Greensburg City Administrator Steve Hewitt lost his home and everything he owned. However, he also felt the "the tornado had a silver lining, for it made this town and some 1,400 people regroup and reinvent itself" (Nguyen & Morris, 2009, para. 2). He explained further that "it forced people to make a change. It forced people to say, You know what—we have an opportunity unlike any other community gets" (Nguyen & Morris, 2009, para. 3). In this case, Steve Hewitt began to see a tabula rasa from which to recreate and reinvent the town of Greensburg.

Less than 2 days after the tornado, as the wreckage was being excavated from local buildings, School Superintendent Darren Hedrick provided a similar description to Steve Hewitt's of how Greensburg could capitalize on the effect of the disaster. He explained, "Towns are about people, they are not about buildings. And it's a huge opportunity to rebuild—not just rebuild it the way it was but maybe rebuild it a little bit better than it was" (Morris, 2007, para. 4).

These initial thoughts and communication by leaders began to instigate conversations by citizens through community forums held periodically to discuss the recovery process, including any problems or frustrations that people may be experiencing. Because most people were living in FEMA trailers and were anxious to move into more permanent housing, developing a plan for moving forward was very important. However, through community forums, people began to talk about the disaster as a way to reinvigorate the town and solve the problem of its declining population. These people hoped to "reverse the trend. To not lose the kids, but to bring our kids back. To invest back in the community so that after they graduate they can have new jobs and new opportunities" (Nguyen & Morris, 2009, para. 4). In doing so, "the tornado was something that bonded people, which . . . is a natural element of shared adversity, and the community was able to tap into that in a big way" (Phelps, 2009, para. 21).

The Greensburg city council met regularly to discuss what businesses would continue to do business in Greensburg and when they would be reopening. This group also led many of the community forums and listened to the concerns and frustrations about the uncertain future that current residents faced. However, through city council meetings and community forums, a vision of creating a green city that could be a model for the entire world of energy conservation began to emerge. Danny Wallach, who headed a nonprofit group leading the push for environmental sustainability in Greensburg, began rallying residents to consider making Greensburg an example of what an energy- and environmentally sound community could be. He explained, "I mean, it literally struck me, green—Greensburg—and at the time, I wasn't aware of just how perfect the timing in the national green movement was" (Morris, 2007, para. 14). Steve Hewitt said that Greensburg could come back stronger than ever. "Before the tornado, Greensburg was shedding 2% of its population every year. Those who left for college rarely returned to stay. It was a death by a thousand cuts" (Morris, 2007, para. 22). The leadership of the community began to see the potential and opportunity that the crisis created. Ultimately, these early visions and discussions led to the Greensburg City Council resolving that all new city buildings should meet the very highest environmental standard—LEED platinum" (Morris, 2007, para. 23).

CONSEQUENCES OF A BOLD ENVIRONMENTAL VISION FOLLOWING THE TORNADO

Steve Hewitt was thinking big after the disaster. He focused on creating "office space for new businesses, a high school and an art center designed to be LEED platinum" (Morris, 2007, para. 23). He explained that building a green community would not be easy. "Maybe it's a little bit crazy. There are only 14 platinum buildings in the country. When it's all said and done, I'd like 4 or 5 here in Greensburg" (Morris, 2007, para. 25). When word got out about the vision Greensburg had created, several unintended outcomes developed. The Discovery Channel began filming a television series called *Greensburg Eco-Town* and ultimately created a television series called *Greensburg: A Story of Community Rebuilding*, which chronicled the entire renewal process.

By 2009, Greensburg was well on its way to becoming "a green community of the future . . . making Greensburg a national model for environmentally conscious living" (Nguyen & Morris, 2009, para. 5).

▸ Greensburg developed a series of eco-homes to educate people about energy-efficient construction. The eco-homes feature ground source heating and cooling, solar hot water, and even vegetable gardens on the roofs. They are about 70% more energy efficient than the average house and have been tested for safety in the event of future tornadoes (Nguyen & Morris, 2009).

▸ Greensburg developed buildings with solid concrete, using more natural light, and installing better insulation and state-of-the-art windows.

▸ The community developed solar and wind technologies to harness power and geothermal heat.

▸ The town's John Deere dealership created a state-of-the-art facility that is energy efficient by employing oil and heat to cool its floors and wind turbines to power the building. The owner believes he will save $25,000 a year with these improvements (Nguyen & Morris, 2009).

COMMUNITY RESPONSE

It appears that Greensburg's approach to interpret the crisis as an opportunity to reinvigorate the town has been effective. School superintendent Hedrick explains, "A lot of towns are dying a slow death. We had a fork put in us pretty hard. We have to find a way to resurrect and we hope we're making good decisions to do that" (Morris, 2007). Fifteen-year-old Levi Schmidt described the recovery this way: "Before the tornado, I was not going to come back. I was going to go to college, and who knows where. This community was dying. Now I'm definitely coming back, and I know a good majority of my friends are" (Morris, 2007, para. 34). This certainly does not mean that everyone stayed following the tornado but does suggest that Greensburg is able, for the time being, to stem the tide of its decline in population. For more information on this case, take a look at the Greensburg, Kansas, website: www.greensburgks.org. The new slogan on the home page of the town's website reads *Greensburg: Better, Stronger, Greener!* (Nguyen & Morris, 2009).

YOU MAKE THE CALL

After examining this case, it is time to determine whether the leadership of Greensburg, Kansas, communicated effectively with the many stakeholders involved in the crisis. First, take a moment to refresh in your mind the lessons established in Chapter 3 on communicating effectively and ineffectively during crises. These lessons should guide you in evaluating the strengths and weaknesses of Greensburg's crisis response. As you contemplate the questions that follow, consider whether the leadership of Greensburg was effective or ineffective in coping with the added constraints it faced during its crisis response.

Lessons on Producing Effective Crisis Communication

Lesson 1: Determine your goals for crisis communication.

▶ In what ways did Greensburg leaders illustrate clear goals in their crisis communication?

Lesson 2: Before a crisis, develop true equal partnerships with organizations and groups that are important to the organization.

▶ Did relationships established before the tornado aid in Greensburg's response?

Lesson 3:   Acknowledge your stakeholders, including the media, as partners when managing a crisis.

▶ In what ways did Greensburg leaders include stakeholders in their renewal efforts?

Lesson 4:   Organizations need to develop strong, positive primary and secondary stakeholder relationships.

▶ In what ways did Greensburg leaders establish new stakeholder relationships that helped them create the new vision for their town?

Lesson 5:   Effective crisis communication involves listening to your stakeholders.

▶ Did the leadership of Greensburg include residents in decision making about the new vision for the town?

Lesson 6:   Communicate early about the crisis, acknowledge uncertainty, and assure the public that you will maintain contact with them about current and future risk.

▶ How and how often did Greensburg leadership communicate with the public about the crisis?

Lesson 7:   Avoid certain or absolute answers to the public and media until sufficient information is available.

▶ Did Greensburg leaders communicate with excessive certainty about the crisis?

Lesson 8:   Do not overreassure stakeholders about the impact the crisis will have on them.

▶ Did Greensburg leaders overreassure about the potential for renewal following the crisis?

Lesson 9:   The public needs useful and practical statements of self-efficacy during a crisis.

▶ Did Greensburg leaders communicate statements of self-efficacy following the crisis?

Lesson 10:   Effective crisis communicators acknowledge that positive factors can arise from organizational crises.

▶ In what ways did leaders in Greensburg community acknowledge that positive factors could arise as a result of the crisis?

SUMMARY

The 2007 tornado in Greensburg, Kansas, caught everyone by surprise. The leadership in Greensburg quickly considered the potential opportunities associated with the disaster and framed it this way for citizens. This new prospective vision focused on making Greensburg a model of environmentally sensitive building and housing and set a plan for moving Greensburg forward. Greensburg engaged environmentally savvy stakeholders to help it create its vision and support its relief efforts. Through effective communication, Greensburg, Kansas, was able to effectively respond to a dramatic and tragic crisis.

EXAMPLE 4.6. A COSTLY YOUTUBE HOAX FOR DOMINO'S PIZZA

The simple combination of a video camera, two unsupervised restaurant employees with vulgar senses of humor, and access to the video sharing website YouTube created a cascade of problems for Domino's Pizza, Inc. In April of 2009, two Domino's employees, Kristy Hammonds and Michael Setzer, both in their 30s, posted a grotesque video to YouTube. The two created the video in the kitchen of a Domino's franchise located in Conover, North Carolina. In the video, Hammonds narrates as Setzer is seen violating standard health codes by intentionally contacting food with several of his orifices. Although the video was truly disgusting and juvenile, it piqued the interest of the online community. The video, seen by nearly a million viewers before it was taken down, created a public relations and financial crisis for Domino's (Clifford, 2009).

UNUSUAL CHALLENGES FOR DOMINO'S

The Domino's YouTube crisis created two unusual challenges. First, the crisis was created by a hoax. Second, the perpetrators used a social media outlet to publicize their mischief. We will discuss each of these challenges individually.

Hoaxes, by their nature, create contradicting demands for organizations. Hoaxes begin with an accusation against an organization. In this case, the hoaxers, Setzer and Hammonds, falsely claimed to have served the food that had been contaminated by Setzer. Even if an organization suspects that the claims are false, as was the case with the Domino's hoax, the organization must take every precaution against the threat at hand and display a capacity for dealing with similar threats that may occur in the future. Thus, organizations must simultaneously

> ▶ argue they have a plan in place, either preestablished or spontaneously generated, that can mitigate or manage any crisis emerging from the threat; and

▶ scrutinize available evidence in order to recognize and refute false claims at the earliest point possible (Sellnow, Littlefield, Vidoloff, & Webb, 2010, p. 142).

For Domino's, the primary objectives were to emphasize its commitment to food safety and hiring reputable staff, while discrediting the claims brought against the organization in the YouTube video.

Domino's second challenge was caused by the popularity and accessibility of YouTube. Awareness of the hoax video spread in a virtually exponential manner. Within hours, thousands saw the video. Within 2 days, that number climbed to a million. Even after YouTube agreed to remove the video from its site, the video was posted and made accessible by bloggers at a variety of alternative sites. For Domino's, the challenge was to gain control of a story that proliferated extensively overnight and did so completely independent of the standard media sources, such as television and newspapers.

Screenshot of the Domino's Pizza YouTube hoax video

DOMINO'S CRISIS RESPONSE

This case accentuates the need for organizations to monitor social media to detect potential crisis situations. Domino's was ineffective in such monitoring. In fact, Domino's did not detect the video on its own. Rather, a blogger alerted the company to the condemning video. Domino's initially failed to grasp the urgency of the situation. The company first responded with standard press releases denying that the company had served contaminated food.

Unfortunately, this routine response failed to account for the fact that the crisis emerged on a social media site. Consequently, many who viewed the hoax video never saw Domino's initial response. The company did not provide a formal statement from Domino's USA President Patrick Doyle until 48 hours after realizing the video was on YouTube. During this lapse of time, bloggers speculated openly about Domino's credibility and capacity for managing the crisis (Levinsohn & Gibson, 2009).

Domino's spokesperson Tim McIntyre expressed his dismay as the crisis unfolded in a conversation with the *New York Times*. "We got blindsided by two idiots with a video camera and an awful idea," McIntyre said (Clifford, 2009, p. 1B). "Even people who've been with us as loyal customers for 10, 15, 20 years, people are second-guessing their relationship with Domino's, and that's not fair," he lamented (Clifford, 2009, p. 1B).

With their reputation reeling, Domino's did what it had never done before—address a crisis situation via a social media site. Dressed in a shirt with an open collar, Doyle read a 2-minute crisis response seated in front of a single camera. The statement was straightforward and apologetic. Doyle began by saying, "We sincerely apologize for this incident. We thank members of the online community who quickly alerted us and allowed us to take immediate action. Although the individuals in question claim it's a hoax, we are taking this incredibly seriously." Doyle also indicated that the facility in Conover had been temporarily closed and thoroughly disinfected. After claiming that customer trust is "sacred" to Domino's, Doyle vowed to reexamine the company's hiring practices to "make sure people like this don't make it into our stores." Doyle ended the video by saying he was "sickened" by the damage this incident had done to the Domino's brand and the harm it had done to the reputation of the company's 125,000 employees worldwide (Domino's president, n.d.).

News of Doyle's YouTube response spread quickly. His message was viewed extensively, and many of the websites that had criticized Domino's for its slow and routine response offered critiques of the video—some favorable, some unfavorable. Unlike Domino's initial effort, the YouTube apology garnered the much-needed attention that had been missing. *Business Week* heralded the Domino's response as a lesson for all major companies, saying, "If there's a lesson here, experts say, it's that companies must have an active presence on the web—to monitor their brands continuously, perhaps enlisting loyal customers to help deal immediately with any damage" (Levinsohn & Gibson, 2009, p. 15). Another lesson from this case concerns the communication approach that organizations select for their crisis communication. Clearly, using standard press releases through traditional media venues did not reach the audience of the hoax video. Not until Doyle communicated through the same medium selected by the hoaxers was he able to reach his relevant audience.

YOU MAKE THE CALL

After examining this case, it is time to determine whether Domino's communicated effectively with the stakeholders involved in the crisis. First, take a moment to refresh in your mind the lessons established in Chapter 3 for communicating effectively and ineffectively during crises. These lessons should guide you in evaluating the strengths and weaknesses of Domino's crisis response. As you contemplate the questions that follow, consider whether Domino's was effective or ineffective in coping with the added constraints of the hoax and the use of social media it faced during its crisis response.

Lessons on Producing Effective Crisis Communication

Lesson 1:   Determine your goals for crisis communication.

▶ Did Domino's exemplify clear goals in its crisis communication?

Lesson 2:   Before a crisis, develop true equal partnerships with organizations and groups that are important to the organization.

▶ In what ways did Domino's develop partnerships with stakeholders?

Lesson 3:   Acknowledge your stakeholders, including the media, as partners when managing a crisis.

▶ How did Domino's acknowledge its stakeholders following the crisis?

Lesson 4:   Organizations need to develop strong, positive primary and secondary stakeholder relationships.

▶ Is there evidence that Domino's established relationships with its stakeholders?

Lesson 5:   Effective crisis communication involves listening to your stakeholders.

▶ Is there evidence that Domino's listened to its stakeholders?

(Continued)

(Continued)

Lesson 6:   Communicate early about the crisis, acknowledge uncertainty, and assure the public that you will maintain contact with them about current and future risk.

▶ In what ways did Domino's maintain contact with the public?

Lesson 7:   Avoid certain or absolute answers to the public and media until sufficient information is available.

▶ Did Domino's provide certain or absolute answers about the cause of the crisis?

Lesson 8:   Do not overreassure stakeholders about the impact the crisis will have on them.

▶ Did Domino's overreassure about the impact of the crisis?

Lesson 9:   The public needs useful and practical statements of self-efficacy during a crisis.

▶ In what way did Domino's provide statements of self-efficacy following the crisis?

Lesson 10:   Effective crisis communicators acknowledge that positive factors can arise from organizational crises.

▶ Was there evidence that positive factors could arise from this crisis?

SUMMARY

The Domino's case offers valuable lessons for responding to hoaxes. First, hoaxes can cause notable damage to an organization's financial well-being. The YouTube incident caused extensive damage to Domino's brand and to consumer confidence. Second, responding to hoaxes is complex. Organizations must, at once, discredit the hoaxers while establishing that the company takes all such threats seriously. At times, this type of crisis places an organization in a seemingly contradictory position. Third, the Domino's case clearly exemplifies the increasing importance of alternative media such as YouTube in preventing and managing crises. Organizations would be wise to study the Domino's case and consider their own levels of preparedness for such an attack.

REFERENCES

Calo, B. (Producer). (1996, August 25). Labor of love. *Dateline NBC* [Television broadcast]. Universal City, CA: National Broadcasting Company.

Clifford, S. (2009, April 6). Video prank at Domino's taints brand. *New York Times*, p. 1B.

De Lisser, E. (1998, September 22). FDA is putting the squeeze on makers of fresh juice: New warning labels are sparking safety concerns among customers. *The Wall Street Journal*, p. 1.

Domino's president responds to prank video. (n.d.). Retrieved from http://www .youtube.com/watch?v=dem6eA7-A2I

Keating, F. (2001, August). Catastrophic terrorism—Local response to a national threat. Journal of Homeland Security. Retrieved February 28, 2006, from http://www.homelandsecurity.org/journal/

Levinsohn, B., & Gibson, E. (2009, May 4). An unwelcome delivery. *Business Week, 4129,* 15.

Martinelli, K., & Briggs, W. (1998). Integrating public relations and legal responses during a crisis: The case of Odwalla, Inc. *Public Relations Review, 24,* 443–460.

Milne, J. (1995, December 15). Mill owner says he'll pay workers for a month. *The Boston Globe*, p. B50.

Milne, J., & Aucoin, D. (1995, December 13). In flicker of flames, mill owner vows to rebuild. *The Boston Globe*, p. B1.

Moore, B. L. (1998, August 19). Time may be right to take bite of Odwalla. *The Wall Street Journal*, p. CA1.

Morris, F. (2007). Kansas town's green dreams could save its future. NPR.com. Retrieved from http://www.npr.com

Nguyen, B., & Morris, J. (2009). After tornado, town rebuilds by going green. CNN .com. Retrieved from http://cnn.com

Odwalla pleads guilty, to pay $1.5 million in tainted-juice case. (1998, July 24). *The Wall Street Journal*, p. 1.

Odwalla, Inc. crisis management. (1997, August 22). *The Wall Street Journal*, p. A6.

Phelps, M. (2009). Building a model green community in Greensburg, KS. *Mother Earth News*. Retrieved from http://www.motherearthnews.com/Nature -Community/Greensburg-Kansas-Daniel-Wallach.aspx

Pyle, A. (2011). Effective Crisis Communication: Lessons learned from the Deepwater Horizon Oil Spill. Master's Paper. University of Arkansas at Little Rock, Little Rock, AR.

Reierson, J. L., Sellnow, T. L., & Ulmer, R. R. (2009). Complexities of crisis renewal over time: Learning from the case of tainted Odwalla apple juice. *Communication Studies, 60,* 114–129.

Sellnow, T. L., Littlefield, R. S., Vidoloff, K. G., & Webb, E. M. (2010). The inter-acting arguments of risk communication in response to terrorist hoaxes. *Argumentation and Advocacy, 45,* 139–154.

Thomsen, S., & Rawson, B. (1998). Purifying a tainted corporate image: Odwalla's response to an E. coli poisoning. *Public Relations Quarterly, 43,* 35–46.

Ulmer, R. R. (2001). Effective crisis management through established stakeholder relationships: Malden Mills as a case study. *Management Communication Quarterly, 14,* 590–615.

Lessons on Managing Crisis Uncertainty Effectively

Every crisis carries with it some level of uncertainty. Following a crisis, questions often surface about how to communicate during the uncertainty of a crisis. Whether the crisis is a natural disaster, a food-borne illness outbreak, or a plant explosion, a crisis communicator has to manage uncertainty. Consider that the cases in the last chapter, BP and the United States Coast Guard; Malden Mills; Odwalla; the terrorist attack in Oklahoma City; the tornado in Greensburg, Kansas; and Dominos, all experienced high levels of uncertainty during their crises. Uncertainty makes communicating complex because the crisis communicators must speak publicly without always having clear or accurate information. This chapter, then, provides some highly specialized approaches that go beyond effective crisis communication to meet the needs of high uncertainty crises. Our goal in this chapter is to provide some constructive advice about how to communicate in the presence of uncertainty. We identify 10 lessons for effectively managing the uncertainty of crisis. These lessons serve as guideposts for both students and practitioners of crisis communication.

To provide a quick overview of the chapter, we begin by providing a definition of uncertainty and discussing its link to our initial definition of crisis. The first four lessons characterize uncertainty as a potential challenge for crisis communicators, who can expect some frustration when initially communicating following a crisis. The next six lessons focus on proven communication strategies for changing uncertainty from a challenge to an opportunity. We conclude with a discussion of communication strategies that we believe either intensify or reduce the inherent uncertainty of crisis events. After reading this chapter, you should be better able to transform the constraints of uncertainty into opportunities.

DEFINING UNCERTAINTY

Uncertainty is the inability to determine the present or predict the future. Kramer (2004) suggests, "We may experience uncertainty due to lack of information, due to the complexity of the information, or due to questions about the quality of the information" (pp. 8–9).

We live in a world constrained by uncertainty. Uncertainty is a common experience regardless of your position in life, your job, or your age. For students, there is uncertainty about their next semester courses, their grades, and their futures. Organizations also experience uncertainty. They must plan for market upturns and downturns and try to predict, in a fickle market, what products or services their customers will purchase.

Crisis-induced uncertainty is quite different from the type of uncertainty people and organizations experience on a daily basis. To better understand the scope of crisis uncertainty, we illustrate its role through our definition of crisis discussed in Chapter 1. We defined crisis as an unexpected, nonroutine event that threatens the ultimate goals of the organization. Uncertainty is related to each of the elements of this definition and exemplifies the communication demands during crisis. Taleb (2010) explains that crises often create epistemological and ontological uncertainty. He defines *epistemological uncertainty* as the lack of knowledge we have following a crisis. Because crisis events are so new, complex, and subject to change, there is often little knowledge available about how to manage them. For this reason, crises often create gaps in knowledge for extended periods of time that constrain decision making and understanding. *Ontological uncertainty* refers to the type of uncertainty in which the future has little or no relationship to the past. Crisis events are often described as creating a new normal for all impacted by the event. This new normal is highly uncertain, because people's beliefs about how the world operates change dramatically. Consider the new normal we experienced following 9/11 regarding airport security. As a society, we knew there would be changes; in the time that has passed since 9/11 there has been—and still is—considerable debate, discussion, and uncertainty about what this new normal will ultimately look like.

UNEXPECTED CRISES AND UNCERTAINTY

Crises happen when least expected, are shocking, and create a great deal of uncertainty for everyone concerned. To better understand the unexpected nature of crises, consider the Malden Mills case from the last chapter. In the middle of the night, Malden Mills erupted into flames for no apparent reason. The explosion and fire startled citizens of the community, as many wondered what would happen to their jobs. Some company executives first learned of the blaze as they walked through an airport and saw CNN's live report of the fire on terminal television monitors. Aaron Feuerstein, Malden Mills's CEO, was at his 70th birthday party when he received a call about the fire. Clearly, crises are unexpected and can raise many different uncertainties.

<table>
<tr><td>**LESSON 1**</td></tr>
<tr><td>Organization members must accept that a crisis can start quickly and unexpectedly.</td></tr>
</table>

Learning from a television report that your property is on fire is obviously a surreal and unexpected experience. In this case, for Malden Mills's executives, there was great uncertainty about the extent of the damage, whether or not people were hurt, and how the fire started.

NONROUTINE CRISIS EVENTS AND UNCERTAINTY

Crises are dramatic and chaotic events. One goal after a crisis is to get the organization back into operation. Organizational leaders have several options when responding to a crisis: They can respond with routine procedures, such as firing the person responsible for the crisis, minimizing the scope of the crisis, or shifting the blame. Alternatively, they can respond with unique solutions that directly rectify the crisis. Although routine solutions can be effective, they rarely rectify systematic problems in the organization. In the last chapter we examined the BP oil spill and the high levels of uncertainty the crisis created for Public Information Officers and the public. However, one of the largest oil spills in United States history before the BP oil spill was by Exxon in Alaska. Exxon's CEO Lawrence Rawl responded to the 1987 Exxon *Valdez* oil spill in Prince William Sound by saying, while one of its ships gushed oil into the water, that the spill was not severe and that Exxon had a good record of cleaning up much worse spills (Small, 1991). However, Rawl did not take into account that the currents in the sound were stronger than any Exxon had handled before, and the dispersants that Exxon had used in other cleanups were not going to be as effective in this cleanup effort. Exxon failed, in part, because it did not address the uncertainty and novelty of the situation. Conversely, Rawl used routine solutions—minimizing the crisis and firing the intoxicated *Valdez* captain—to handle a nonroutine crisis event. As a result, Exxon received justified criticism for failing to effectively manage the spill.

Exxon would have done better had it examined the oil spill quickly and developed original solutions to protect the wildlife and environment. Exxon had been pressed for years by environmental groups to adapt its cleanup efforts to meet the unique needs of Alaska and Prince William Sound. However, the company decided to go with the routine solutions they had developed companywide.

LESSON 2

Organizations should not respond to crises with routine solutions.

THREAT PERCEPTION AND UNCERTAINTY

A key characteristic of crisis is the threat to the organization's ultimate goals. Remember, in the first chapter, we argued that organizations should not focus solely on the threat associated with crises and should also consider the opportunities inherent to these events. Threat and uncertainty are linked because there is doubt about whether organizational goals will be met as a result of the crisis. In addition, there is uncertainty about the level of threat the organization is experiencing. If you remember the definition of crisis provided in Chapter 1, you recall that we discussed perceived threat. The fact that threat is perceptual contributes to the overall uncertainty of the event: Some people in the organization may view a situation as a potential crisis, and others may not. The computer code problem, Y2K, which was expected to disable many computers prior to the new millennium, was not viewed by many organizations as a potential crisis when it was first identified. The threat was not taken seriously until it was certain that the code problem could have an impact on banking, organizational record keeping, and even personal computers.

Organizations must be able to manage uncertainty associated with a crisis threat. Addressing this uncertainty involves developing consensus with stakeholders about potential threats. As a result, communication about potential threats helps reduce uncertainty about potential risks in the organization.

LESSON 3

Threat is perceptual.

SHORT RESPONSE TIME AND UNCERTAINTY

Once an organization has experienced a crisis, it must communicate to its stakeholders. This process is inherently uncertain because the organization typically does not have accurate or readily available information to provide to these groups. In addition, the organization may not know what is appropriate to communicate about the crisis. At times, this is due to a lack of basic crisis preparation. However, at other times, the event is so dramatic and ill defined that it shocks the organization so severely that little information is available. This is particularly true in the initial moments after a crisis.

When Rudy Giuliani, the former mayor of New York City, first spoke after the terrorist attacks in September of 2001, he was only able to acknowledge and confirm what the whole world had seen on television—that the World Trade Center towers had fallen. He had no other information to provide at the time. As a result, he did not speculate or predict what would happen next. All he could do was discuss what he had witnessed and answer any questions the media had for him.

One of the key tenets of crisis communication is that, following the onset of a crisis, the organization should make a statement to stakeholders in order to reduce the stakeholders' uncertainty and to avoid any appearance of not wanting to answer questions or stonewalling. There are many questions that need answering following a crisis, which is one reason the media are so attracted to these events. Often, in the presence of tremendous uncertainty created by a crisis, the affected organization is left to answer the following questions:

- ▶ What happened?
- ▶ Who is responsible?
- ▶ Why did it happen?
- ▶ Who is affected?
- ▶ What should we do?
- ▶ Who can we trust?
- ▶ What should we say?
- ▶ How should we say it?

Although this is not an exhaustive list, these are questions that every crisis communicator should be prepared to answer. In the context of the uncertainty following a crisis, it is important to reiterate that, immediately following the event, there may not be answers for many of these questions. Crisis communicators must be able to have a clear and consistent message and present this message quickly and regularly following a crisis event. If the organization is not prepared to provide definitive answers and explanations related to the crisis, the spokesperson must be able to provide information, such as the organization's latest safety records, its measures for collecting information about the crisis, and a timeline for how it is going to handle the crisis in the future. Good advice for crisis communicators is to tell people what you know, what you do not know, and what you are going to do to find answers to the still unanswered questions about the crisis.

As discussed, the surprising, nonroutine, and threatening nature of crisis creates tremendous uncertainty for crisis communicators. However, the short response time associated with crisis creates even greater uncertainty because crisis communicators must communicate about events with

LESSON 4

Crisis communicators must communicate early and often following a crisis, regardless of whether they have critical information about the crisis.

little, no, or competing information about how the crisis happened, who is affected, and whether the event was managed effectively.

THE IMPACT OF CRISIS-INDUCED UNCERTAINTY ON STAKEHOLDERS

The next six lessons focus on how crisis communicators can turn uncertainty from a challenge into an opportunity when communicating with stakeholders. As we have discussed, because a crisis is sudden and unforeseen, uncertainty about what to say and how to make sense of the situation is a key communication challenge. Furthermore, crises often create public debates about responsibility, cause, and the impact on stakeholders. This next section focuses on the public debates that arise following a crisis and how they should be resolved ethically and responsibly. Before we go any further, here is our definition of *stakeholders*:

> Stakeholders are any groups of people internal or external to an organization who have a stake in the actions of the organization, such as employees, customers, creditors, government regulatory agencies, the media, competitors, or community members.

Stakeholders are very vocal following a crisis because they seek information and ask questions about the crisis. They want to know who is responsible, why the crisis happened, and how they can protect themselves, along with many of the other questions we presented earlier in this chapter. Stakeholders typically want clear and quick answers to these questions to protect themselves and make sense of the crisis. However, this is a difficult standard to meet. The question of who is responsible, for instance, can take weeks and sometimes years to answer. Typically, the greatest uncertainty involves determining who is at fault. Organizations and their lawyers often fight endlessly trying to determine responsibility.

In addition to determining fault, examples of the uncertainty in crises are plentiful. Consider the meltdown that took place on April 26, 1986, at the former Soviet Union's Chernobyl nuclear power plant. The meltdown, instigated by several explosions damaging the nuclear reactor, is described as the worst-ever nuclear accident. Following the crisis, there was great uncertainty regarding who was impacted and to what extent. For instance, pregnant mothers and their unborn children became critical stakeholders as birth defects heightened significantly in the years following the meltdown. In addition, there were varying estimates on the incidence of cancer by those who may have been exposed to the radiation. In this case, the ultimate impact of the crisis on stakeholders was uncertain, complex, and open to public debate and argument.

Determining the extent of the damage of a crisis can be complicated and open to debate. Researchers are still contesting whether Exxon has fully cleaned up its 1989 oil spill or whether the oil is still having a negative impact on the sound's ecosystem. Sixteen years after the spill, both the U.S. government and Exxon commissioned scientists who conducted studies and debated whether the ecosystem was still contaminated or whether the food supply had become safe (Guterman, 2004). Twenty years after a 1984 toxic gas leak at a Union Carbide pesticide plant in Bhopal, India, Amnesty International reported that Indian residents continued to experience health problems associated with the event. Union Carbide, which was purchased by Dow Chemical after the crisis, argued that the site had been cleaned and there were no lasting effects from the explosion. The two groups continue to disagree about what caused the gas leak, the impact the leak had on Indian residents, and how to compensate those impacted by the crisis (Sharma, 2005). As you can see, even 15 to 20 years after a crisis, uncertainty is still an important variable (for information about the current status in Bhopal, see "International Campaign," n.d.).

As was illustrated in the foregoing examples, public arguments will be made by many stakeholders concerning who is responsible, what people should do, who is affected, and how the victims should be compensated. Uncertainty and confusion can be increased when stakeholders disagree about important questions surrounding the crisis.

Adding to the complexity are regulatory and safety decisions that need to be made regarding the crisis. For instance, when a chemical plant explodes, there are many competing claims regarding air safety, the cleanliness of the water supply, and the relative levels of harm associated with each potential hazard. When there are conflicting claims, the organization, independent contractors, and government regulators, such as the health departments, may conduct their own tests. It is not uncommon for each group to arrive at divergent answers, which in turn often heighten the uncertainty associated with the crisis. Such heightened uncertainty and disagreements about important questions regarding the crisis can create multiple interpretations about the same event or what we refer to as *communication ambiguity*.

MANAGING COMMUNICATION AMBIGUITY ETHICALLY DURING CRISIS

Organizations and stakeholders may not be able to fully ascertain clear answers to key questions about the crisis until an investigation is completed. As we just discussed, investigations and disagreements about the crisis can proceed for decades. In the meantime, the uncertainty surrounding the crisis is likely to make communication about causation and responsibility ambiguous. Weick (1995) defines ambiguity as "an ongoing stream that supports several different interpretations at the same time" (pp. 91–92).

Similarly to Weick (1995), we define *communication ambiguity* as multiple interpretations of a crisis event. In the simplest terms, due to the uncertainty of crisis, there is not a clear-cut, precise answer to every important question following a crisis. As a result, each stakeholder group, including customers, workers, and the impacted public, may hold and express differing viewpoints of the event.

As a result, the inherent uncertainty related to any crisis allows for multiple interpretations. Organizations then can select an interpretation of a crisis that reflects more favorably on their actions than competing interpretations. Moreover, it would also be possible for organizations to increase the degree of ambiguity of a crisis in an effort to produce competing perspectives on the event. We believe that intentionally heightening the level of ambiguity in a crisis is unethical and irresponsible for any crisis communicator. However, we acknowledge that ambiguity is inherent to any crisis situation. So, in order to assess the ethicality of ambiguity in crisis situations, we maintain that

▸ ambiguity is ethical when it contributes to the complete understanding of an issue by posing alternative views that are based on complete and unbiased data that aim to inform, and

▸ ambiguity is unethical if it poses alternative interpretations using biased or incomplete information that aims to deceive.

In this case, how one interprets and communicates critical information about a crisis can serve to reduce, maintain, or increase the level of ambiguity inherent to that situation. A now classic case of capitalizing unethically on the inherent uncertainty of crisis and intentionally heightening its ambiguity took place in 1994 when Dr. David Kessler

(Ulmer & Sellnow, 1997) contended publicly that nicotine was an addictive drug. This announcement created a crisis for the tobacco industry. The tobacco industry's response, by the presidents or chairmen (all were male) of the seven largest tobacco companies, was to interject as much ambiguity into the situation as possible. They described Kessler as an extremist, downplayed and lied about the known addictiveness of nicotine, and used biased research to support their contentions (see Ulmer & Sellnow, 1997). The tobacco industry's goal was to create and add as much uncertainty to the debate as possible. By increasing the uncertainty about the addictiveness of nicotine, they hoped to complicate the issue enough to escape blame.

LESSON 5

Organizations should not purposely heighten the ambiguity of a crisis to deceive or distract the public.

CONSISTENT QUESTIONS OF AMBIGUITY

After investigating and studying communication ambiguity in crisis situations, we believe you should prepare for three areas of ambiguity where multiple interpretations often arise after an organizational crisis: questions of evidence, questions of intent, and questions of responsibility (Ulmer & Sellnow, 2000) (see Table 5.1).

Questions of evidence refer to ambiguity created as a result of complex legal battles or scientific debates concerning crisis evidence. For instance, when women began coming forward with complaints regarding their Dow Corning silicone breast implants, the company downplayed these complaints with their own evidence that even a punctured implant would not cause notable distress to a woman's body. In this case, the general public was left with the question of whom to believe.

Table 5.1 Consistent Questions of Ambiguity in Organizational Crisis

Ambiguity Example	Common Public Questions
Evidence	Whose scientific evidence should the public believe?
Intent	Did the organization knowingly commit the crisis?
Responsibility	Did the crisis originate within or outside of the organization?

Questions of evidence focus on how complexity breeds uncertainty and ambiguity because of the multiple interpretations available in the data collection process following the crisis. Because science can be

LESSON 6

Be prepared to defend your interpretation of the evidence surrounding a crisis.

subjective regarding how data are collected and interpreted, the results are often debated. We assert that those debates create uncertainty and ambiguity for a public trying to make sense of the crisis. A consistent debate, then, in crisis situations is one between stakeholders who view crisis evidence differently.

Questions of intent refer to whether a crisis was an accident or whether an organization knowingly put its workers or the public in danger. It may seem ridiculous that an organization would knowingly put itself in a crisis; however, history suggests that the reality of the matter is quite different. For instance, Ford Motor Company sold the Pinto (1971–1980), a car that they knew had life-threatening defects, to an unsuspecting public. The rationale for their decision was that paying settlements to individuals or families whose loved ones were injured or killed in the vehicle would cost the company less than a recall or redesign (Larsen, 1998). Questions of intent refer to whether an organization knew about potential problems and failed to correct them before a crisis or whether the crisis happened as an accident in an otherwise socially responsible system.

Whether an organization intended to cause a crisis is a critical aspect of moving beyond the crisis. There is a clear difference between an organization having an accident and an organization knowingly causing or allowing a crisis to occur. If the crisis was an accident, the public and the organization's stakeholders are much more likely to forgive the organization and potentially even help it reestablish itself. However, when an organization has been knowingly unethical or irresponsible in its business practices, the public is much less likely to forgive and forget. Many people still refuse to buy Exxon gasoline or support an organization that has destructively and knowingly abused its business responsibilities.

LESSON 7

Without good intentions prior to a crisis, recovery is difficult or impossible.

Questions of responsibility refer to the level and placement of blame that should be attributed to the organization for a crisis. Should responsibility rest within or outside the organization? In 1993, Jack in the Box, a fast-food chain, experienced a food-borne illness outbreak in the form of *E. coli* bacteria. During this crisis, three children died and hundreds of

Jack in the Box customers were infected (see the discussion in Ulmer & Sellnow, 2000). When asked about the crisis, Jack in the Box spokespersons insisted that meat-testing procedures at the United States Department of Agriculture (USDA) were much more responsible for the crisis than were Jack in the Box restaurants. In this case, Jack in the Box was placing blame for the crisis outside the purview of its organization. However, after an internal communication audit, Jack in the Box found that it had not acted on a state health department memo instructing the restaurant to increase grill temperatures in order to kill the *E. coli* bacteria in hamburger.

Whether the organization or an outside agency is responsible for the crisis is a constant and recurring type of ambiguity that contributes to the uncertainty of a crisis. One of the key communication strategies for organizations following a crisis is to deny responsibility for the event. However, shifting the blame to another organization is most often a more effective strategy. Clearly, it is more effective to say, "We are not responsible, but we know who is" rather than just saying, "We did not do it." In this case, a debate often results in which organizations cast accusations at one another, trying to place blame on the other party for the crisis. This heightens the uncertainty about who is responsible for the event.

> **LESSON 8**
>
> If you believe you are not responsible for a crisis, you need to build a case for who is responsible and why.

Communication ambiguity is a key factor in understanding uncertainty associated with crisis events. We have focused on three types of communication ambiguity—evidence, intent, and responsibility—that arise after a crisis and often create more uncertainty because of the complex nature of the crisis and the multiple ways of understanding the event. Although crises are inherently complicated, there are times when communication can be open and honest and still somewhat ambiguous. This is discussed in depth in the next chapter.

To recap, communication ambiguity is a central factor in managing any type of crisis. Due to the inherent uncertainty of crises, there will be multiple interpretations and arguments made about the severity of the crisis, how the crisis was caused, who is affected, and whether the organization is responsible for the event (see Table 5.2). The lessons in this section suggest that crisis communicators should be ready and willing to defend their interpretation of a crisis; to practice good, honest, ethical conduct before and after a crisis develops; and to make sure they build a case for why they are not responsible for the crisis if indeed they are not.

Table 5.2	Crisis and Uncertainty	

Key Issues in Uncertainty	Organization	Stakeholder
Unanswered questions	Who, what, why, how	Who, what, why, how
Need for Information	High	High
Ambiguity	High	Confusion surrounding evidence, intent, locus
Personal Beliefs	Collapsed	Collapsed

TRAINING, SIMULATIONS, AND UNCERTAINTY

One of the conditions of crisis is that the established organizational structure collapses following the event. When an organizational structure collapses, people are further traumatized by the lack of resources to help them make sense of the situation. For instance, after an airline crash, air patterns are disrupted making it difficult to predict when flights will take off and land. Similarly, after a toxic release in the air or water, evacuations often disrupt families and their day-to-day functioning. Obviously, large-scale crises like 9/11 create a further collapsing of communication and other established structures, increasing the difficulty of collecting helpful information about the event.

Weick (1993) argues that the breakdown in established organizational structures is a key issue in the failure to respond appropriately to crisis situations. He argues that crises "thrust people into unfamiliar roles, leave some key roles unfilled, make the task more ambiguous, discredit the role system, and make all of these changes in a context in which small events can combine into something monstrous" (p. 638). In this case, structures are not as rigid or invulnerable as many organizations would like to think. The demands of crisis on an organization and its stakeholders can bring established structures to their knees (see Table 5.2 once again). Organizations need to train and prepare for the uncertainty, threat, and communication demands before a crisis hits. Organizations often do tabletop exercises and mock simulations to prepare for the uncertainty and destruction of crisis. Many people have seen televised accounts of New York City and other metropolitan areas training and preparing for future terrorist attacks and other crises. These simulations may include a dirty bomb placed in a sports stadium or a chemical release in a subway. These simulations help federal agencies understand

LESSON 9

Organizations need to prepare for uncertainty through simulations and training.

how well they are able to coordinate and communicate in a crisis. As we discuss further in the next chapter, establishing strong stakeholder relationships can help prevent breakdowns in established structures.

BELIEF STRUCTURES AND UNCERTAINTY

During a crisis, the public as well as the organization experience high levels of uncertainty. Due to uncertainty during and following a crisis, stakeholders often experience what Weick (1993) refers to as *cosmology episodes*, wherein uncertainty creates a disorienting experience in which beliefs and sensemaking structures are severely hampered. These belief structures are severely impacted by the epistemic uncertainty we discussed at the beginning of this chapter. For example, following the 1997 North Dakota floods, many people experienced shock and terror as the high-cresting Red River washed away their homes. They described themselves as being traumatized by the crisis (see the discussion in Sellnow, Seeger, & Ulmer, 2002). Others mentioned that the only time they had experienced something so disturbing was in Vietnam. When people are suffering from collapses in their belief structures or are going through very traumatic times, effective communication can become increasingly complicated.

Along with the high uncertainty and threat associated with a crisis, organizations also experience collapses in their belief structures. Crises are often so disturbing that they change the way we think about the world. This type of uncertainty relates to the ontological uncertainty we discussed at the outset of this chapter. Just think how things have changed since 9/11. The airlines' beliefs about cockpit, passenger, and baggage safety have changed forever. Vicki Freimuth, director of the CDC during 9/11 and the anthrax letters crisis, explained that the CDC had to change its beliefs about the world twice, once after 9/11 and once after they failed to communicate effectively about the 2001 anthrax contaminations. These two events, she suggests, forced the "CDC [to] permanently alter its strategy for communicating publicly during crises" (Sellnow, Seeger, & Ulmer, 2005, p. 178). These cases are illustrative of the dramatic shifts in beliefs organizations must manage while handling a crisis.

Crisis situations, then, create interesting and unconventional contexts in which both organizations and stakeholders need critical information to reduce their uncertainty. As a result, both organizations and stakeholders search for information. However, they rarely speak to one another. The organization in crisis often stonewalls and explains that if it had any information that information would be shared publicly. On the other hand, the organization's stakeholders often are left wondering if they will receive the necessary information to protect themselves and to find out what happened.

LESSON 10
Crises challenge the way organizations think about and conduct their business.

Related to this vacuum of communication is the media, which often speculate on questions concerning the crisis, as information is not readily available and company spokespersons are not often available for comment.

SUMMARY

Communicating in the midst or the wake of a crisis is unlike communicating during any other time. Effective communication can become very difficult. During crisis situations, there are tremendous constraints on an organization to communicate effectively, yet the organization's stakeholders need critical information in order to make informed decisions. These constraints may include lack of knowledge about the severity of the problem, difficulty in identifying those affected by the crisis, and unavailability of accurate and appropriate information. In addition, decisions have to be made under stressful conditions—all this while the image and credibility of the organization are at risk. Our next chapter examines how organizations can overcome these difficulties and communicate effectively and appropriately in crisis situations.

Lessons on Uncertainty and Crisis Communication
Lesson 1:   Organization members must accept that a crisis can start quickly and unexpectedly.
Lesson 2:   Organizations should not respond to crises with routine solutions.
Lesson 3:   Threat is perceptual.
Lesson 4:   Crisis communicators must communicate early and often following a crisis regardless of whether they have critical information about the crisis.
Lesson 5:   Organizations should not purposely heighten the ambiguity of a crisis to deceive or distract the public.
(Continued)

(Continued)

Lesson 6:   Be prepared to defend your interpretation of the evidence surrounding a crisis.

Lesson 7:   Without good intentions prior to a crisis, recovery is difficult or impossible.

Lesson 8:   If you believe you are not responsible for a crisis, you need to build a case for who is responsible and why.

Lesson 9:   Organizations need to prepare for uncertainty through simulations and training.

Lesson 10: Crises challenge the way organizations think about and conduct their business.

REFERENCES

Guterman, L. (2004). Slippery science. *Chronicle of Higher Education, 51*(5), A12–A17.

International campaign for justice in Bhopal. (n.d.). Retrieved from http://www.bhopal.net

Kramer, M. W. (2004). *Managing uncertainty in organizational communication.* Mahwah, NJ: Lawrence Erlbaum.

Larsen, S. (1998). Safety last. *Mother Jones.* Retrieved from http://www.motherjones.com

Sellnow, T. L., Seeger, M. W., & Ulmer, R. R. (2002). Chaos theory, informational needs, and natural disasters. *Journal of Applied Communication Research, 30,* 269–292.

Sellnow, T. L., Seeger, M. W., & Ulmer, R. R. (2005). Constructing the "new normal" through post crisis discourse. In D. O'Hair, R. L. Heath, & G. R. Ledlow (Eds.), *Community preparedness and response to terrorism: Communication and the media* (Vol. 3, pp. 167–189). Westport, CT: Praeger.

Sharma, D. (2005). Bhopal: 20 years on. *Lancet, 365,* 111–113.

Small, W. (1991). Exxon *Valdez*: How to spend billions and still get a black eye. *Public Relations Review, 17,* 9–26.

Taleb, N. N. (2010). *The black swan: The impact of the highly improbable* (2nd ed.). New York, NY: Random House.

Ulmer, R. R., & Sellnow, T. L. (1997). Strategic ambiguity and the ethic of significant choice in the tobacco industry's crisis communication. *Communication Studies, 48,* 215–233.

Ulmer, R. R., & Sellnow, T. L. (2000). Consistent questions of ambiguity in organizational crisis communication: Jack in the Box as a case study. *Journal of Business Ethics, 25,* 143–155.

Weick, K. E. (1993). The collapse of sensemaking in organizations: The Mann Gulch disaster. *Administrative Science Quarterly, 38,* 628–652.

Weick, K. E. (1995). *Sensemaking in organizations.* Thousand Oaks, CA: Sage.

Applying the Lessons for Managing Crisis Uncertainty Effectively

M anaging crisis-induced uncertainty is one of the most important skills of an effective crisis communicator. It is a highly specialized skill that allows crisis communicators to be ethical and responsible in their communication practices yet still provide accurate information to stakeholders. Every crisis has some level of uncertainty and as a result the effective crisis communicator must respond appropriately. After reading the last chapter you now understand the key elements of managing uncertainty through effective crisis communication. However, as you will see in the following cases, the practice of managing uncertainty takes considerable practice and experience. The following five cases examine managing crisis uncertainty during an environmental disaster, a natural disaster, a terrorist attack, an international food-borne illness crisis, and a corporate meltdown. Each case provides examples of key elements of crisis uncertainty. Good luck with working through these cases while developing your crisis communication skills and experience at the same time.

EXAMPLE 6.1. TENNESSEE VALLEY AUTHORITY AND THE KINGSTON ASH SLIDE

The Emory River would never meander along the same peaceful path after the morning of December 22, 2008. The river flowed near the Kingston Fossil Plant, located near Knoxville, Tennessee. The plant, operated by the Tennessee Valley Authority (TVA), burns coal to generate "10 billion kilowatt-hours of electricity a year" to serve "670,000 homes" (Tennessee Valley Authority, n.d., para. 2). In doing so, the plant creates tons of fly ash, a coal-combustion waste product. The ash, combined with water to form sludge, is stored in enormous containment ponds.

The ponds, surrounded by earthen walls built by TVA, hold the ash until a portion of it can be dried and recycled into building products. On this rainy December morning, ash began to ooze from a wall of one of the ponds. The leak weakened the wall until it crumbled, discharging "5.4 million cubic yards of coal ash into the river and into a nearby community, destroying several houses and forcing families to leave the area" ("Welcome to a new year," 2010, para. 6).

MISSED OPPORTUNITIES IN CRISIS PREPARATION AND PLANNING

Simply put, TVA failed to accept the uncertainty related to storing the volume of fly ash contained in the Kingston facility. In his testimony before Congress, TVA Chief Executive Officer, Tom Kilgore (2009), admitted that the crisis was the result of "long-evolving conditions" that the organization failed to recognize or consider as it heaped more and more ash into the fragile pond (para. 12). Kilgore acknowledged TVA overlooked "the existence of an unusual bottom layer of ash and silt, the high water content of the wet ash, the increasing height of ash, and the construction of the sloping dikes over the wet ash" (para. 12). Perhaps the most puzzling lapse was TVA's failure to respond to a preliminary report 2 months before the spill that "described a wet spot on one retaining wall that might be associated with a leak" (National Aeronautics and Space Administration, n.d., para. 5). By their nature, leaks

Removing ash from the Emory River near the TVA Kingston Fossil Plant

SOURCE: AP Photo/Wade Payne.

in earthen containment systems are a sign that the moisture is eroding the integrity of the structure. Still, TVA continued to add ash to the Kingston pond without question.

TENNESSEE VALLEY AUTHORITY'S RESPONSE TO AN UNCERTAIN CRISIS

To its credit, TVA accepted blame for the spill, obtained emergency permission to begin dredging the Emory River—portions of which literally disappeared under the thick layer of ash—and conducted an extensive internal investigation into the organization's failures.

Some criticized the timing of the dredging process undertaken by TVA. For example, Gregory Button, an anthropologist on faculty at the University of Tennessee, told the *Knoxville News Sentinel*, a major newspaper in the region, that, although the cleanup was launched relatively soon after the spill, he was "worried about the haste in cleaning up the waste" ("Vines," 2009, para. 9). Button and others were concerned that no independent party was allowed to assess the dredging plan before it was launched. Button insisted that including hearings with a third party about the cleanup would be to "TVA's advantage" because "it will haunt TVA if it doesn't work out" (para. 10).

Despite criticism, the dredging continued through 2009 and into 2010. Cleanup of the land impacted by the spill began after the Emory River was cleared of ash. The *Knoxville News Sentinel* emphasized the notoriety of the spill that was "called one of the worst environmental disasters in the nation by the federal Environmental Protection Agency," and has a projected cleanup cost that is "expected to exceed $1.2 billion, not including lawsuits filed against TVA" ("Welcome to a new year," 2010, para. 7).

TVA's internal investigation into the organization's failures leading up to the crisis was extensive. In addition to conducting its own review, the TVA board of directors commissioned the law firm of McKenna Long & Aldridge (MLA) to look at any "management, controls, and standards issues that may have contributed to the event and to make recommendations on culture and organizational effectiveness" (Kilgore, 2009, para. 10). The law firm identified six primary failures in TVA's "systems, controls, standards, and culture" (Ide & Blanco, 2009, p. 2) in place at the Kingston plant:

▶ *"Lack of Clarity and Accountability for Ultimate Responsibility."* Multiple group involvement in decision making and frequent reorganization created a "lack of accountability" (p. 3).

▶ *"Lack of Standardization, Training and Metrics."* TVA had "no standard procedures" in place for managing ash ponds (p. 4). Separate manuals existed for each facility, and in many cases the manuals were not updated.

▶ *"Siloed Responsibilities and Poor Communication."* TVA had four separate divisions sharing responsibilities for maintaining ash retention facilities. Communication among these divisions was "strained and in some instances, nonexistent" (p. 4). The report noted one example where engineers failed to instruct workers to suspend work on the pond due to excessive moisture. When the engineers were asked why they failed to provide this instruction, they responded, "no one had asked" (p. 4).

▶ *"Lack of Checks and Balances."* TVA failed to create a quality assurance or quality control plan. Thus, employees failed to perform routine inspections "to ensure that the pond was constructed pursuant to the engineered specifications" (p. 4). The report found "the lack of a Quality Assurance/Quality Control [plan] created an environment where employees felt empowered to ignore engineers and 'build it better' than the drawings" (p. 4).

▶ *"Lack of Prevention Priority and Resources."* TVA facilities failed to provide the necessary upkeep on the walls of their retention ponds. The report indicated that this failure was due to a lack of prioritization of preventive activities, such as mowing the earthen walls and removing tree growth that could weaken them. Overall, TVA's funding "was inadequate for routine maintenance, creating a situation in which adequate inspections were impossible because the sides of the dikes were overgrown and maintenance needs compounded over time" (p. 5).

▶ *"Reactive Instead of Proactive."* When seeps or leaks were found in the dike's walls, they were patched without "investigating the cause of incidents beyond the specific physical occurrences" (p. 5). As similar warning signs were seen, "no effort was made to leverage the lessons learned across" the fleet of similar ponds managed by TVA (p. 5).

This extensive list of failures provides a clear overview of how TVA failed to respond to warning signs and actually heighted uncertainty by its internal communication or lack thereof.

In his testimony before Congress, Tom Kilgore acknowledged the findings of the MLA report and pledged to create a more safety-conscious culture and to improve internal communication. To improve the organization's culture, Kilgore (2009) vowed to act on "several lessons learned about the challenges facing us" (para. 29). He summarized these lessons as follows:

▸ Storage facilities and structures should not be built in areas where stability cannot be assured and verified.

▸ Aggressive, rigorous inspections and structural analysis of all coal-combustion product storage have been initiated and will be kept current.

▸ Management will visibly demonstrate and emphasize the need for self-assessments to promote objective and fact-based reporting, inspections, and auditing.

▸ Safety-related risks must be given the highest priority to identify, minimize, and eliminate risks.

▸ Engineering design philosophy, design, and construction of ash management facilities must be standardized.

▸ The handling, storage, and disposal operations for coal-combustion products must be standardized.

Each of these strategies was designed to overcome the organization's failure to respond proactively and accurately to the warning signs the company failed to heed.

Kilgore (2009) also recognized that poor communication, unclear accountability, and a lack of follow-through contributed notably to the crisis. As such, he promised to make the following changes at TVA (para. 30):

▸ Clear accountabilities

▸ Strong governance

▸ Robust self-assessment

▸ Independent reviews for quality and compliance

▸ A culture of personal responsibility and problem solving

Through these substantial changes, Kilgore (2009) hoped to use the Kingston crisis as a "wake-up call for TVA" and to "rebuild the public's trust" (para. 5).

As the cleanup and organizational changes continue, some residents worry about the long-term impact of the spill. For example, lingering uncertainty about possible contamination of the ground water supply, loss of property values in the entire region, and fears that, as the spilled ash begins to dry, airborne pollutants will place residents at risk remain largely unaddressed by the current TVA crisis response plan. Consequently, area residents have organized to bring a lawsuit against TVA. Oak Ridge attorney, Michael Ritter, said "the figure of $165 million is just the tip of the iceberg" (Huotari, 2009, para. 2). The lawsuit alleges "that the spill hurt family incomes, destroyed property or property values, created potential future medical expenses, probably hurt property sales for years, and caused severe mental anguish and a loss of 'the right to enjoy life'" (para. 13). Rather than addressing these concerns directly, TVA largely ignored them in its response plan. Although lawsuits are common in crises such as the Kingston ash slide, at least one plaintiff insists he would not have sued if TVA had addressed his concerns. At a press conference announcing the lawsuit, this plaintiff said bluntly, "had the TVA done what the TVA should, we wouldn't be here" (para. 23).

YOU MAKE THE CALL

After examining this case, it is time to determine how the TVA handled the uncertainty we discussed in Chapter 5. First, take a moment to refresh in your mind the lessons established on managing uncertainty. Second, note that these lessons serve as touchstones and discussion points for what we believe are key aspects of any crisis response. As you answer the questions that follow, consider whether the TVA was effective or ineffective in its managing of uncertainty surrounding the crisis. We have rephrased the lessons into questions so that you are better able to address the key issues in the case.

Lessons on Managing Crisis Uncertainty

Lesson 1:   Organizational members must accept that a crisis can start quickly and unexpectedly.

▶ Did the Kingston ash slide happen quickly? Was it unexpected?

Lesson 2:   Organizations should not respond to crises with routine solutions.

▶ Did TVA respond to the crisis in a routine manner? Did their response address the problems with their organizational culture?

Lesson 3:   Threat is perceptual.

> ▶ In what way was the threat associated with this crisis perceptual? How did perceptions differ among stakeholders?

Lesson 4:   Crisis communicators must communicate early and often following a crisis regardless of whether they have critical information about the crisis.

> ▶ Did Tom Kilgore communicate early and often about the crisis? Was he effective or ineffective?

Lesson 5:   Organizations should not purposely heighten the ambiguity of a crisis to deceive or distract the public.

> ▶ Were there issues that were uncertain or ambiguous for stakeholders after the crisis?

> ▶ Did TVA contribute to the uncertainty surrounding the crisis?

Lesson 6:   Be prepared to defend your interpretation of the evidence surrounding a crisis.

> ▶ Did TVA defend its interpretation of evidence surrounding the crisis? Was TVA effective or ineffective?

Lesson 7:   Without good intentions prior to a crisis, recovery is difficult or impossible.

> ▶ Did TVA have good intentions with stakeholders prior to the Kingston ash slide?

Lesson 8:   If you believe you are not responsible for a crisis, you need to build a case for who is responsible and why.

> ▶ Did TVA build a case for why it was or was not responsible for the crisis? Was TVA effective or ineffective?

Lesson 9:   Organizations need to prepare for uncertainty through simulations and training.

> ▶ Did TVA prepare adequately for the risk of a major ash spill?

Lesson 10:   Crises challenge the way organizations think about their business.

> ▶ Should this crisis have changed TVA's management style? If so, how?

SUMMARY

The Kingston ash slide is a clear example of the peril an organization can create by failing to accept uncertainty in crisis planning and response. TVA did not have an organizational structure or culture that was prepared to respond to warning signs. The efficiency of the recovery process was hampered by TVA's need to undergo extensive innovations in its organizational communication patterns and its organizational culture regarding safety. Warning signs were either missed altogether or observed and not shared among relevant parties in the organization. Although TVA responded to these deficiencies in earnest, its cleanup plan fails to address the uncertainty residents feel about the long-term danger of toxins in the fly ash and dwindling property values. As of 2010, the public and environmentalists had not forgotten this crisis.

What follows is a discussion of the 1997 Red River Valley Floods. Consider the lessons on effective communication in Chapter 5 when reading this case.

EXAMPLE 6.2. 1997 RED RIVER VALLEY FLOODS

In 1997, the cities of Fargo and Grand Forks, North Dakota, and Moorhead and East Grand Forks, Minnesota, worked to manage one of the most costly and damaging floods in recent history. The Red River Valley, located along the border of North Dakota and Minnesota, had a record snowfall during the winter of 1996–1997. The valley is actually an ancient lake bed that has a tendency to return to its ancient state during the spring. Following the heavy winter snowfall, the spring thaw unleashed incredible amounts of water into the north-flowing Red River. Although the cities had planned for flooding that year, the National Weather Service's (NWS) flood predictions were considerably lower than what the region experienced (Sellnow, Seeger, & Ulmer, 2002). This discrepancy between the predictions and what was experienced created great uncertainty for North Dakota and Minnesota residents. Complicating the matter was the confidence placed in the NWS's highly variable crest levels communicated to the public. This information was crucial for community members, because they used these announcements to sandbag areas and construct levees.

A view of the Red River in Grand Forks

SOURCE: Ken Gardner, U.S. Army Corps of Engineers/Wikimedia.

PREDICTING FLOODWATERS IN THE RED RIVER VALLEY

Faced with record snowfalls and the prospect of significant flooding, residents of Minnesota and North Dakota looked for information about area flood levels. Conventional water measurements and Red River predictions were based on the NWS's series of gauges that provided specific water depth measurements. Historically, these quantitative measurements were effective in predicting water levels for normal spring flooding. However, the complexity of the overall system was dramatically different because of an unprecedented runoff. In this case, the runoff interacted with roadbeds, bridges, and even levees to make predictions of river crest levels difficult. There were several factors that negatively influenced the NWS's ability to predict the levels of the floodwaters (Sellnow, Seeger, & Ulmer, 2002):

> During the winter, snow measured 30 inches in area fields—more than twice the normal levels.
>
> Floating ice damaged the gauges in the river.
>
> Heavy rain and fluctuating temperatures made it difficult to keep pace with the fluctuating water levels. (pp. 275–278)

Each of these factors affected the NWS's ability to use their gauges effectively. The snowfields created a dramatic amount of water runoff into the Red River. Floating ice routinely damaged the river gauges, leading to incorrect crest level readings being announced to the public. In addition, heavy rain and fluctuating temperatures created shifts in water levels. Clearly, each of these factors made communicating about the flood difficult, particularly because the NWS could not be certain at any time that their gauges were accurately reading the levels of the river. In addition, there were many factors that could change readings from day to day.

COMMUNICATING TO THE PUBLIC ABOUT CREST LEVELS

While the cities in North Dakota and Minnesota were uncertain about the level of floodwaters, the NWS had a difficult time communicating flood information because of the complexity of the crisis. Here are some of the key communication issues during the flooding (Sellnow, Seeger, & Ulmer, 2002, pp. 276–280):

▸ Early in the flood, residents of Fargo were advised to prepare for flood crests as high as 38 feet. Before the flood, 38 feet was thought to be generous.

▸ On April 10, 1997, the NWS increased its predicted crests to between 39 and 39.5 feet.

▸ Two days later, on April 12, 1997, this prediction was changed. The new prediction was 37.5 feet. Residents were frustrated by the erratic 2-foot difference in the predictions.

▸ The gauges were blamed for the faulty readings. The malfunctions were blamed on floating ice and extreme temperatures.

The NWS changed its predictions many times during the crisis. However, each prediction failed to take into account the amount of variance. The NWS routinely gave specific and precise measurements to the public and then had to go back and correct earlier predictions. This inconsistency became a source of frustration for citizens sandbagging and building dikes. The constant corrections, coupled with the public's lack of confidence in the gauges, actually created more uncertainty in an already complex situation.

Ultimately, the water reached levels that had not been seen for more than 100 years. The city of Grand Forks saw its permanent dikes overwhelmed by the floodwater. The population of 50,000 was evacuated because nearly every part of the city was flooded. The financial impact was estimated at "$5 billion, making it one of the most expensive floods in U.S. history" (Sellnow & Seeger, 2001, p. 156).

UNDERSTANDING THE NATIONAL WEATHER SERVICE'S RESPONSE TO THE RED RIVER VALLEY FLOODS

Several lessons were learned from the NWS's response to the 1997 Red River Valley Floods. Most of them focus on the role of communication during complex crises, such as natural disasters. Some of the key issues are as follows:

▸ The NWS admitted that "forecasters could have stressed the uncertainties of their predictions in stronger terms" ("No evidence," 1997, p. C1).

▸ Both the NWS's and community leaders' crest level communications were excessively overconfident.

▸ The region's flood preparation was hampered by both measurement procedures and communication failures.

▸ Meteorologists deemphasized the uncertainties of their science in their communication to the public.

▶ Both the NWS's and meteorologists' communication did not take into account the variability and uncertainty caused by other factors, such as snowpack and temperature fluctuation (Sellnow, Seeger, & Ulmer, 2002, pp. 275–287).

These lessons suggest that communication about the facts surrounding a crisis can be difficult. This case provides an example of the role of uncertainty during natural disasters and some of the pitfalls related to managing that uncertainty. Even with quantitative measurement, effective crisis communicators would be wise to incorporate some of the natural uncertainty of the crisis into their communication.

YOU MAKE THE CALL

After examining this case, it is time to determine whether the NWS dealt effectively with the type of uncertainty we described in Chapter 5. First, take a moment to refresh in your mind the lessons established on managing uncertainty. These lessons should help you identify the strengths and weaknesses of NWS's crisis response. As you answer the questions that follow, consider whether the NWS was effective or ineffective in addressing the crisis from beginning to end. We have rephrased the lessons into questions so that you are better able to address the key issues in the case.

Lessons on Managing Crisis Uncertainty

Lesson 1: Organization members must accept that a crisis can start quickly and unexpectedly.

▶ In what ways was the 1997 Red River Valley flood a surprise? Was it unexpected?

Lesson 2: Organizations should not respond to crises with routine solutions.

▶ Were the responses to the flood routine?

Lesson 3: Threat is perceptual.

▶ In what ways was the threat associated with the flood perceptual? How did perceptions differ among stakeholders?

(Continued)

(Continued)

Lesson 4:   Crisis communicators must communicate early and often following a crisis regardless of whether they have critical information about the crisis.

▶ Did the NWS communicate early and often about the flood?

Lesson 5:   Organizations should not purposely heighten the ambiguity of a crisis to deceive or distract the public.

▶ Were there issues that were uncertain or ambiguous for the public after the crisis?

▶ Did the NWS heighten the ambiguity surrounding the crisis?

Lesson 6:   Be prepared to defend your interpretation of the evidence surrounding a crisis.

▶ Did the NWS defend its interpretation of the flood levels?

Lesson 7:   Without good intentions prior to a crisis, recovery is difficult or impossible.

▶ Had the NWS developed strong relationships with the public prior to the flood?

Lesson 8:   If you believe you are not responsible for a crisis, you need to build a case for who is responsible and why.

▶ Was there a need to build a case regarding responsibility during this crisis?

Lesson 9:   Organizations need to prepare for uncertainty through simulations and training.

▶ Was there any evidence that any of the involved organizations prepared for the crisis through simulations and training?

Lesson 10:   Crises challenge the way organizations think about and conduct their business.

▶ Did the 1997 Red River Valley floods challenge the way the NWS communicated crisis information to the public?

SUMMARY

The 1997 Red River Valley floods illustrate the role of uncertainty and unpredictability in crisis communication. Due to the complexity of natural disasters, it is difficult if not impossible to predict the impact of these events on a community. The NWS failed to take into account the variance of the flood levels in its communication. As a result, its certain communication did not take into account the unpredictability of the flood or the potential inaccuracy of the flood gauges. Therefore, the public was confused and frustrated by the inaccuracies communicated by the NWS during a stressful and threatening event.

EXAMPLE 6.3. THE CASE OF 9/11

The 9/11 attacks have changed the world in fundamental ways. Basic understandings of what constitutes normal have been altered. Before 9/11, security in airports, for example, was usually minimal. Most travelers resented the intrusions of security checks. Now, air travelers go through multiple levels of security checks before boarding, and most take comfort in the added security. Before 9/11, most people thought a terrorist attack on American soil was highly unlikely. Today, a great deal of effort goes into preparing for the possibility of a major terrorist attack. While 9/11 presents a number of important lessons for effective crisis communication, one of the most important issues concerns uncertainty.

The twin towers where CF's world headquarters were located

SOURCE: Jeffmock/ Wikimedia.

Initially, the cause and the scope of the attack were unclear. In fact, initial news reports indicated that the event involved a small plane and that it was an accident. People in the immediate area, even those in the World Trade Center, were unaware that a plane was involved. Even when the second plane hit the second tower, most people still thought it was an accident. NBC's *Today Show* host, Matt Lauer, even speculated on the air that these crashes were caused by some failure in the air traffic control system.

Among the uncertainties were questions of who had died, how many had died, and who was responsible for the attacks. There was also a great deal of uncertainty about the possibility of additional attacks, whether air travel was safe, what people should do, and what the attacks meant. Information about missing family members and friends was not available, and many people resorted to handing out flyers or posting notices

Rudy Giuliani maintaining communication with the public following 9/11

SOURCE: R. D. Ward/Department of Defense/Wikimedia.

requesting information about their missing loved ones. It became clear over time that many of the missing had died in the attacks.

One study of the 9/11 attacks reported that the information most wanted by the public related to the cause of the disaster, additional threats, the levels of damage, and the events' implications. The same study found that the average person spent over 8 hours on that day searching for information about the disasters by watching television news reports, listening to the radio, searching the Internet, or talking to friends and family. Many people wanted to be with friends and family as they watched the news reports (Seeger, Venette, Ulmer, & Sellnow, 2002).

Even when it became clear that the 9/11 crisis was an act of terrorism, it was still unclear who was responsible. In fact, it was still unclear a day after the event when President George Bush first spoke to the nation. The president simply called the attackers *evil terrorists*. An additional factor contributing to the uncertainty and lack of information was that many cellular telephone towers and broadcast antennas for Lower Manhattan had been located on the top of the World Trade Center. The loss of these towers rendered cell phones and much of the radio communication in the area useless.

One of the important figures in this crisis was New York City Mayor Rudolph Giuliani. Although the attacks occurred with little or no warning and created very high levels of uncertainty and confusion, the city of New York was not entirely unprepared. "As shocking as this crash was," Mayor Giuliani later explained, "we had planned for just such a catastrophe. My administration had built a state-of-the-art command center for the emergencies that inevitably befall a city like New York" (Giuliani & Kurson, 2002, p. 4). New York City first responders, fire, police, and emergency personnel practiced for crises frequently and had experience dealing with many crises, such as West Nile virus outbreaks and power blackouts.

Upon hearing of the first plane crash, Mayor Giuliani immediately traveled to see the site. "I needed to see with my own eyes the disaster site and our rescue operation and get a sense of what we would be dealing with in the months to come" (Giuliani & Kurson, 2002, p. 22). He also held frequent news conferences from close to the World Trade Center site, sometimes speaking to the press several times a day. In fact, his first appearance in the media occurred during a walking news conference while debris was still falling from the collapsed towers. Often, he had little or no new information other than reports of how many bodies had been recovered and how the recovery effort was proceeding. He would report on how many people were working on recovery or how operations were proceeding to remove debris. He was also very emotional, often very angry, when he talked about the attacks. As time went on and more information became available, he shared the emerging details with the public. His reassuring tone and manner helped New Yorkers and the rest of the country. In one of his first news conferences, he said, "Tomorrow New York is going to be here. And we're going to rebuild, and we're going to be stronger than we were before. . . . I want the people of New York to be an example to the rest of the country, and the rest of the world, that terrorism can't stop us" (Giuliani, n.d.). He attended hundreds of funerals and spent time with the families of victims. He coordinated the activities of emergency responders and was involved in almost all aspects of the disaster, from recovery to planning memorial services. Most of all, Mayor Giuliani spoke to a wide variety of groups about the events, what they meant, and how New York was going to recover.

In his book *Leadership*, Mayor Giuliani described the important role of communicating strong values and beliefs, particularly following major crises like the 9/11 attacks. Giuliani described how he had spoken plainly and directly about values: "I tried to explain the enormity of what happened and hold accountable those who were responsible" (Giuliani & Kurson, 2002, p. 186). In a speech before the United Nations, he said, "This was not just an attack on the City of New York or on the United States of America. It was an attack on the very idea of a free, inclusive, civil society. . . . Terrorism is based on the persistent and deliberate violation of fundamental human rights" (p. 184). This and other clear and direct statements of values helped Mayor Giuliani rally support for New York as it struggled to recover. He also described his communication style as "available and candid," even "blunt" (p. 188).

Mayor Giuliani is widely recognized as a very successful crisis leader. Many people watching him on television took a great deal of comfort in his straightforward statements. His attitudes and approaches came to symbolize the response of New York and most of America to this devastating terrorist attack.

YOU MAKE THE CALL

After examining this case, it is time to determine whether Mayor Rudy Giuliani dealt effectively with the type of uncertainty we described in Chapter 5. First, take a moment to refresh in your mind the lessons established on managing uncertainty. These lessons should help you identify the strengths and weaknesses of Rudy Giuliani's crisis response. As you contemplate the questions that follow, consider whether the mayor was effective or ineffective in addressing the crisis from beginning to end. We have rephrased the lessons into questions so that you are better able to address the key issues in the case.

Lessons on Managing Crisis Uncertainty

Lesson 1: Organization members must accept that a crisis can start quickly and unexpectedly.

▶ How did the unexpected nature of this crisis influence how it was perceived?

Lesson 2: Organizations should not respond to crises with routine solutions.

▶ Which of Mayor Giuliani's responses would you characterize as nonroutine? How did Mayor Giuliani's responses reflect the nonroutine nature of the situation?

Lesson 3: Threat is perceptual.

▶ How did the public perceive the threat of the 9/11 attacks?

Lesson 4: Crisis communicators must communicate early and often following a crisis regardless of whether they have critical information about it.

▶ How did Rudy Giuliani's early presence and frequent news conferences influence the way the crisis developed?

Lesson 5: Organizations should not purposely heighten the ambiguity of a crisis to deceive or distract the public.

▶ Would you characterize Rudy Giuliani's communication about the 9/11 attacks as honest? If so, what was the result of an honest response?

Lesson 6:   Be prepared to defend your interpretation of the evidence surrounding a crisis.

 ▶ Rudy Giuliani spent a great deal of time talking about the toughness and resilience of New Yorkers. He said that the city would come back strong. Would you agree with this characterization?

Lesson 7:   Without good intentions prior to a crisis, recovery is difficult or impossible.

 ▶ How did Mayor Giuliani use established American values to help generate support for New York?

Lesson 8:   If you believe you are not responsible for a crisis, you need to build a case for who is responsible and why.

 ▶ How did Mayor Giuliani describe those who were to blame for the 9/11 attacks? How did this help him rally support?

Lesson 9:   Organizations need to prepare for uncertainty through simulations and training.

 ▶ How did New York prepare for events such as 9/11?

Lesson 10:   Crises challenge the way organizations think about and conduct their business.

 ▶ How did the events of 9/11 change the way U.S. citizens think about New York? Did Mayor Giuliani's actions help change the way you think about New York and New Yorkers?

SUMMARY

The events of 9/11 have changed basic understandings regarding the threats of terrorist attacks. In many ways, 9/11 created a new sense of normal. Most of U.S. society pulled together following the 9/11 events. In part, this was because leaders like Mayor Giuliani spoke directly and often to the public. Even though there was tremendous uncertainty about who caused the crisis and what would happen next, Mayor Giuliani was able to manage this uncertainty effectively.

EXAMPLE 6.4. KING CAR'S RESPONSE TO THE 2008 MELAMINE CRISIS

In August 2008, the Asian food industry experienced a widespread crisis. Chinese food companies were implicated with increasing the amount of protein in their nondairy milk products by adding melamine to inflate their apparent protein contents. The crisis originally began in 2007 when dogs and cats began to experience kidney failure after eating pet food that contained high levels of melamine. The crisis expanded when nearly 300,000 infants became ill and six died after consuming melamine-contaminated baby formula produced by Chinese dairy product company Sanlu. At this time, there was heightened uncertainty among companies worldwide regarding the safety of Chinese food ingredients. Initially, the Chinese government was slow to respond and denied any problems with their food products. This created more uncertainty and doubt about the safety of products originating from China. For instance, the USDA and the Food and Drug Administration (FDA) subjected all imported food products from China to physical examination before they could enter the United States.

REDUCING CRISIS UNCERTAINTY

King Car, a Taiwanese food company, responded immediately to the melamine crisis, because it imported many Chinese-based ingredients for its milk products. At the time of the crisis, the Taiwanese Department of Health emphasized its strong food testing system in their initial communications and tried to minimize concern and reassure the public about its strong food safety regulations. However, there was considerable public unrest and uncertainty about whether Taiwanese products were safe. On Saturday, September 13, 2008, King Car called an emergency meeting and decided to hold a media conference to discuss product safety (Ku, 2009). At this time, Mr. Lee, the chairman of King Car, explained that the only way to ensure public trust was to have King Car test its products for excessive melamine levels in addition to the government testing to ensure their safety (Chen, 2008; Ku, 2009). After testing of its products was complete, King Car determined that in fact its milk products contained unacceptably high levels of melamine even though the Taiwanese government tested these products.

A GUIDING VISION FOR KING CAR'S CRISIS COMMUNICATION

At the outset of the crisis, Chairman Lee set a guiding philosophy for King Car's response. He told his senior management there were no limits on the budget for fixing the crisis (Wu, Hsieh, & Peng, 2008). Chairman Lee explained that customer trust was of the utmost importance to King Car. He noted that King Car had worked for 50 years to gain the trust of its customers and that the company would do everything in its power to maintain this trust throughout the crisis.

After learning through its own investigation that its products were contaminated, King Car immediately sent these results to a second laboratory to have the results quickly checked again. King Car could have taken the word of the Taiwanese government, but it decided to take matters into its own hands and test its products independently to ensure the safety of its customers.

INITIAL CRISIS COMMUNICATION

When King Car's second round of testing came back positive for high levels of melamine, the company immediately engaged the public with its information. First, King Car notified the Taiwanese Department of Health about the contamination it had found independently of the Taiwanese government tests. Second, the general manager for King Car personally called media reporters to make them aware of the contamination and to inform the public. In this case, the public was under the impression that government tests were adequate and Taiwanese products were safe. King Car wanted to apologize for the unsafe products and make sure that the public had information about how to protect themselves. Lin (2008) explains that King Car chose to publicize its contaminated products before the Taiwanese government's tests had identified high levels of melamine. Without King Car's own testing and quick communication, the crisis would have most certainly been much worse. At this time, King Car also informed all its retailers that King Car was recalling all its nondairy milk powder.

THE RECALL

After King Car had determined its product was not safe for consumption, they communicated to retailers across Taiwan about a recall. Over time, King Car had developed strong, positive relationships with these retailers that made communication easier and more productive. As a result, the company was able to recall over 95% of its product in 3 days. To help with the recall, King Car provided unconditional refunds to all its customers even

Taiwanese customers check King Car products for a new safety stamp

SOURCE: AP Photo/Chen qianjun.

without a receipt. As a result, within a week, almost 100% of its product was recalled. King Car also announced that it would soon have safe products for consumption with a different package and a certification of safety stamp on it. The repackaging and certification enabled King Car to differentiate its products from those that were not tested or certified. King Car also set up toll-free service lines to answer any and all customer questions about the recall and the safety of the products. The company also made product tests public via its website so consumers could check to see if the products they had purchased were safe (Young, Lo, Lee, & Chu, 2008). Finally, King Car invited reporters to its plant to see the recalled products being destroyed. The cost of the recall was estimated at over $3 million dollars. These actions received widespread critical acclaim from the Taiwanese public, media, and scholars (Lin, 2008).

CRITICAL ACCLAIM

King Car received widespread critical acclaim for its response to the melamine crisis. In fact, King Car was able to quickly restore trust with the public and its stakeholders as a result of its response. On the other hand, companies like Nestle and United, which refused to admit the use of contaminated ingredients until a month later, struggled for public acceptance. A Taiwanese business magazine, *Business Today*, explained that the melamine crisis upset everybody, yet King Car was the only organization willing to apologize and fix the problem. Their attitude makes them the model for other companies (Ku, 2009). *Apple Daily*, a Taiwanese newspaper, explained King Car is probably the only company that's going to be forgiven by the public throughout this Chinese poisoned-milk crisis (Ku, 2009).

YOU MAKE THE CALL

After examining this case, it is time to determine whether King Car dealt effectively with the type of uncertainty we described in Chapter 5. First, take a moment to refresh in your mind the lessons established on managing uncertainty. These lessons should help you identify the strengths and weaknesses of King Car's crisis response. As you contemplate the questions that follow, consider whether King Car was effective or ineffective in addressing the crisis from beginning to end. We have rephrased the lessons into questions so that you are better able to address the key issues in the case.

Lessons on Managing Crisis Uncertainty

Lesson 1:   Organization members must accept that a crisis can start quickly and unexpectedly.

▶ In what ways did King Car's crisis start quickly and with uncertainty?

Lesson 2:   Organizations should not respond to crises with routine solutions.

▶ Did King Car respond to the crisis in a routine manner? Was their response effective?

Lesson 3:   Threat is perceptual.

▶ In what ways was the threat associated with this crisis perceptual? How did perceptions differ among stakeholders?

Lesson 4:   Crisis communicators must communicate early and often following a crisis regardless of whether they have critical information about the crisis.

▶ Did King Car communicate early and often following the crisis? Were they effective or ineffective?

Lesson 5:   Organizations should not purposely heighten the ambiguity of a crisis to deceive or distract the public.

▶ Were there issues that were uncertain or ambiguous for stakeholders following the crisis? Did King Car heighten or reduce the ambiguity surrounding the crisis?

Lesson 6:   Be prepared to defend your interpretation of the evidence surrounding a crisis.

▶ Did King Car defend its interpretation of evidence surrounding the crisis? Was King Car effective or ineffective?

Lesson 7:   Without good intentions prior to a crisis, recovery is difficult or impossible.

▶ Had King Car developed good relationships with stakeholders prior to the crisis?

Lesson 8:   If you believe you are not responsible for a crisis, you need to build a case for who is responsible and why.

▶ Did responsibility emerge as a key factor in King Car's response to the melamine crisis? Was King Car's response effective or ineffective?

(Continued)

(Continued)

Lesson 9:   Organizations need to prepare for uncertainty through simulations and training.

▶ Is there evidence that King Car was prepared to respond to the crisis?

Lesson 10:   Crises challenge the way organizations think about and conduct their business.

▶ In what ways did King Car and the food industry change the way it conducts its business following the melamine crisis?

SUMMARY

The King Car crisis is a classic case of how threat, surprise, short response time, and uncertainty can impact decision making and communication following a crisis. Under the stress and uncertainty of the crisis, King Car made a critical mistake by shifting blame for the crisis outside the organization when the company had not checked to make sure that it was not responsible. King Car capitalized on the uncertainty of the situation in the short term, but when an internal investigation revealed that the company's headquarters had received the new state standard, it quickly moved to accepting responsibility and learning from the crisis.

EXAMPLE 6.5. ENRON

The Enron case has been widely publicized as an example of corporate greed, excessive risk taking, and unethical business practices (Lyon, 2008; Seeger & Ulmer, 2003). At the center of the case are Kenneth Lay, CEO and founder of Enron; Jeffery Skilling, president; Andrew Fastow, chief financial officer; and David Duncan, Enron's chief auditor for Arthur Andersen, the accounting firm that was required to check Enron's accounting practices. Much of Enron's early success was attributable to deregulation of the energy industry and free market commodity trading of natural gas and electricity. Enron's clout, success, aggressiveness, and business context of little or no oversight allowed it to expand its commodity trading businesses to weather derivatives, Internet bandwidth, and bankruptcy protection. Enron was quickly changing the business of what commodities could be traded and how they could be traded. While Enron manipulated energy rates, its profits, and its losses, few questioned the implications of these complex financial instruments and the inherent risk associated with them. In fact, from 1996 to 2000 Enron was named by *Fortune Magazine* as "America's most innovative company" (Stein, 2000). In addition, in 2000, Enron was named by *Fortune Magazine* as number 24 on the list of the "100 best companies to work for" ("Best companies list," 2000). Yet by the end of 2001 Enron would be surrounded by controversy in the middle of one of the worst corporate crises in history and on the verge of bankruptcy. In 15 years, Enron grew to the 7th largest company in the world with a staff of 21,000 in over 40 countries. Enron was also one of the hottest stocks on Wall Street, hitting its high in 2000 at $90 a share. By 2001, Enron's stock was worthless and had plummeted to under $1 a share.

Kenneth Lay following the Enron crisis

SOURCE: Dave Einsel/Getty Images News/Getty Images.

LEADERSHIP COMMUNICATION

To achieve success, Enron leaders failed in communicating appropriate values to employees, failed to be informed about the organization's business practices, and failed to be open to signs of problems (Seeger & Ulmer, 2003). Each of these leadership failures contributed to Enron's eventual demise.

DIVERGENT CORPORATE VALUES

From the inception of the company, Enron was known as a highly competitive company and had an entrepreneurial vision based on values that emphasized innovation and creativity over traditional thinking and standard business models. However, Enron had established a formal code of ethics that described their values and key mission with respect to how they would conduct business. Every employee was required to sign that they had read the Rice Code and agreed to comply with it.

Over time, Enron moved from an entrepreneurial vision and approach to business to higher and higher levels of excess, risk, and hubris. However, the hidden values of these were kept largely out of view from stakeholders. Initially, in its natural gas operation, Enron had used traditional and widely accepted accounting practices to determine its earnings. Basically, they would subtract the costs of selling the natural gas to customers from the revenues earned from selling it. However, over time, Enron took on even more complicated, risky, and ethically questionable accounting processes that ultimately served to increase profits and hide any losses. These complex accounting processes made accurate reporting of their quarterly earnings more difficult to explain, more prone to error, and less reliable. Rather than the Rice Code being the standards from which success or failure was measured at Enron, profitability became the barometer for Enron's success. This new value was illustrated as Enron executives modeled conspicuous displays of power, excess, risk taking, and wealth at the organization. Employees understood that profitability at any cost was the dominant value position at Enron (Fox, 2003).

Rice Code of Ethics for Enron

Respect: We treat others, as we would like to be treated ourselves. We do not tolerate abusive or disrespectful treatment. Ruthlessness, callousness, and arrogance don't belong here.

Integrity: We work with customers and prospects openly, honestly, and sincerely. When we say we will do something, we will do it; when we say we cannot or will not do something, then we won't do it.

Communication: We have an obligation to communicate. Here, we take time to talk with one another . . . and to listen. We believe that information is meant to move and that information moves people.

Excellence: We are satisfied with nothing less than the very best in everything we do. We will continue to raise the bar for everyone. The great fun here will be for all of us to discover just how good we really can be. ("Enron statement," 1996)

RESPONSIBILITY TO BE INFORMED

Part of the Enron culture involved the organization being highly decentralized. Employees were encouraged to be very independent and worked with little supervision. The more money employees made for Enron, the more independence and responsibility they were given. Kenneth Lay developed this very decentralized organizational structure (Seeger & Ulmer, 2003). When Jeffrey Skilling ultimately took the company over from Kenneth Lay, he flattened the levels of supervision at Enron from 13 to four. Skilling traded oversight and control for flexibility, agility, and innovation. He felt that, with fewer levels of oversight, employees could act more quickly with fewer meetings and reviews by superiors. This radically decentralized structure made it difficult and ultimately impossible to have direct knowledge of business operations, particularly with employees who were generating profits for Enron. Over time, Skilling took this lack of accountability to the extreme by approving deals verbally without any paperwork or even taking notes. Without any knowledge of business operations, Enron's leaders could also declare plausible deniability about their knowledge of any unethical business practices. An SEC chief enforcement officer would later describe Enron's leadership behavior as willful blindness (Witt & Behr, 2002).

OPENNESS TO SIGNS OF PROBLEMS

Enron had created a culture of innovation, risk tolerance, and positivity at all costs. Employees soon recognized that negative information was not valued. The best example of squelching bad news was Sharron Watkins, the now celebrated Enron whistle-blower, who worked for CFO Andrew Fastow and wrote an anonymous letter to Kenneth Lay expressing her concerns about Enron's accounting practices and public financial statements. Watkins eventually met with Kenneth Lay in person about her concerns. After their meeting, Kenneth Lay hired an outside law firm to examine some of Enron's business transactions. The law firm concluded that some restatement of earnings would be necessary. Even though Sharron Watkins's warning was useful and accurate, Enron tried to fire her (Fox, 2003; Morse & Bower, 2003). Ultimately, Watkins resigned from Enron in 2002. The failure to be open to signs of problems and Enron's culture of no bad news created self-censorship, denial, and often belligerence toward those who tried to uncover problems at Enron. Skilling, for example, once called an analyst an "asshole" for suggesting Enron's financial statements were incomplete (Cruver, 2002). At the height of the accusations against Enron and mounting losses, Enron executives continued to deny problems and regularly promoted buying Enron stock to their employees and stockholders.

Enron filed for bankruptcy on December 2, 2001, which was the largest on record until WorldCom declared bankruptcy in 2002. Several pieces of legislation, such as the Sarbanes-Oxley Act, were put into place to protect shareholders and stakeholders from being defrauded and to increase the accountability of accounting firms to be objective and independent of their clients. Enron's collapse illustrates the importance of managing uncertainty effectively before, during, and after an organizational crisis. Organizational leaders should place a premium on making sure that they do not willfully accentuate ambiguity and uncertainty through their leadership communication. Organizations should pay attention to their espoused values and codes of ethics and make sure that the organization's leadership models those values. Enron had a strong code of ethics, but the countervalues of greed, excess, and profitability overrode any of the values espoused there. Finally, leaders need to be obligated to be open to bad news and signs of problems. Leaders who fail to be open to warning signs of problems are likely to increase uncertainty and ambiguity within an organization.

YOU MAKE THE CALL

After examining this case, it is time to determine whether Enron communicated effectively with the stakeholders involved in the crisis. First, take a moment to refresh in your mind the lessons established in Chapter 5 for managing crisis uncertainty. These lessons should guide you in evaluating the strengths and weaknesses of Enron's crisis response.

Lessons on Managing Crisis Uncertainty

Lesson 1: Organization members must accept that a crisis can start quickly and unexpectedly.

▶ In what ways was the financial crisis at Enron a surprise? Was it unexpected?

Lesson 2: Organizations should not respond to crises with routine solutions.

▶ Were the responses to the crisis by Enron's leaders routine?

Lesson 3: Threat is perceptual.

▶ In what ways was the threat associated with Enron's financial crisis perceptual? How did perceptions differ among stakeholders?

Lesson 4: Crisis communicators must communicate early and often following a crisis regardless of whether they have critical information about the crisis.

▶ Did Enron or any of its stakeholders communicate early and often about the financial crisis?

Lesson 5:   Organizations should not purposely heighten the ambiguity of a crisis to deceive or distract the public.

▶ Were there issues that were uncertain or ambiguous for the public during or after the crisis?

▶ Did Enron heighten the ambiguity surrounding the crisis?

Lesson 6:   Be prepared to defend your interpretation of the evidence surrounding a crisis.

▶ Did Enron ethically defend its interpretation of the financial crisis?

Lesson 7:   Without good intentions prior to a crisis, recovery is difficult or impossible.

▶ Had Enron developed strong, ethical relationships with their stakeholders prior to the crisis?

Lesson 8:   If you believe you are not responsible for a crisis, you need to build a case for who is responsible and why.

▶ Was there a need to build a case regarding responsibility during this crisis?

Lesson 9:   Organizations need to prepare for uncertainty through simulations and training.

▶ Was there any evidence that training for crises could have prevented this event?

Lesson 10: Crises challenge the way organizations think about and conduct their business.

▶ Did Enron's financial crisis challenge the way these types of crises will be handled in the future?

SUMMARY

The Enron case offers valuable lessons for understanding financial crises. First, financial crises are difficult to identify if the company is not forthcoming about its financial problems. Arthur Andersen, the accounting agency responsible for auditing and checking Enron's financial viability, was not effective and did not fulfill its professional responsibilities. Second, extreme decentralization and lack of oversight in this case led to increased uncertainty and fewer checks and balances regarding Enron business deals. Decentralization can be effective and can distribute power and control broadly, but organizations should maintain consistent updates about organizational activities if they are to avoid making the same mistakes as Enron. Third, organizations should be open to signs of problems and address those problems as quickly as possible. Finally, organizations should work to establish codes of ethics and make sure that those values are driving everyday business operations and decisions. Organizations that deviate from established values and codes are likely to make decisions they will regret later.

EXAMPLE 6.6. FUKASHIMA DAIICHI: UNCERTAINTY CREATED BY THREE INTERRELATED CRISIS EVENTS

The Fukushima Daiichi disaster on March 11, 2011, was among the most significant nuclear accidents in recent history. The disaster was really three events that interacted with each other. First came the Tōhoku magnitude 9 earthquake that created a tsunami. The tsunami then resulted in an industrial accident at the Tokyo Electric Power Company (TEPCO), Fukushima Nuclear Power Plant.

According to the International Nuclear Event Scale, the disaster was a Level 7 event, the most severe. Equipment failures at the plant occurred because generators, located in the basement, were flooded and failed. Without electricity, pumps to circulate water to cool the reactor could not be operated. This lead to a nuclear meltdown and ultimately to releases of radioactive materials into the air and water. The disaster went on for some time and it was not until December 16 that the plant was declared stable. Several workers were seriously hurt and many were exposed to high levels of radiation. Almost 18,500 people died from the devastation of the Tōhoku earthquake and tsunami. Only a few were immediately hurt by the Fukushima disaster but the broader and long-term impact of the radiation exposure is unknown.

The greatest concern of a radiological event is the impact of public health through exposure. Evacuations and shelter in place are the most typical ways in which exposure can be limited. A four-level evacuation process was put in

Fukushima Daiichi nuclear disaster

SOURCE: © AFLO/Mainichi Newspaper/epa/Corbis.

place, but the Japanese government changed evacuation notices as the crisis developed.

On the first day, 134,000 people were evacuated, and 4 days later an additional 354,000 were evacuated. Information released by the Japanese government was delayed and in some cases inaccurate. Some suggested that the government and the plant's owner, the Tokyo Electric Power Company, sought to downplay the risks. The government's final report on the disaster found a number of problems with the way information was provided to the public. Initially the government tried to downplay the disaster for fear of creating panic and even disputed the use of the term "reactor meltdown" by the media.

Most observers agree that the company operating the plant, TEPCO, was not well prepared and was too slow in its response. The government and TEPCO did not coordinate their communication, and the crisis communication plans seemed inadequate and incomplete. There were few appropriate guidelines for how to communicate with the public about radiological events. Japan in general takes disasters very seriously because the country is so prone to earthquakes. September 1 is designated Disaster Preparedness day and is set aside for drills and exercises for organizations and government agencies. For the first 10 days of the Fukushima Daiichi event, little information was available, and then when the information was provided about the level of radiation exposure, it was highly technical and could not easily be understood by the public. Japanese scientists were also reluctant to discuss the disaster for fear of creating yet more confusion and uncertainty.

In addition, radiation exposure is generally very frightening to people because it is both unseen and exotic. It can persist for a very long time and come through the air, water, and food. Low levels of exposure generally pose very limited risks while high levels of exposure for extended periods of time can create a number of serious health problems including birth defects and cancer. We are all exposed to radiation every day. Cell phones, security scans, smoke detectors, microwaves, and power lines all emit radiation. Most of us have had x-rays taken for medical purposes. Despite the fact that we are all exposed to radiation, most people become concerned, some would say unduly concerned, about radiation.

The fear about radiation, the uncertainty about the levels of release, the exposure, trauma, and destruction from the earthquake and tsunami created a very challenging context for communication. The confusion about who should provide information resulted in the public being denied access to critical information.

YOU MAKE THE CALL

The Fukushima Daiichi disaster is generally described as a complex event because it involved natural disasters and an industrial accident. It also created a great deal of uncertainty. What were some of the other factors that made this event so uncertain? Can you think of other cases where a crisis may involve the interactions of risks that create high uncertainty? First, take a moment to refresh in your mind the lessons established in Chapter 5 for managing crisis uncertainty. These lessons should guide you in evaluating the strengths and weaknesses of Fukushima's crisis response.

Lessons on Managing Crisis Uncertainty

Lesson 1: Organization members must accept that a crisis can start quickly and unexpectedly.

▶ How did the Fukushima crisis create uncertainty through a quick and unexpected start to the crisis?

Lesson 2: Organizations should not respond to crises with routine solutions.

▶ Were there routine responses available for the Fukushima disaster?

Lesson 3: Threat is perceptual.

▶ How did perceptions about the dangers of radiation contamination impact this event?

Lesson 4: Crisis communicators must communicate early and often following a crisis regardless of whether they have critical information about the crisis.

▶ Did the TEPCO officials communicate early and often? What were some of the factors influencing how quickly and often they communicated?

Lesson 5: Organizations should not purposely heighten the ambiguity of a crisis to deceive or distract the public.

▶ How did the complexity of this event impact the ambiguity of the situation? What communication approaches would be most helpful in a case such as the Fukushima

Daiichi disaster where there is high uncertainty and the situation is changing?

Lesson 6:   Be prepared to defend your interpretation of the evidence surrounding a crisis.

▶ How should TEMPCO and Japanese officials have defended their interpretations regarding safe levels of radiation exposure? How should they have discussed their interpretations of evacuations?

Lesson 7:   Without good intentions prior to a crisis, recovery is difficult or impossible.

▶ What is the perception of the nuclear power industry? Have other events called the intentions of the industry into question?

Lesson 8:   If you believe you are not responsible for a crisis, you need to build a case for who is responsible and why.

▶ Was there a need to build a case regarding responsibility during this crisis?

Lesson 9:   Organizations need to prepare for uncertainty through simulations and training.

▶ How would you describe Japan's level of preparedness for this disaster?

Lesson 10:   Crises challenge the way organizations think about and conduct their business.

▶ Did the Fukushima Daiichi disaster change the way people think about nuclear energy? If so, how?

SUMMARY

The complexity and unusual precipitating events for the start of the crisis at Fukashima initiated great uncertainty during this crisis. The lack of preparedness by the nuclear power plant followed by the high uncertainty of the crisis led to several missteps by TEPCO, the company that managed the Fukushima Daiichi nuclear power plant. The lack of preparation and ineffective communication skills for managing the uncertainty of the crisis enraged the general public and the global audience. The response also created industry-wide questions about the role of nuclear power and radiation levels in our lives.

REFERENCES

Best companies list. (2000). Retrieved from http://www.greatplacetowork.com/what_we_do/lists-us-bestusa-2000.htm

Chen, F. Y. (2008). Honesty is a basic human moral. *Business Weekly, 1089*. Retrieved from http://www.businessweekly.com.tw/article.php?id=34532

Cruver, B. (2002). *Anatomy of greed: The unshredded truth from an Enron insider.* New York, NY: Carroll & Graf.

Enron statement of human rights. (1996). Retrieved from http://www.ethics-governance.com/article/enronstatement-of-human-rights-principles.html

Fox, L. (2003). *Enron: The rise and fall.* Hoboken, NJ: Wiley.

Giuliani, R. (n.d.). Wikipedia. Retrieved from http://en.wikipedia.org/wiki/Rudy_Giuliani

Giuliani, R. W., & Kurson, K. (2002). *Leadership* (1st ed.). New York, NY: Hyperion.

Huotari, J. (2009, January 1). $165M TVA lawsuit could get bigger. *Oakridger.* Retrieved from http://www.oakridger.com/news/x1277304648/-165M-TVA-lawsuit-could-get-bigger

Ide, W. R., & Blanco, J. O. (2009, July 21). *A report to the board of directors of the Tennessee Valley Authority regarding Kingston factual findings.* Retrieved from http://www.tva.gov/kingston/board_report/index.htm

Kilgore, T. (2009, July 28). Statement of Tom Kilgore President and Chief Executive Officer Tennessee Valley Authority. *FDCH Congressional Testimony.* Retrieved from http://search.ebscohost.com/login.aspx?direct=true&db=ulh&AN=32Y0398551033&site-ehost-live&scope=site

Ku, F. (2009). *Organizational renewal: A case study of King Car's crisis communication strategies.* Unpublished Master's Thesis. University of Arkansas at Little Rock.

Lin, Y. (2008). King Car: Consumers are way more important than profits. *Awakening News Networks.* Retrieved from http://www.awakeningtw.com/awakening/news_center/show.php?itemid=755

Lyon, A. (2008). The Mis/recognition of Enron executives' competence as cultural and social capital. *Communication Studies, 59,* 371–387.

Morse, J., & Bower, A. (2003, December 30, 2002/January 6). The party crasher. *Time,* 53–56.

National Aeronautics and Space Administration (NASA). (n.d.). Coal ash spill, Tennessee. *Earth Observatory.* Retrieved from http://earthobservatory.nasa.gov/NaturalHazards/view.php?id=36352

No evidence feds bungled flood forecast. (1997, May 19). *The Forum,* p. C1.

Seeger, M. W., & Ulmer, R. R. (2003). Explaining Enron: Communication and responsible leadership. *Management Communication Quarterly, 17,* 58–84.

Seeger, M.W., Venette, S., Ulmer, R. R., & Sellnow, T. L. (2002). Media use, information seeking, and reported needs in post crisis contexts. In B. S. Greenberg (Ed.), *Communication and terrorism: Public and media responses to 9/11* (pp. 53–63). Cresskill, NJ: Hampton Press.

Sellnow, T. L., & Seeger, M. W. (2001). Exploring the boundaries of crisis communication: The case of the 1997 Red River Valley flood. *Communication Studies, 52,* 154–169.

Sellnow, T. L., Seeger, M. W., & Ulmer, R. R. (2002). Chaos theory, informational needs, and natural disasters. *Journal of Applied Communication Research, 30,* 269–292.

Stein, N. (2000). *The world's most admired companies. How do you make the most admired list? Innovate, innovate, innovate. The winners on this year's list, compiled by the Hay Group consultancy, tell how they do it.* Retrieved from http://money.cnn.com/magazines/fortune/fortune_archive/2000/10/02/288448/index.htm

Tennessee Valley Authority (TVA). (n.d.). *Kingston fossil plant.* Retrieved from http://www.tva.gov/sites/kingston.htm

Vines: Conference tackles TVA cleanup plan. (2009, April 4). Knoxnews.com. Retrieved from http://www.knoxnews.com/news/2009/apr/04/conference-tackles-tva-cleanup-plan/

Welcome to a new year. (2010, January 1). Knoxnews.com. Retrieved from http://www.knoxnews.com/news/2010/ja

Witt, A., & Behr, P. (2002, July 29). Dream job turns into nightmare. *The Washington Post,* p. A1.

Wu, Y., Hsieh, M., Peng Y. (2008). Crisis management: Interview with King Car chairman Mr. Lee. *Common Wealth, 407.* Retrieved from http://www.cw.com.tw/article/index.jsp?id=35825

Young, Y., Lo, C., Lee, L., & Chu, H. (2008). King Car recalls 2.1 million packaged products. *Liberty Times.* Retrieved from http://www.libertytimes.com.tw/2008/new/sep/22/today-fo3.htm

Lessons on Effective Crisis Leadership

The third content chapter in this section of our book explains and describes effective leadership during crisis. Previously we discussed lessons on producing effective crisis communication along with managing uncertainty effectively. We believe that the ability to manage a crisis is a critical leadership skill and that, in the future, leaders will be called on more and more to respond to the threat and opportunity of crises. Crisis leadership, then, is a critical management skill. We begin this chapter by defining and describing leadership and crisis leadership. We then focus on 10 strategies particular to crisis leadership. The first set of lessons focuses on some of the functions of leadership during crisis. For instance, leaders need to be visible and engaged following a crisis; they need to develop strong, positive relationships with stakeholders; their responses need to create opportunities for transformation and renewal; and they should build cooperation following a crisis. The next group of lessons provides some advice and guidance for managing crises. Specifically, this section examines how poor leadership can make a crisis much worse, how leadership styles are much different during times of crisis, and how leaders have specific communication obligations in responding to, managing, resolving, and learning from crisis.

THE IMPORTANCE OF EFFECTIVE LEADERSHIP

Most of us place a great deal of faith in our leaders. Whether they are business leaders, political leaders, or leaders of religious or social groups, leaders are important representatives of their groups, organizations, and communities. We look to our leaders for direction, inspiration, motivation, resources, and comfort. Leaders establish a clear vision, communicate that vision with others, collect and distribute information and knowledge, and coordinate the efforts of others. They represent the organization. They select, train, coach, and mentor employees. Leaders reflect and strengthen the organizational culture and serve as a model. Leaders give us clues about how to behave, about what is right, and about what things mean. They promote ethical conduct and serve as moral guides. Sometimes, we expect our leaders to be almost superhuman in their abilities to solve problems and create positive outcomes.

Many definitions of leadership exist, and these definitions have changed over time as society has changed. Communication researcher Peter Northouse (2012) identified four characteristics that most definitions of leadership share. First, it is a process, suggesting it is ongoing and changing. Second, leadership involves influence of follower behaviors and perceptions. Leadership also occurs in groups, organizations, or community contexts. Finally, leadership is directed toward goals. We define *leadership* as a communication and influence process directed toward followers who are members of a group, organization, or community to assist in achieving some goal or outcome.

While leaders are always important to the success of organizations, during crisis, they take on particularly critical roles. They help reduce the turmoil of crises and reassert order and control, in part, by being visible to employees, members of the community, and the media. They oversee responses and help others understand and cope with what is happening. During a crisis, the leader may become an emergency manager coordinating response efforts, providing comfort and reassurance, disseminating information, speaking to the media, and providing a vision for response, recovery, and renewal. The goals in the case of a crisis are to contain and limit harm, assist those who have been harmed, move beyond the crisis in an appropriate manner, and learn and grow from the experience. We describe 10 lessons of effective leadership during a crisis.

> **LESSON 1**
>
> Effective leadership is critical to a crisis response.

WHY VISIBILITY FOLLOWING A CRISIS IS IMPORTANT

As you read in the case on 9/11 in Chapter 6, one well-known example of crisis leadership is the role played by New York City Mayor Rudolph Giuliani during the World Trade Center attacks (Giuliani & Kurson, 2002). Mayor Giuliani was a calm and steady presence during the chaos following the attacks. He organized much of the response, spoke to the public several times a day through the media, and came to represent the strong spirit of New Yorkers. Giuliani offered comfort to those who lost friends or family, and he was also comforting to those of us who were upset, angry, scared, and confused by the crisis. His calm presence and direct manner were reassuring to everyone affected by the attacks including the emergency workers, police, firefighters, and volunteers working to recover victims. And almost as soon as the dust had settled from the attacks, he made public commitments to rebuild.

There are many other examples of successful crisis leaders. In one of the most thoroughly studied examples of public relations and crisis management, Johnson & Johnson CEO James Burke took decisive action that helped save his company in 1982 after 13 people died from Tylenol capsules laced with cyanide. Sales of Tylenol capsules, the company's most profitable product, were decimated by the product-tampering crisis. Moving fast to save its product, the company withdrew all the Tylenol from stores. CEO Burke then appeared on the *Phil Donahue Show*, the most popular television talk show at that time, to explain that the company had nothing to do with the poisoning. He also openly described detailed plans to ensure that no such tampering could ever occur again. The company soon introduced a redesigned, tamper-proof, triple-sealed package (Benson, 1988; Snyder & Foster, 1983).

Tylenol sales rebounded, largely because of the credibility of Burke's remarks and the personal reassurance he offered. His direct and honest communication to the public was widely recognized as an example of effective crisis public relations. He built credibility and goodwill through his appearance on the *Phil Donahue Show*, and this goodwill helped the company survive.

These cases illustrate that leaders must be actively engaged during a crisis. They should be visible and accessible to the media. They should be responsive to the needs of victims. They should be actively engaged in the response. This communication helps create the impression that the crisis is being actively managed and reduces the impression that the company has something to hide. In fact, it is often appropriate for the leader to serve as the crisis spokesperson, although he or she should work with other members of the crisis team and be trained in crisis communication.

One of the questions leaders must face during crises is how visible they should be. Leaders sometimes feel the impulse to withdraw during crises, particularly when they believe that they might be blamed. This tendency to circle the wagons is understandable but can make the crisis much worse. When leaders withdraw, they cut themselves off from important information and increase the uncertainty. They may enhance the impression that there is something to hide. Some leaders may also be hesitant to honestly and openly discuss the circumstances of the crises for fear of making the situation worse. However, the actions of leaders like Rudolph Giuliani and James Burke illustrate that being open and honest are important leadership behaviors during a crisis. Transparency and honesty also build trust, credibility, and support.

The glare of the media spotlight during a crisis can be very stressful for a leader who isn't prepared or is inexperienced. One reason organizations sometimes choose to circle the wagons is because they are afraid to face the media. There are some strategies that can increase the chances of communicating successfully with the media. First, recognize that you have no choice but to face the media. A crisis is usually news, and the media will cover the story with or without you. Second, if you are open, honest, and courteous with reporters, then they will usually respond in similar ways. Finally, always be sure to express concern for those harmed by the crisis. This does not mean that you are accepting responsibility or blame; it simply means your organization is human, empathetic, and caring.

> **LESSON 2**
>
> Leaders should be visible during a crisis.

DEVELOPING NETWORKS OF SUPPORT

In another famous case, Lee Iacocca was able to bring the Chrysler Corporation back from bankruptcy through his effective crisis leadership. In 1982, Chrysler was essentially broke. In a last-ditch effort, the company brought in Iacocca as its new CEO. Iacocca moved quickly to build support for loans from the federal government. He spoke to workers, banks, and suppliers and was open, honest, and even blunt in his assessment of the company's situation. He also received help from state and local governments, community groups, and political organizations. The network of support he built helped the company secure government loans and make one of the most spectacular crisis recoveries ever. Customers reported buying Chryslers because they wanted to support Iacocca's efforts to save the company.

As with Burke in the Johnson & Johnson case, Iacocca was visible in his efforts to build widespread support for the company. He was honest and direct in explaining the situation Chrysler faced. He also described his plans for saving the company and asked directly for the public's support. Although Chrysler had fallen on hard times, it had long-established relationships with customers, communities, suppliers, unions, banks, and even competitors. Chrysler had been a good corporate citizen, providing jobs and supporting communities, and for many years, building solid products. These relationships and the company's long history of success represented a kind of reservoir of goodwill and legitimacy that it used during the crisis. This reservoir of goodwill, positive reputation, and credibility is often essential to surviving a crisis. Lee Iacocca was a very effective and natural communicator, and his communication saved the company.

In another example, CEO of the Canadian company Maple Leafs Foods, Michael McCain, managed a 2008 recall of it products linked to a serious outbreak of food-borne illness. The outbreak was linked to 9 confirmed and 11 suspected deaths. Rather than try to deny responsibility and limit the recall, McCann actually voluntarily expanded the recall of 23 of its products, to all 220 packaged meat products produced at the plant, where the contamination occurred. McCain was highly visible holding several press conferences. Company spokespersons did interviews, and the CEO posted a public apology on its website. In it he said, "To those people who have become ill, and to the families who have lost loved ones, I want to express my deepest and most sincere sympathies. Words cannot begin to express our sadness for your pain" (McCain, 2008).

> **LESSON 3**
>
> Leaders should work to develop a positive company reputation during normal times to build a reservoir of goodwill.

BEING AVAILABLE, OPEN, AND HONEST

These examples show that crisis leadership is a critical skill for many managers. Leadership is important for managing and recovering from all kinds of crises, including product tampering, near bankruptcy, and even terrorist attacks. In all cases and in all organizational contexts, engaged, open, and honest leadership is critical to successful crisis management.

James Lee Witt, former director of FEMA, explains however, that crisis "communication is more than talking—it's the honest and open exchange of personal views" (Witt & Morgan, 2002, p. 49). Honesty and openness can be difficult during a crisis if the organization has done something wrong. As we described earlier, there is a natural tendency to circle the wagons or batten down the hatches during a crisis. Where there is a history of wrongdoing, the natural first impulse may be to hide the wrongdoing. Company attorneys often advise leaders to say as little as possible following a crisis. They typically argue that any statement about the crisis can be used against the organization and may increase the organization's liability. In the case of Maple Leaf Foods, CEO Michael McCain specifically noted that he ignored the advice of both his lawyers and accountants in deciding how to respond to the crisis. Failure to be open and honest usually compounds the crisis and makes the

> **LESSON 4**
>
> Leaders should be open and honest following a crisis.

media even more aggressive and the public more suspicious. Stakeholders may also become angry if they think an organization is trying to shift blame and avoid responsibility. In the long run, failure to be open, honest, and forthcoming usually makes matters worse for a company.

THE IMPACT OF LEADERSHIP ON RENEWAL FOLLOWING A CRISIS

The experiences of Chrysler, Johnson & Johnson, and Maple Leaf Foods are examples of organizations that were able to recreate themselves, not just surviving their crises but subsequently thriving and achieving even more success. Chrysler went on to become one of the most profitable car companies during the 1980s. Johnson & Johnson actually built market share after the poisonings. Michael McCain was named CEO of the year, and his company also added market share. These examples illustrates that when a crisis is managed successfully and when managers are open and honest and draw on a set of strong core values crises can actually serve as renewing forces.

Companies facing crisis are forced to reexamine basic goals and values. Support regarding money, resources, and goodwill may come to an organization following a crisis if it is managed successfully. A crisis can create an opportunity to change fundamental operations and activities. Fires or explosions, for example, provide opportunities to rebuild facilities and acquire new, modern equipment. A crisis may create opportunities for a company to be more visible. In some cases, customers choose to buy products to help out a company facing a crisis. General Motors went through a devastating bankruptcy in 2009 when it was caught in a very significant economic downturn. The company came out of bankruptcy a much leaner, stronger, and profitable company. The crisis created an opportunity for renewal.

> **LESSON 5**
>
> Leaders who manage crises successfully may create opportunities for renewal.

INEFFECTIVE LEADERSHIP DURING A CRISIS

While the cases of Michael McCain, James Burke, and Lee Iacocca are success stories, there are many more cases of leaders failing to successfully communicate and manage crises. In fact, leaders are often part of the crisis; when this is true, their efforts may actually backfire and make things worse.

As we discussed in Chapter 5, when Exxon's tanker *Valdez* ran into an Alaskan reef in 1989, spilling 1.5 million gallons of crude oil, Exxon CEO Lawrence Rawl's response made the environmental damage much worse.

He decided early on not to visit the scene of the spill, thereby indicating to many observers that he thought the problem was insignificant. He then sought to shift blame for the spill to the *Valdez* captain and blame for cleanup failure to decisions made by the State of Alaska. At the very time when cooperation was needed, Rawl became engaged in a public dispute with Alaska's Governor Cowper. The Exxon *Valdez* oil spill is generally recognized as a public relations disaster, one compounded by Rawl's behavior.

In 2010, Tony Hayward, CEO of BP, during the Gulf Coast oil spill crisis received much criticism for his crisis communication. Hayward's ineffective leadership communication started with a delayed response that minimized the severity of the spill. He also made mistakes by stating that "he wanted his life back" in a public interview about the crisis (Chen, 2010, para. 5). Not only was the content of Hayward's message ineffective but so too was the form of his response. While the Gulf Coast fishermen and residents suffered the effects of the oil spill, Hayward was photographed at a glitzy yacht race in England. Ultimately, Hayward was criticized for his lack of transparency, a lack of crisis planning, a delayed response that initially minimized the scope of the crisis, and a lack of empathy to those impacted by the crisis.

In another classic example of poor crisis leadership, Firestone CEO John Lampe and Ford CEO Jack Nassar became involved in a public fight over a series of accidents involving Ford Explorers equipped with Firestone tires. Lampe blamed the Ford Explorer for a series of rollover accidents; Nassar blamed Firestone tires (see Venette, Sellnow, & Lang, 2003). The public brawl not only ended a 95-year relationship between the two companies, but it also seriously damaged the reputations of both firms. As Ford and Firestone exchanged charges and countercharges, the public was left with the impression that both companies were more interested in avoiding responsibility than in solving the problem or protecting consumers. Negative publicity was prolonged for many months, and the public squabble made it almost impossible to find the real cause of the problem.

LESSON 6

Leaders should cooperate with stakeholders during a crisis and should work to build consensus.

During the recent economic downturn that reached economic proportions in 2008, many Wall Street executives failed to acknowledge the crisis until it was too late, failed in their responsibilities to be visible and engaged, and in many cases, failed to change their usual approaches to doing business. The result was several bankruptcies and further damage to Wall Street's already very negative reputation.

In another well-publicized crisis, the Catholic Church faced a series of scandals beginning in 2001–2002 regarding accusation of sexual abuse on the part of priests. In many cases, church leaders had covered up the abuse, even when it was reported to them and even when the allegations involved children. According to BostonGlobe.com, "Victims who came forward with abuse claims were ignored or paid off, while accused priests were quietly transferred from parish to parish or sent for brief periods of psychological counseling" ("Spotlight investigation," para. 2). In 2002, the United State Conference of Catholic Bishops passed new rules and guidelines for dealing with accusations of abuse. Critics pointed out, however, that many of these bishops had at one point covered up accusations of abuse. The failure of the Catholic Church to protect children and young people from abuse and the long-term practice of cover-ups seriously damaged the reputation of the church. Many victims sued, and many Catholics withheld their donations.

Leaders who deny that problems exist, who seek to cover up problems, or who simply to try to minimize the crisis or shift the blame risk creating more damage. If a problem is not fixed, it may become much worse. If leaders do not act to take responsibility and to actively manage crises, they can create the impression that they do not care about those who have been harmed and are only concerned about profits and avoiding blame.

> **LESSON 7**
>
> Poor leadership, including denials, cover-ups, or lack of response, can make a crisis much worse.

WHAT MAKES AN EFFECTIVE CRISIS LEADER?

Leadership has been the object of study for thousands of years. Even the ancient Egyptians were fascinated by leadership. The ancient Chinese military leader Sun Tzu wrote about the qualities of a successful leader, as did the medieval European writer Machiavelli. Modern researchers in management, political science, sociology, psychology, and communication have continued to study leadership using a variety of methods. This research has developed over time as society has changed. A number of theories of leadership have been developed to help explain leadership. Three general approaches to crisis leadership are discussed here.

LEADERSHIP STYLES

Researchers have examined the ways leaders behave and how they communicate (Northouse, 2012). They have found that all leaders do not behave the same way and that there is a great deal of variance from leader to leader. Various kinds of leader behavior and communication have been classified as specific styles of leadership.

For example, some leaders are very directive in giving orders and issuing instructions. They generally ask for little input from followers and make decisions based largely on their own opinions and information. This is generally described as an *authoritarian leadership style*. Authoritarian leaders are much more directive in telling followers what to do and very specific when describing how tasks should be done.

In other cases, leaders are more open to the ideas and suggestions of others. They rarely make decisions without asking for input and suggestions. These leaders are also less likely to be directive and are more likely to offer suggestions or come up with more general goals for followers. This is called a *democratic leadership style*.

A third form of leadership is called *laissez faire* or *nonleadership style*. In this style, the leader exhibits few of the characteristics associated with leadership and may be a leader in name only, generally allowing followers to do whatever they want without direction or, in many cases, without supervision.

There is some evidence to suggest that during a crisis, authoritarian leadership styles are more effective than other styles. Mayor Giuliani had been criticized for his authoritarian approach before 9/11, but after the attack, his style of leadership was seen as appropriate. People may want more directive leadership to counteract the uncertainty and confusion associated with a crisis situation. An authoritarian leader may create a stronger impression of control; however, they may also risk alienating followers and other stakeholders.

While the styles of leadership are useful in explaining what a leader actually does, many particularly effective leaders do not act the same in every context. This conclusion leads to another view of leadership: the contingency approach.

CONTINGENCY APPROACH TO LEADERSHIP

Contingency leadership suggests that different leadership situations require different kinds of leadership. For example, when the leader has good relationships with followers, the situation may call for a different style of leadership than in circumstances when the leader has poor follower relationships. In some situations, a task may be clearly structured with easily identifiable steps to achieving a desired goal, while in others, the situation is unclear and uncertain. Again, the style of leadership in these

LESSON 8

Leaders must adapt their leadership styles and contingencies during crises.

cases may be different. A third factor in contingency models of leadership is the power of the leader. Often during a crisis, leaders are given extra authority and power so they may quickly contain and limit the harm.

Crises are unique situations and require different leadership approaches. As mentioned earlier, during a crisis, the situation is usually uncertain and confusing. In some instances, authoritarian leadership may be seen as an appropriate effort to take control, particularly when there are clear and simple actions that must be undertaken quickly, such as evacuation. When the situation is seen as an emergency, leaders often have more power to move quickly and take action. In other situations, the leader may need to build cooperation and support through more democratic styles. Getting input and building consensus take time, so a democratic approach is more common after the immediacy of the crisis is over. As described earlier, leaders with positive reputations and high credibility are generally given more support by followers during crisis situations.

TRANSFORMATIONAL LEADERSHIP

A third approach to understanding crisis leadership is called *transformational leadership*. This approach to leadership was developed by researchers studying political leaders and has expanded to many organizational contexts. James MacGregor Burns (1978) described transformational leadership as both leaders and followers coming to agree on a shared vision and goals. By creating agreement on core values, priorities, and what should be done, leaders can motivate their followers to achieve extraordinary outcomes. The success of transformational leadership is associated with the communication skill of the leader and the importance of the shared goals.

Earlier, we described leadership as a transformational situation when we discussed renewal. Crises can create great changes, and although most people see them as negative, these changes can also create very positive transformations. In 1999, an explosion and fire in the massive Ford Rouge River plant near Detroit killed one worker and injured 30 others. While the accident could have resulted in major criticism of the company and questions about safety, William Clay Ford Jr., Ford Motor's chairman and the great-grandson of the founder, came to the plant less than 2 hours after the explosion. Even while firefighters were still trying to control the flames, Ford expressed his deep condolences and concerns for the workers, whom he described as members of his Ford family. Later, he went to the hospital to meet with those who had been injured, express his concerns, and offer his help. While the crisis could have been a public relations disaster, Ford's leadership was transformational by demonstrating that the most important value was the safety of workers and that the priority was taking care of the victims.

We believe most crises create opportunities for transformational leadership. Sometimes, this is due to a silver lining that is created by a crisis. In other cases, an entire organization can be recreated and renewed by a crisis. Renewal usually happens because a leader has stepped forward and communicated a clear set of values, a sense of common purpose, and a way forward.

LEADERSHIP VIRTUES

Another general approach to understanding leadership comes from the concept of virtues. *Virtues* can be understood as a predisposition to act in a positive or ethical way. A person who has the virtues of honesty and responsibility, for example, is a person who tends to act in an honest and responsible manner. This virtue ethics approach has been used since the time of Aristotle to study and teach people about moral and ethical behavior.

Virtues have also been applied to leadership and crisis leadership (Seeger & Ulmer, 2001). Returning to an earlier example, Aaron Feuerstein was the CEO of the textile company Malden Mills when it experienced a devastating fire. While the fire still burned, he made a public commitment to continue to pay his workers and rebuild the plant. This response was very consistent with earlier decisions Feuerstein had made and helped him generate the support necessary to rebuild his company. When asked why he had decided to rebuild, Feuerstein noted that it was the right thing to do (see Ulmer, 2001). The examples of William Ford Jr. and Michael McCain discussed earlier are other examples of a corporate leader acting in virtuous ways following a crisis.

Many effective responses to crisis are based on a personal set of values and a commitment to do the right thing. Crises are highly uncertain and stressful events, and during these kinds of circumstances, leaders can fall back on values, ethics, and virtues to determine how to respond. A virtuous response to a crisis is likely to generate support from stakeholders and is much more defensible than a response based in the need to avoid lawsuits or protect profits. A virtuous response to a crisis may enhance an organization's reputation and help a company renew itself.

MANAGING UNCERTAINTY, RESPONDING, RESOLVING, AND LEARNING FROM CRISIS

In Chapter 1, four consistent communication demands of crisis were described: managing uncertainty, responding to the crisis, resolving it, and learning from it. Each of these demands requires leaders to act and communicate effectively.

Managing uncertainty, for example, requires a consistent voice, usually in the form of a crisis spokesperson, and necessitates creating and maintaining open channels of communication and information flow. As mentioned earlier, we look to leaders to actively manage a crisis, and followers expect the leader to be visible during a crisis. One of the critical behaviors of the crisis leader is to serve as a spokesperson.

Speaking as a representative of the organization to aggressive and demanding media while the uncertainty of a crisis still prevails is not easy. Many leaders are not well prepared to serve as spokespersons. Many CEOs will undergo media training before a crisis. This training usually focuses on responding to intense media questioning, understanding the needs of the media during a crisis, and strategies for how to respond to questions effectively even when all the facts aren't known and where questions of responsibility and liability may be raised. Training will often put leaders in mock press conferences or staged interviews where reporters ask tough questions. The Centers for Disease Control and Prevention has conducted extensive interviews with community leaders who have managed crises. They recommend following the six principles of STARCC: (1) Simple messages are important during a crisis when people may have difficulty processing information. (2) Timely messages are critical during a crisis. (3) Accuracy requires straightforward direct messages. (4) Relevant messages address the most immediate concerns. (5) Credibility builds trust that is essential to effective crisis communication. Finally, (6) consistency is the hallmark of effective crisis communication. Additional guidelines for a crisis spokesperson are presented below.

SUGGESTIONS FOR THE LEADER AS SPOKESPERSON

▸ Don't let the media push you into saying things that you do not want to say, but don't become angry with the media.

▸ Express concern for anyone harmed by the crisis.

▸ Avoid the phrase "no comment."

▸ If you don't have the answer to a question, say so, but indicate that you are working to find the answer.

▸ Don't speak with certainty unless you are absolutely sure of all the facts.

▸ Be sure to point out the uncertainty of situations with phrases such as, "The situation is evolving" or "We don't have all the facts yet."

▸ Don't hesitate to involve others on the crisis team when you don't know the answer.

As described earlier, many leaders withdraw and limit external contact during a crisis situation. Sometimes managers may believe they should circle the wagons or batten down the hatches during crises. But one of the principal features of managing uncertainty is to facilitate the flow of information. Crisis leaders should reach out to a variety of groups and agencies during a crisis. Often, this simply means making phone calls, asking for help, giving an update, or offering to coordinate. At times, this outreach means identifying liaisons or creating coordinating groups so that everyone has access to information. What is most important is that the leader remains open to information and is willing to share information with others.

Maintaining openness can also assist with the second consistent communication requirement: responding to the crisis. Part of responding to a crisis is building coalitions of support through leader openness and accessibility. In addition, crisis leaders need to be honest and forthright in their discussion of the crisis. Lawrence Rawl, CEO of Exxon, initially tried to deny the harm caused by the *Valdez* oil spill and blame others for the spill. This only served to reduce the company's credibility and prolong the damage. The effort to shift the blame to others created additional harm and resentment.

As described earlier, one way to generate support for a crisis is to use a virtuous, value-based response reflecting values that most stakeholders admire. For example, a response that is focused primarily on helping those who have been harmed by a crisis is likely to generate more support than those responses designed to shift or avoid blame. In the case of 2005's Hurricane Katrina, which is discussed in more depth in the next chapter, much of the communication by public officials was directed toward shifting blame among FEMA, the State of Louisiana, and the City of New Orleans. The needs of the victims were secondary. A virtuous response by leaders grounded more fully in the values of helping those who had lost their homes and livelihoods may have been more effective. In addition, a virtuous response may have helped generate more support and cooperation for rebuilding and renewal.

LESSON 9

A virtuous response to a crisis by the organization's leaders may be the most effective in generating support and renewal.

Resolving the crisis, the third consistent communication demand, usually requires specific actions to offset the harm. Action may need to be taken to limit the injury to consumers, employees, or members of the community. Leaders may need to apologize publicly. During and after a crisis, leaders have specific obligations and duties to others. These may include victims, employees, stockholders, regulatory agencies, members of the community, and other crisis stakeholders. In general, crisis resolution may also require that there be an agreed-upon explanation of what caused the crisis.

Determination of blame and responsibility usually impacts insurance settlements and legal liability. Sometimes, renewal and rebuilding are postponed until questions of blame are resolved. If the leader is associated with the cause, he or she may also be held responsible for the crisis. It is not uncommon for leaders to step down from their positions following crises.

> ### LESSON 10
>
> Leaders have specific communication obligations and duties for managing and learning from crises.

A final crisis communication demand is to learn from the crisis. Unfortunately, many organizations fail to learn from the crises they experience and repeat the same mistakes again and again. After a crisis has been resolved, leaders have the important responsibility of interpreting the lessons of the crisis and communicating them throughout the organization. For leaders such as Lee Iacocca, Rudolph Giuliani, and Aaron Feuerstein, crises are life-changing experiences that include fundamental lessons about how to manage and lead, how to avoid risk, how to respond to crisis, and what is most important. By communicating the lessons, leaders enhance safety and prevention, increase an organization's vigilance, and demonstrate its values.

SUMMARY

Even during the best of times and the most normal of circumstances, leadership is a demanding and complex process. During the stress, uncertainty, and harm the demands, obligations, and duties of leadership are even more complex. This chapter explains that effective crisis leadership can create opportunities for renewal. Conversely, ineffective leadership can cause a crisis or make a crisis much worse. Crisis leadership can be understood by studying approaches or styles or by examining crisis situations as contingencies of leadership. In addition, crisis leadership may be understood as a set of specific activities. Regardless of how crisis leadership is approached, leaders should be visible, open, and honest. They should cooperate with others, work to build a reservoir of goodwill, and explore opportunities for renewal.

Lessons on Effective Crisis Leadership

Lesson 1:   Effective leadership is critical to overcoming a crisis.

Lesson 2:   Leaders should be visible during a crisis.

(Continued)

(Continued)

Lesson 3:   Leaders should work to develop a positive company reputation during normal times to build a reservoir of goodwill.

Lesson 4:   Leaders should be open and honest following a crisis.

Lesson 5:   Leaders who manage crises successfully may create opportunities for renewal.

Lesson 6:   Leaders should cooperate with stakeholders during a crisis and should work to build consensus.

Lesson 7:   Poor leadership, including denials, cover-ups, or lack of response, can make a crisis much worse.

Lesson 8:   Leaders must adapt their leadership styles and contingencies during crises.

Lesson 9:   A virtuous response to a crisis by the organization's leaders may be the most effective in generating support and renewal.

Lesson 10:   Leaders have specific communication obligations for managing and learning from crises.

REFERENCES

Benson, J. A. (1988). Crisis revisited: An analysis of strategies used by Tylenol in the second tampering episode. *Central States Speech Journal, 39*, 49–66.

Burns, J. M. (1978). *Leadership*. New York, NY: Harper & Row.

Chen, S. (2010). Crisis management 101: What can BP CEO Hayward's mistakes teach us? CNN.com. Retrieved from http://www.cnn.com/2010/LIVING/07/27/bp.tony.hayward.mistakes/index.html

Giuliani, R. W., & Kurson, K. (2002). *Leadership* (1st ed.). New York, NY: Hyperion.

McCain, M. (2008). *Maple Leaf CEO Michael H. McCain responds to determination of link to plant*. Retrieved from http://investor.mapleleaf.ca/phoenix.zhtml?c=88490&p=irol-newsArticle&ID=1189861&highlight=

Northouse, P. (2012). *Leadership: Theory and practice* (6th ed.). Thousand Oaks, CA: Sage.

Seeger, M. W., & Ulmer, R. R. (2001). Virtuous responses to organizational crisis: Aaron Feuerstein and Milt Cole. *Journal of Business Ethics, 31*, 369–376.

Snyder, L., & Foster, L. G. (1983). An anniversary review and critique: The Tylenol crisis. *Public Relations Review, 9*, 24–34.

Spotlight investigation: Abuse in the Catholic Church. (n.d.). BostonGlobe.com. Retrieved from http://www.boston.com/globe/spotlight/abuse/scandal

Ulmer, R. R. (2001). Effective crisis management through established stakeholder relationships: Malden Mills as a case study. *Management Communication Quarterly, 14,* 590–615.

Venette, S. J., Sellnow, T. L., & Lang, P. A. (2003). Metanarration's role in restructuring perceptions of crisis: NHTSA's failure in the Ford-Firestone crisis. *Journal of Business Communication, 40,* 219–236.

Witt, J. L., & Morgan, G. (2002). *Stronger in broken places: Nine lessons for turning crisis into triumph.* New York, NY: Times Books.

Applying the Lessons for Developing Effective Crisis Leadership

ffective leadership is critical to producing effective crisis communication. The previous chapter outlined the key crisis communication functions of an effective leader. What follows are five cases that examine in depth the role of leadership in crisis communication. This chapter begins with a case of the Peanut Butter Corporation's response to its devastating salmonella outbreak in 2008 and 2009. The second case examines a fire at a lumber mill and the owner's virtuous leadership response to the crisis. The third case describes a food-borne illness outbreak at a frozen food company and how a guiding vision by the owner set effective crisis communication in motion. The fourth case presents Cantor Fitzgerald, a NYC bond trading company and its leader's response to 9/11. The fifth case explains the myriad leadership failures during Hurricane Katrina. In this case, the reader is able to apply the lessons to a case of ineffective and maladaptive leadership practices. Finally, this chapter presents an examination of how General Motors' leadership responded during the 2008 financial crisis. Good luck with working through these cases while developing your crisis communication skills and experience at the same time.

EXAMPLE 8.1. THE SWEEPING IMPACT OF A CONTAMINATED FOOD INGREDIENT: PEANUT CORPORATION OF AMERICA

The first set of tests returned to plant managers of Peanut Corporation of America (PCA) indicated that the peanut product was contaminated with salmonella. Rather than discarding the tainted product, PCA sent additional samples to another testing facility. When the second set of tests failed to detect salmonella, PCA officials made the decision to ship the tainted product to various food makers where it was used in 2008 as an ingredient in other products. The Centers for Disease Control and Prevention (CDC) in the United States explains that salmonella is a form of bacteria that is transferred to humans when food items are contaminated with animal feces. Those who ingest salmonella can develop salmonellosis, leading to "diarrhea, fever, and abdominal cramps" (CDC, 2009, para. 1). After experiencing extreme discomfort for 4 to 7 days, most victims of salmonellosis fully recover. The condition can be fatal, however, in the very young and the very old. Salmonellosis is also life-threatening to people with some pre-existing health conditions. Investigations conducted later revealed that the retesting and eventual shipment of products initially identified as contaminated was done repeatedly at the PCA plant (Millner, 2011).

PCA was a major producer of peanut meal, peanut butter, and peanut paste for use as ingredients in a wide variety of products. When the contaminated ingredients left the PCA processing plant, the managers knew it would be an ingredient in such food items as "brownies, cakes, pies, many types of candy, cereals, cookies, crackers, donuts, dressings and seasonings, prepared fruit and vegetable precuts, ice creams, peanut butter and products, pet foods, prepackaged meals, snack bars, snack mixes, and toppings" (Wittenberger & Dohlman, 2010, p. 4). With such a diversity of products and companies receiving the contaminated product, it was only a matter of time before a major crisis would erupt.

In September of 2008, the CDC identified a pattern of salmonellosis cases in a dozen states. Further investigations revealed the peanut ingredients shipped earlier by PCA were the source of the outbreak. In December of 2008, the first death caused by the outbreak occurred. By this point, the Food and Drug Administration (FDA) was engaged in a widespread investigation of PCA trying to determine the full reach of the contaminated ingredients. In January of 2009, PCA recalled all products shipped from its plant beginning in the summer of 2008.

PERVASIVENESS OF THE PRODUCT

Unlike many recalls, the PCA salmonella crisis was not limited to a single product. If the company had only produced an end user product such as peanut butter purchased directly by consumers, the focus of the recall could have been limited to that product. Instead, PCA produced an ingredient that was purchased by a host of companies and included in hundreds of different products purchased by consumers. By the end of February 2009, over 1,550 assorted peanut products were "removed from store shelves," and the CDC reported that over 500 people across 43 states had contracted salmonellosis, eight of whom had died (Hartman & Barrett, 2009). In its final update on the crisis, the CDC (2010) reported a total of 714 confirmed cases of salmonellosis in 46 states. The communication challenges associated with the crisis expanded and intensified with the discovery of every new contaminated product (Millner & Sellnow, 2013, p. 264).

PCA'S CRISIS RESPONSE

Aside from announcing the recall, PCA remained largely silent through the crisis, offering no "instructing information, apology, remorse, or even an explanation" (Millner, Veil, & Sellnow, 2011). Instructing information is helpful during a food-borne crisis such as this because without a clear explanation of which products are safe the consumers lack the information needed to protect themselves (Sellnow, Sellnow, Lane, & Littlefield, 2012). Hallman and Cuite (2009) explain that when consumers "cannot successfully distinguish affected from unaffected products, they are likely to either underreact by assuming that they do not own any of the recalled products or overreact by discarding or avoiding the purchase of anything that resembles it" (p. 4). PCA's reticence contributed to two problems as the recall expanded. First, the ingredient was used in so many products that consumers had a difficult time comprehending the full extent of the recall. Second, many consumers incorrectly assumed that peanut butter sold under such names as Jif or Peter Pan were contaminated with salmonella. In response, the FDA launched a website that listed all contaminated products. For efficiency, the site was designed so that consumers could also enter the name of a product in a search box on the webpage to see if it was listed. The FDA updated the website regularly, and the CDC frequently issued reports on the outbreak, including instructions for identifying and responding to the symptoms of salmonellosis. This process continued for both the FDA and CDC until the CDC announced that it was issuing its final report about the outbreak in May of 2010. Organizational leaders responsible for products such as Jif and Peter Pan peanut butter "began costly ad campaigns to reassure the public" (Phillips,

Representative Greg Walden, right, holds up a container of food items recalled due to the salmonella outbreak associated with peanut products manufactured by the Peanut Corporation of America

SOURCE: AP Photo/J. Scott Applewhite.

2009) alerting the public that their products were not associated with PCA in any way and were never part of the recall.

PCA's silence continued as the investigation into the contamination deepened. Notably, during a February 2009 congressional hearing, PCA's owner and the plant manager both refused to testify, pleading the Fifth Amendment (CNN, 2009). The CDC, FDA, and some industry leaders such as Jif and Peter Pan communicated admirably in the absence of information from PCA. Millner, Veil, and Sellnow (2011) label such third party sources of critical information during crises *proxy communicators*. Although proxy communicators can effectively fill the void created when an organization in crisis chooses to remain mute, this substitution is not without problems. For example, proxy communicators such as CDC and FDA lacked immediate access to critical information about where products were shipped and when. Thus, as third parties involved in the crisis, proxy communicators face inherent delays that can allow the crisis to intensify (Millner, Veil, & Sellnow, 2011). As for the PCA owner and plant managers involved in shipping the tainted product, all pleaded not guilty and their trials were still underway when this book went into production. As you contemplate the questions that follow, consider the extent to which the proxy communicators were eventually able to satisfy the informational needs of consumers during the crisis.

YOU MAKE THE CALL

After examining this case, it is time to determine whether PCA or the proxy communicators communicated effectively with consumers. First, take a moment to refresh in your mind the lessons established in Chapter 7 for effective leadership during crises. These lessons should guide you in evaluating the strengths, weaknesses, and challenges in the leadership response by PCA and the proxy communicators.

Lessons on Developing Effective Leadership

Lesson 1: Effective leadership is critical to overcoming a crisis.
  ▶ Was the PCA or proxy communicators leadership useful during the crisis?

Lesson 2: Leaders should be visible during a crisis.
  ▶ Was the PCA or proxy communicators visible during the crisis?

(Continued)

(Continued)

Lesson 3: Leaders should work to develop a positive company reputation during normal times to build a reservoir of goodwill.

▶ Had the PCA worked to develop strong positive stakeholder relationships before the crisis?

Lesson 4: Leaders should be open and honest following a crisis.

▶ Was the PCA open and honest in its crisis response?

Lesson 5: Leaders who manage crises successfully may create opportunities for renewal.

▶ Did the PCA create opportunities for renewal following its crisis?

Lesson 6: Leaders should cooperate with stakeholders during a crisis and should work to build consensus.

▶ Did the PCA cooperate with stakeholders following the crisis?

Lesson 7: Poor leadership, including denials, cover-ups, or lack of response, can make a crisis much worse.

▶ Did the PCA's leadership make the crisis better or worse?

Lesson 8: Leaders must adapt their leadership styles and contingencies during crises.

▶ Did the PCA adapt its leadership style during the crisis?

Lesson 9: A virtuous response to a crisis by the organization's leaders may be the most effective in generating support and renewal.

▶ Would you describe the PCA's leadership as virtuous?

Lesson 10: Leaders have specific communication obligations for managing and learning from crises.

▶ How did the PCA manage the communication obligations following the crisis? Do you believe any learning took place?

SUMMARY

The PCA case offers valuable lessons for responding to food-borne illness crises. First, failure to communicate following a crisis has serious implications for the health and wellness of your customers and the industry in which you operate. Second, when an organization fails to communicate it puts pressure on proxy communicators to fill that void. These proxy communicators are at a serious disadvantage when responding to crises because they do not have direct access to information or the facts surrounding the crisis. Organizations would be wise to study the PCA case and consider the implications of silence as a strategy in crisis communication.

EXAMPLE 8.2. A FIRE AT COLE HARDWOOD

On Saturday, June 13, 1998, Cole Hardwood, a lumber mill in Logansport, Indiana, that processes green lumber from several regional lumber mills, burned. The fire, described as the largest in Indiana history, burned for over 6 days, putting 110 employees out of work. The fire destroyed roughly 140,000 square feet of inventory, equipment, and warehousing capacity. Milt Cole, the CEO and owner of Cole Hardwood, was well known in the community for supporting his workers and the community. What follows are some key characteristics of sole owner Milt Cole's leadership style and character.

CRISIS PLANNING AND PREPARATION

Milt Cole described himself as a simple man who has been blessed with success and friendship. He mentioned that employees are key to his business: "I have lots of confidence in people, people make the company. [Our key to success is to] keep people informed and have good communications" (Seeger & Ulmer, 2002, p. 133). Mr. Cole took the relationships that he developed over time with his workers and the community very seriously.

Milt Cole (personal communication, June 9, 1999) explained that the lumber industry is largely built on personal trust and credibility rather than on contractual obligations. Personal loyalty and commitment, interpersonal trust, and credibility represented Milt Cole's core business values. "I believe in taking care of people," he said. "I have a profit-sharing plan and employees have never missed a year. They made the company; I can't do it myself" (M. Cole, personal communication, June 9, 1999). Beyond the respect and responsibility Cole had for his workers, he believed in the community as well.

Milt Cole at his lumber mill in Logansport, IN

SOURCE: Photo Courtesy of Cole Hardwood.

Milt Cole was an active community leader and philanthropist. He donated several scholarships to local colleges and chaired the local United Way fundraising campaign.

Milt Cole's leadership characteristics were obviously well established before the crisis. What follows is a description of his leadership communication following one of the most devastating experiences for his organization.

LEADING INSTINCTIVELY AFTER A DISASTER

Because of the fire, the company's entire stock of green and processed lumber was lost. The good news was that no one was injured; however, the main offices, along with a small retail outlet, were destroyed. In the wake of the severe damage to the buildings, equipment, and inventory, many of the workers were concerned about their jobs. Milt Cole took several communication actions following the crisis.

Watching the fires, Mr. Cole reported, "I felt gutted. That night I slept like a baby and the next day we started planning to rebuild, even before the fire was out" (Seeger & Ulmer, 2002, p. 135). It appeared as though Milt Cole knew immediately how he was going to respond to the crisis. At about 8:00 a.m. on Monday morning, while firefighters from 31 counties fought the blaze, Milt Cole announced in front of an assembly of his employees that he would pay salaries and benefits while they were unemployed and while the lumber mill was being rebuilt. "I knew it was the right thing to do," he reported (Seeger & Ulmer, 2002, p. 132).

The rebuilding effort began immediately, and the workers were split into two shifts to accommodate the lack of equipment. Over a year after the fire, Cole Hardwood was making record profits and was continuing to grow (Seeger & Ulmer, 2002). Mr. Cole was able to mobilize his workforce quickly following the crisis. Once he had assembled the workers, he explained how they were going to proceed: "We never looked back. . . . There was no consideration of not rebuilding" (Seeger & Ulmer, 2001, p. 373).

Over the next year, Cole Hardwood rebuilt their lumber mill. The previous mill had been hampered by a lack of warehouse space and equipment. One consequence of Cole's response to the crisis was the opportunity to reconstruct the business in a more efficient manner, allowing for more profitability on less volume. Milt Cole capitalized on his years of experience with the old mill and made changes accordingly. The fire allowed Cole to update his mill with state-of-the-art equipment.

When asked about the plant fire after the lumber mill was rebuilt, Milt Cole explained that he experienced "the highest highs and lowest lows but I've never been prouder of anything in my life" (Seeger & Ulmer, 2001, p. 373).

YOU MAKE THE CALL

After examining this case, it is time to determine whether Milt Cole exhibited the leadership qualities identified in Chapter 7. First, take a moment to refresh in your mind these leadership lessons. Second, note that these lessons serve as touchstones and discussion points for what we believe are key aspects of any approach to crisis leadership. As you answer the questions that follow, consider whether Milt Cole was effective or ineffective in his crisis leadership. We rephrased the lessons into question format so that you are better able to address the key issues in the case.

Lessons on Developing Effective Leadership

Lesson 1:   Effective leadership is critical to overcoming a crisis.

▶ In what ways was Milt Cole's leadership critical to overcoming the crisis?

Lesson 2:   Leaders should be visible during a crisis.

▶ In what ways was Milt Cole visible following the fire?

Lesson 3:   Leaders should work to develop a positive company reputation during normal times to build a reservoir of goodwill.

▶ How did Milt Cole work to develop a positive reputation for his company before the fire?

Lesson 4:   Leaders should be open and honest following a crisis.

▶ In what ways was Milt Cole open and honest following the crisis?

Lesson 5:   Leaders who manage crises successfully may create opportunities for renewal.

▶ How did Milt Cole create opportunities for renewal following the fire?

Lesson 6:   Leaders should cooperate with stakeholders during a crisis and should work to build consensus.

▶ Did Milt Cole cooperate with stakeholders following the fire?

(Continued)

(Continued)

Lesson 7:   Poor leadership, including denials, cover-ups, or lack of response, can make a crisis much worse.

▶ Did Milt Cole's leadership make the crisis better or worse?

Lesson 8:   Leaders must adapt their leadership styles and contingencies during crises.

▶ Did Milt Cole adapt his leadership style to the nature of the crisis?

Lesson 9:   A virtuous response to a crisis by the organization's leaders may be the most effective in generating support and renewal.

▶ In what ways was Milt Cole's communication virtuous?

Lesson 10:   Leaders have specific communication obligations for managing and learning from crises.

▶ How did Milt Cole manage the communication obligations following the fire? Did learning take place?

SUMMARY

Milt Cole displayed outstanding leadership following the 1998 fire at his lumber mill. It is no surprise that, following the fire, Mr. Cole displayed the character and integrity that his stakeholders had been accustomed to before the event. Milt Cole communicated consistently and early following the crisis and made himself available to his stakeholders. These characteristics and actions created a reservoir of goodwill and support for Cole Hardwood following the crisis. In addition, Milt Cole's leadership enabled the company to move beyond the plant fire. The focus following the crisis was not on blame and responsibility but rather on the opportunity for the company to renew, prosper, and grow.

EXAMPLE 8.3. THE LARGEST FOOD-BORNE ILLNESS OUTBREAK IN HISTORY: SCHWAN'S SALES ENTERPRISES

In September 1994, a tanker truck owned and operated by Cliff Viessman, Incorporated, returned to the company's Minnesota facility after hauling a load of raw eggs which, unknown to Viessman employees, were infected with salmonella bacteria. The truck was parked and scrubbed internally by high-pressure washers. The washing, however, did not completely eliminate the bacteria, and as the contaminated truck sat idle, waiting for its next load, the bacteria multiplied. Unfortunately, for Schwan's Sales Enterprises (Schwan's), the contaminated truck's next assignment was to haul ice cream mix to the Schwan's plant in Marshall, Minnesota. The ice cream mix was severely contaminated by the time it was delivered to Schwan's. In turn, the mix contaminated every part of the Schwan's ice cream processing system that it touched.

Egg-associated salmonella infections are a serious health problem. The CDC explains that persons infected with salmonella experience "fever, abdominal cramps, and diarrhea beginning 12 to 72 hours after consuming a contaminated food or beverage" (Centers for Disease Control and Prevention, 2010). The illness typically lasts 4 to 7 days. Antibiotic treatment is sometimes prescribed and, in some cases, "the diarrhea can be severe, and the person may be ill enough to require hospitalization" (Centers for Disease Control and Prevention, 2009). Like other food-borne illnesses, salmonella bacteria are most dangerous for the very young and the very old. The bacteria can be killed by thoroughly cooking or pasteurizing infected eggs. The eggs in the Viessman truck were raw and unpasteurized.

In 1994, Schwan's was a private company believed to be earning between $1.2 billion and $1.5 billion annually. Schwan's products were, and still are, shipped throughout the United States. As has been the case since the company began in 1952, Schwan's ice cream and other frozen foods are sold door-to-door by drivers in yellow, refrigerated trucks. Some of Schwan's products are also distributed to grocery stores throughout the country. Schwan's drivers tend to establish friendly relationships with their customers, because the drivers deliver products several times per month.

In the middle lane, Schwan's trucks are on their way to supply frozen food throughout the nation

SOURCE: Photo Courtesy of the Schwan Food Company.

The popularity and broad distribution of Schwan's products meant that, in a short time, a wide network of customers had purchased infected ice cream. The subsequent outbreak was enormous. At least 224,000 people in 35 states became ill, making the Schwan's crisis the largest food-borne illness outbreak in history ("Ice cream poisoning," 1996).

A GUIDING PHILOSOPHY

From Schwan's perspective, the crisis began on October 7, 1994. An epidemiologist from the Minnesota Department of Health contacted Schwan's, telling them that there was a "very, very big statistical relationship" between Schwan's ice cream and a widespread salmonella outbreak (Sievers & Yost, 1994, p. 1). Once this information was received, the company leaders met immediately to discuss their strategy. Schwan's had a crisis management plan in place, but the guiding philosophy for the company came from a statement made by company president Alfred Schwan. Schwan's manager of public affairs recalled that Schwan asked simply, "If you were a Schwan's customer, what would you expect the company to do?" (D. Jennings, personal communication, January 29, 1996). Jennings went on to say that this statement by Schwan's leader inspired the company to make the "right choices" throughout the crisis.

SCHWAN'S CRISIS RESPONSE

Schwan's did not hesitate to respond to the mounting evidence. Even before the final tests were processed, the company publicly announced that it was recalling the suspected ice cream. In the announcement, Schwan said, "The well-being of our customers is our very first priority at Schwan's, which is why we are willingly withdrawing our ice cream products from distribution and cooperating fully with government agencies" (Sievers & Yost, 1994, p. 1). Schwan's crisis response included apologies and refunds delivered by drivers, a consumer hotline, and compensation for medical treatment.

Schwan's had an advantage over most distributors in that the company's drivers had face-to-face contact with customers. Drivers apologized to customers, collected the recalled ice cream, and refunded them for the cost. Because the drivers had delivered the product, they were able to identify and contact a majority of the people who had purchased the tainted ice cream. Most food processing companies have no idea, beyond delivery to a grocery store or restaurant, who has purchased their products.

Schwan's managed the expansive nature of the outbreak by establishing a customer hotline. The company spared no expense with its hotline. Rather than using prerecorded messages, calls were answered in person. Jennings recalled that the hotline received "15,000 [calls] a day at its peak" (D. Jennings, personal communication, November 19, 1996). The hotline gave customers another means of speaking directly with the company to get answers to their questions.

A third strategy in Schwan's crisis response was to compensate customers for any medical expenses they may have incurred due to eating the infected ice cream. The company mailed a letter to customers offering to pay for diagnostic medical exams. The crucial paragraph in the letter reads,

> If you believe you may have persisting symptoms of salmonella and have eaten any of our ice cream products mentioned, we want to encourage you to see your physician and get the tests necessary to confirm it one way or the other and get the treatment you need. The information on the reverse side of this letter will explain what the symptoms might include and how to go about getting the test. We will pay for the test. (D. Jennings, personal communication, October 14, 1996)

The letter clearly indicated that Schwan's valued the well-being of its customers over all other considerations. The letter, like all Schwan's correspondence with its customers, emphasized the guiding philosophy established by Alfred Schwan at the onset of the crisis.

LEARNING FROM THE CRISIS

Schwan's immediate and thorough response to the crisis enabled the company to recover quickly without losing its customer base. Schwan's also used the crisis to learn how to make its products safer. In response to the salmonella outbreak, Schwan's made the following changes:

- Schwan's built a new facility allowing the company to repasteurize all products just before final packaging.
- Schwan's contracted to have a dedicated fleet of sealed tanker trucks to transport its products.

Although these changes were costly, Schwan's enacted them voluntarily. These changes established a new standard of safety in the food processing industry.

YOU MAKE THE CALL

After examining this case, it is time to determine whether Alfred Schwan and his company displayed effective leadership in managing the salmonella outbreak. First, take a moment to review the lessons for effective leadership in crisis situations described in Chapter 7. These lessons should guide you in evaluating the strengths and weaknesses of Schwan's crisis response. As you contemplate the questions that follow, consider whether Schwan was effective or ineffective in addressing his customers' needs and concerns.

Lessons on Developing Effective Leadership

Lesson 1: Effective leadership is critical to overcoming a crisis.
  ▶ In what ways was Schwan's leadership critical to overcoming the crisis?

Lesson 2: Leaders should be visible during a crisis.
  ▶ In what ways did Schwan's make itself visible following the crisis?

Lesson 3: Leaders should work to develop a positive company reputation during normal times to build a reservoir of goodwill.
  ▶ How did Schwan's develop a strong reputation prior to the crisis?

Lesson 4: Leaders should be open and honest following a crisis.
  ▶ In what ways was Schwan's open and honest following the crisis?

Lesson 5: Leaders who manage crises successfully may create opportunities for renewal.
  ▶ How did Schwan's create opportunities for renewal following the crisis?

Lesson 6: Leaders should cooperate with stakeholders during a crisis and should work to build consensus.
  ▶ Did Schwan's cooperate with stakeholders during and following the crisis?

Lesson 7: Poor leadership, including denials, cover-ups, or lack of response, can make a crisis much worse.
  ▶ Did Schwan's leadership make the crisis better or worse?

Lesson 8: Leaders must adapt their leadership styles and contingencies during crises.
  ▶ Did Schwan's leadership adapt its leadership style to the nature of the crisis?

Lesson 9:   A virtuous response to a crisis by the organization's leaders may be the most effective in generating support and renewal.

▶ In what ways was the response by Schwan's virtuous?

Lesson 10:   Leaders have specific communication obligations for managing and learning from crises.

▶ How did Schwan's manage the communication obligations following the crisis? Did learning take place?

SUMMARY

The Schwan's salmonella crisis is a classic case of effective crisis communication. It is interesting that the company based its response not on a long and detailed crisis plan but on a guiding philosophy. From this philosophy, Schwan's immediately took responsibility for the crisis and worked to repair relationships with its customers. Schwan's received a tremendous amount of support from its customers following the crisis for its response even though many of its consumers became very ill as a result of the salmonella infection. Schwan's had several opportunities to shift the blame outside the organization. However, the company was determined to take care of its customers and move beyond the crisis.

EXAMPLE 8.4. LEADERSHIP DURING A TERRORIST ATTACK: COPING WITH 9/11 BY REBUILDING

The terrorist attacks of 9/11 were devastating for many industries, companies, communities, and individuals located in New York's financial district. The two airplanes that hit the twin towers demolished both buildings and much of the surrounding area. The financial industry was particularly hard-hit because of where the attack occurred. Many financial firms were located in lower Manhattan, and many were also located in the two towers of the World Trade Center. One of those companies was Cantor Fitzgerald (CF), a bond-trading firm that operated out of the top floors of Tower One (Seeger, Ulmer, Novak, &

The twin towers on fire
SOURCE: ©iStockphoto.com/danhowl.

Sellnow, 2005). CF was impacted particularly hard because, when the plane hit its tower, most of CF's employees were trapped above the initial impact. CF lost a greater percentage of its employees than any other company during the tragedy. Exactly 658 employees died in the attack, including CEO Howard Lutnick's only brother.

CANTOR FITZGERALD'S PRECRISIS REPUTATION

CF was a very successful firm, handling about $200 billion in securities each day (Barbash, 2003). At the time of the attacks, CF was rated as one of the largest bond trading brokerage firms in the world, employing over a 1,000 people, most of whom were housed in the World Trade Center. Wall Street financial firms are known as very competitive workplaces, and bond trading firms are the most competitive of the group. CF had a reputation as a take-no-prisoners firm, where profits came before everything else. The company had at times pushed the limits of financial regulations and come under the scrutiny of the Securities and Exchange Commission (SEC).

Howard Lutnick

SOURCE: Bloomberg/Contributor/
Getty Images.

The CEO of the firm was Howard Lutnick, known as single-minded and even ruthless in his business dealings (Hill, Knight, & Wiggins, 2001). He was very authoritarian and some would even say deceptive in his business practices. In 9 years, by age 29, Lutnick had moved from the bottom of the firm to take over the position of CEO.

HOWARD LUTNICK'S CRISIS RESPONSE

The hijacked American Airlines plane hit Tower One at 8:46 a.m. on the morning of September 11, 2001. At that time, Howard Lutnick was dropping his son off for his first day of kindergarten. Mr. Lutnick's brother, however, was already at work. CF lost about two-thirds of the company's workforce. CF was obviously devastated, and Howard Lutnick was completely overcome by what had happened. In a surprising move, however, he decided to share his grief publicly.

On September 14, 2001, Lutnick was interviewed by ABC's Connie Chung. During the interview, Lutnick broke down in describing the loss of employees. But in this and subsequent interviews, he asked people to help him rebuild his business so that he could help the families of the employees who had died. A tearful Lutnick vowed to stay in business for the sake of "my 700 families" (Russakoff & Eunjung Cha, 2001, p. A24).

RESERVOIR OF GOODWILL

After Howard Lutnick declared that his new American dream was to support the families of his employees who lost their lives in the attack, he had to illustrate that he could maintain business operations with less than one-third of his staff. He also knew he would need help from bond traders around the world to get his company back on its feet. He noted "if every money manager of a pension fund just gave us a little bit of business, then maybe we'll survive" (Dunne, 2001, p. 39). On Monday, September 17, 2001, CF experienced tremendous support, almost too much. Howard Lutnick explained it this way:

> Monday was an amazing thing to witness. All of the accounts— money managers, mutual funds, hedge funds—they reached out to help us. They pumped us up with so much business, and we had one of the busiest days ever. And when I went home that night, I told Alison, "I think we're done. Because we cannot process the trades, and we've got no margin of error here. We were crushed with kindness, I thought." (Barbash, 2003, pp. 60–61)

While some saw Lutnick's public plea for help in saving CF as self-serving effort to save his fortune by exploiting the victims, others believed that he would make good on his promise. On September 19, CF made a public pledge to distribute 25% of the firm's profits for the next 5 years to the families and committed to paying for 10 years of their health care. These funds were taken directly out of the profits that otherwise would have gone to CF's partners.

Due to the support of many who believed his promise, he was able to bring CF back online within a week.

Lutnick was very explicit in explaining that the tragedy had created a specific reason for the company to continue and return to profitability. CF even created a series of ads featuring employees asking for help. In one of these ads, a CF employee says, "We want to make sure that these families can go on. And that's why we're in business today."

POST-9/11: RECOVERY, REMEMBRANCE, AND RENEWAL

CF was able to return to profitability very quickly and remains very profitable today. The company even weathered the economic collapse of 2009 successfully. Some people have suggested this is because of what they learned during 9/11. Howard Lutnick kept his pledge to return a significant part of the company profits to the families of the victims. Additional money was given to other victims of 9/11, and CF today sponsors a program to provide relief to victims of other terrorist attacks, natural disasters, or emergencies.

The CF Memorial website at http://www.cantorfamilies.com/cantor/jsp/index.jsp reads:

> On the morning of September 11th, we lost more than a team. We lost family. We mourn the losses of our siblings, our best friends, and our partners. We cannot imagine work or life without them nor their many unique qualities and characteristics. They have enriched our lives immeasurably, and in us, their spirits shall live on.

YOU MAKE THE CALL

After examining this case, it is time to determine whether Howard Lutnick exemplified effective crisis leadership and crisis communication strategies following 9/11. First, take a moment to review the lessons for effective leadership in crisis situations described in Chapter 7. These lessons should guide you in evaluating the strengths and weaknesses of Howard Lutnick's crisis response.

Lessons on Developing Effective Leadership

Lesson 1:   Effective leadership is critical to overcoming a crisis.

▶ How did leadership function in this case?

Lesson 2:   Leaders should be visible during a crisis.

▶ Describe Lutnick's visibility. Do you think it was appropriate for him to go on TV so soon after the attacks?

Lesson 3:   Leaders should work to develop a positive company reputation during normal times to build a reservoir of goodwill.

▶ Did CF have a positive reputation before the crisis? How did this reputation affect the efforts?

Lesson 4:   Leaders should be open and honest following a crisis.

▶ Do you think Lutnick was open and honest? Why or why not?

Lesson 5:   Leaders who manage crises successfully may create opportunities for renewal.

▶ How were opportunities for renewal created?

Lesson 6:   Leaders should cooperate with stakeholders during a crisis and should work to build consensus.

▶ Was there consensus about the efforts of CF to rebuild?

Lesson 7:   Poor leadership, including denials, cover-ups, or lack of response, can make a crisis much worse.

▶ Was Lutnick's leadership good or bad?

Lesson 8:   Leaders must adapt their leadership styles and contingencies during crises.

▶ What was Lutnick's leadership style before the crisis? Do you think it changed?

Lesson 9:   A virtuous response to a crisis by the organization's leaders may be the most effective in generating support and renewal.

▶ What leadership virtues did Howard Lutnick demonstrate?

Lesson 10: Leaders have specific communication obligations for managing and learning from crises.

▶ What obligations did CF describe after the crisis? Do you think the company learned any important lessons?

SUMMARY

Communication after a crisis such as 9/11 is obviously very emotional and difficult. Howard Lutnick's response illustrated a change in leadership style as well as business philosophy and mission. It is clear that the crisis served as a bifurcation point for Mr. Lutnick's business values and goals. He was quick to act and created a clear vision based on these new business values and goals for the future of CF. This framing of the crisis created a clear vision for his surviving employees and other organization stakeholders for the future.

EXAMPLE 8.5. HURRICANE KATRINA

On August 29, 2005, the worst hurricane to hit the United States in recent history slammed into one of the most vulnerable areas of the country. Hurricane Katrina was the most expensive and one of the most deadly natural disasters to hit the United States ("Katrina may cost," 2005). Some 1,500 people were estimated to have died, and 134 were still missing 2 years after the storm. While the storm was a monster, category 4, it would have been much less devastating had it hit another community. The city of New Orleans, however, was particularly vulnerable.

Disaster managers had long warned that a major hurricane making landfall in New Orleans could result in massive flooding and several thousand deaths. Not only was much of the city actually built below sea level, but the complex network of private and public levees that protected the city from flooding were poorly maintained. The city was often described as a natural bowl, the sides of which were the levees. In addition, the system of natural wetlands and barrier islands that had traditionally protected the city from the full force of storms had been significantly degraded by human activity. Finally, many of the residents of New Orleans were very poor and did not have the resources to prepare for a crisis and, in some cases, to evacuate.

As tropical storm and then Hurricane Katrina churned through the Gulf of Mexico, it was not seen as a major threat. It was not until August 27, after the storm strengthened to category 4 and was clearly heading to the Louisiana coast, that residents of the low-lying areas of New Orleans were ordered to evacuate. While many evacuated, many of the poorer residents either did not receive the notices or simply could not evacuate. Thousands were stranded in the city.

As the storm pushed inland, it was increasingly clear that government officials and agencies were failing to coordinate their messages and their resources. New Orleans Mayor Ray Nagin, Louisiana Governor Kathleen Blanco, and President George W. Bush appeared unprepared, unaware, uninformed, and willing to shift blame for a failure in response.

The Katrina disaster evolved slowly, and the devastation was not clear until the second and third days of the event. This was partly due to the fact that news reports came in slowly and partly due to the fact that the initial effects of the storm seemed to be under control until the protective levees gave way, flooding the city. Eventually, there were over 50 breaches in the levees, and 80% of New Orleans was flooded, with some parts under 15 feet of water.

This confusion was clear in many of the early comments made by the three leaders. The day before the storm hit, Governor Blanco, for example, told the media, "I believe we are prepared. That's the one thing that I've always been able to brag about" (Wilmouth, 2005). The next day, however, she issued a formal disaster declaration, indicating that the hurricane was beyond the ability of the

A view from the Superdome following Hurricane Katrina

SOURCE: FEMA photo/ Andrea Booher.

state government to manage and requested federal disaster aid. Later, she would argue with the Bush administration about the federal government's efforts to take over the management of the disaster. President Bush was reportedly unaware of the disaster unfolding in New Orleans. He was vacationing in Texas at the time the storm hit, and 2 days later, he returned to Washington, DC. On the way back, his plane flew over the flooded city, and President Bush was photographed looking out the window at the disaster below. He commented, "It's devastating; it's got to be doubly devastating on the ground" (Wilmer, 2005). On September 2, President Bush visited Alabama and publicly praised his FEMA director Michael Brown's handling of the disaster, saying, "Brownie, you're doing a heck of a job." Bush seemed to be completely unaware that thousands of people were stranded in New Orleans, many in the large Superdome complex, and were rapidly running out of food and water.

The third leader involved in managing the disaster was New Orleans Mayor Ray Nagin. Mayor Nagin issued an advisory on August 26 encouraging residents to watch the storm's path and prepare for possible evacuation. He made several general statements encouraging residents to leave the city but did not issue an evacuation notice. On the evening of August 27, when it became clear that the city was a likely target of the massive storm, Mayor Nagin issued a call for voluntary evacuation. Some reports indicate that he was worried about issuing an evacuation order because it might disrupt the local economy and result in lawsuits. With fewer than 24 hours left before Hurricane Katrina would make landfall, Nagin declared a mandatory evacuation.

Even with only 24 hours' notice, almost 90% of the residents of New Orleans evacuated. Many experts agree that this was a very high rate and that a 100% evacuation of a major city is almost impossible. Those who remained were the elderly, disabled, and poor. About 30,000 people flocked to the Louisiana Superdome, the shelter of last resort. Media reports from there and images of people stranded on rooftops or wading through the water dominated television. The nation was shocked at the devastation of a major U.S. city, and that government at the local, state, and even federal level seemed unable to help. All three leaders were publicly and severely criticized for their handling of Katrina. The response became a major scandal for the Bush administration. Governor Blanco chose not to run for reelection. Nagin would eventually be voted out of office.

A view of the devastation following Hurricane Katrina

SOURCE: U.S. Coast Guard, Petty Officer 2nd Class Kyle Niemi/Wikimedia.

The long-term impact of Katrina has been devastating. Entire neighborhoods have been destroyed, and several are not being rebuilt because they are too vulnerable to future storms. Significant numbers of people have relocated, and while the population is growing, it still remains at about 25% below its pre-Katrina numbers. The devastation was also a lesson for the rest of the country about what kind of risks communities face and about the need for leaders to prepare for natural disasters and coordinate their efforts when a disaster occurs.

YOU MAKE THE CALL

After examining this case, it is time to determine whether leaders in the Hurricane Katrina case displayed effective leadership in managing the impact of the hurricane. First, take a moment to review the lessons for effective leadership in crisis situations described in Chapter 7. These lessons should guide you in evaluating the strengths and weaknesses of the crisis responses.

Lessons on Developing Effective Leadership

Lesson 1:   Effective leadership is critical to overcoming a crisis.
   ▶ How did leadership function in this case?

Lesson 2:   Leaders should be visible during a crisis.
   ▶ Describe President Bush's visibility. Do you think it was appropriate for him to fly over New Orleans after the crisis?

Lesson 3:   Leaders should work to develop a positive reputation during normal times to build a reservoir of goodwill.

▶ New Orleans had a reputation as a poorly managed city before the crisis. Do you think this impacted the response? How or how not?

Lesson 4:   Leaders should be open and honest following a crisis.

▶ Do you think the three leaders were open and honest?

Lesson 5:   Leaders who manage crises successfully may create opportunities for renewal.

▶ Were there opportunities for renewal missed during this crisis?

Lesson 6:   Leaders should cooperate with stakeholders during a crisis and should work to build consensus.

▶ Describe the ways in which cooperation failed in the case of Katrina.

Lesson 7:   Poor leadership, including denials, cover-ups, or lack of response, can make a crisis much worse.

▶ Describe specific ways in which the leadership of Nagin, Bush, and Blanco failed.

Lesson 8:   Leaders must adapt their leadership styles and contingencies during crises.

▶ Describe the leadership styles of Nagin, Bush, and Blanco as they responded to this crisis.

Lesson 9:   A virtuous response to a crisis by the organization's leaders may be the most effective in generating support and renewal.

▶ What leadership virtues did each of these leaders demonstrate?

Lesson 10:   Leaders have specific communication obligations for managing and learning from crises.

▶ What leadership obligations could have been used following Hurricane Katrina to make the response more effective?

SUMMARY

Hurricane Katrina represents one of the most severe natural disasters in U.S. history. It also represents one of the most poorly handled in terms of crisis communication. Following the crisis, government leaders were more interested in shifting blame and responsibility than helping people evacuate or survive the event. Leadership at all levels of government, including FEMA, failed to respond appropriately to citizen communication needs.

For this reason, Hurricane Katrina is described as a classic case in how not to respond to a natural disaster.

EXAMPLE 8.6. RISING FROM THE WRECKAGE: GENERAL MOTORS AND THE CRASH OF 2008–2009

The United States domestic auto industry has a long history of roller coaster rises and falls. While these boom-to-bust business cycles were normal, the downturn of 2008–2009 was so sudden and so precipitous that the big three, Ford, Chrysler, and GM, were caught largely unprepared. Record high gas prices, rising unemployment, plunging home prices, and a severe credit crunch meant sales of cars all but stopped. By the summer of 2008, it was clear that GM, the largest of the three, was losing cash at a very rapid rate and bankruptcy might be the only option. At the time, GM was run by CEO Rick Wagoner. He had spent his entire career at the company; he was seen as a product of the GM system and was often described as a defender of the system. Wagoner had, however, instituted a number of important changes at GM and had pushed for smaller cars and the new innovative electric car, the Volt. GM, however, was the largest, least flexible, and most out of touch of all the companies.

GENERAL MOTORS' INITIAL RESPONSE TO THE CRISIS

On November 19, 2008, the heads of the big three and the president of the United Auto Workers (UAW) union testified in front of the U.S. House Committee on Banking. They were requesting money to help them avoid bankruptcy and a terrible shock to an economy that was already very unstable. The congressional hearings, however, went poorly for the CEOs. They were severely criticized by members of Congress for years of poor management and for making gas-guzzling, poor-quality products that could not compete with imported cars (Vlasic & Herszenhorn, 2008). They were criticized for giving too many concessions to the UAW. One member of Congress even pointed out that all three executives had flown in on private jets to ask for a government handout (Levs, 2008). The executives talked about saving jobs and protecting communities that had come to depend on the auto companies. They also talked about plans to produce more fuel-efficient cars of higher quality. The executives were sent back to Detroit and asked to come up with detailed turnaround plans that were realistic before Congress would approve any bailout funds (Vlasic & Herszenhorn, 2008).

A SECOND ATTEMPT TO RESPOND TO THE CRISIS

In December of 2008, the three CEOs returned to Washington, DC, for more hearings, and this time they drove hybrid cars (Das, 2008). They asked for a total of $34 billion in help, and while some members of Congress were receptive, others continued to attack the plan. One of the primary complaints was that the UAW simply was not giving up enough. Wagoner offered to resign if it would help save the company. Eventually, the United States taxpayers would invest $60 billion in the domestic auto industry. In March, the Obama Administration Auto Task Force told Rick Wagoner that he would need to step down, and on June 2, 2009, GM, which had just celebrated its 100th anniversary, filed for bankruptcy (King & Stoll, 2009).

BANKRUPTCIES AT GENERAL MOTORS AND CHRYSLER

The Chrysler Corporation was also forced into bankruptcy and was acquired by the Italian car company Fiat. Under bankruptcy and the oversight of government officials, the company quickly moved to reduce its debts and streamline its operations (Vlasic & Bunkley, 2009). Some divisions that were not considered core were dropped, including Saturn, Saab, and Pontiac. The company cut thousands of workers and cut the pay of many more. Many dealers were told they were closing. As 2009 came to an end, a much smaller GM with fewer debts and many managers brought in from outside the company was introducing new, exciting products and reporting higher-than-expected sales numbers.

TELEVISING AND PROMOTING A NEW VISION AT GENERAL MOTORS

Executives began talking about a new GM, and the commercials the company ran talked about a renewed company (Vlasic & Bunkley, 2009). They talked honestly about the pain of bankruptcy and the reinvention that the company was undergoing. Rather that talk about *Chapter 11*, they talked about *Chapter 1*. One senior manager who remained was Bob Lutz, a long-time auto executive who had worked at both Chrysler and GM. The television commercial admitted mistakes that GM had made in the past and delineated learning and changes the company was going to make in the future. In early 2010, Lutz was interviewed about the future of GM. He said, "Going through the crucible for Chapter 11, it really did permit us to fundamentally fix the company. GM's new products are much

GM's new prospective vision following their bankruptcy and the 2008 financial crisis

SOURCE: Photo courtesy of Bill Mattocks.

more fuel efficient, and it appears the company is finally producing many cars that American consumers want to buy. Some of the long-term plans, like the plug-in electric hybrid car, the Volt, and GM products being built and sold in China, are also proving important to the renewal of the company."

Go to http://www.youtube.com/watch?v=30Qnn1oAHQo and watch GM's commercial about reinvention and renewal.

YOU MAKE THE CALL

After examining this case, it is time to determine whether leaders at GM displayed effective leadership in managing their bankruptcy during the financial crisis. First, take a moment to review the lessons for effective leadership in crisis situations described in Chapter 7. These lessons should guide you in evaluating the strengths and weaknesses of the crisis responses. As you contemplate the questions that follow, consider whether GM history and long-standing values hurt or helped its ability to renew following the financial crisis.

Lessons on Developing Effective Leadership

Lesson 1: Effective leadership is critical to overcoming a crisis.
> ▶ What role did the leadership of GM play in this crisis?

Lesson 2: Leaders should be visible during a crisis.
> ▶ How did the appearance of the executives before congress impact this crisis?

Lesson 3: Leaders should work to develop a positive company reputation during normal times to build a reservoir of goodwill.
> ▶ What factors impacted the goodwill of GM?

Lesson 4:   Leaders should be open and honest following a crisis.

▸ Was the commercial GM produced open and honest? Was it effective?

Lesson 5:   Leaders who manage crises successfully may create opportunities for renewal.

▸ What opportunities did Bob Lutz describe? What other opportunities were created by the crisis?

Lesson 6:   Leaders should cooperate with stakeholders during a crisis and should work to build consensus.

▸ Who were the important stakeholders in this case? Why were they important?

Lesson 7:   Poor leadership, including denials, cover-ups, or lack of response, can make a crisis much worse.

▸ What were some examples of poor leadership in this case?

Lesson 8:   Leaders must adapt their leadership styles and contingencies during crises.

▸ How did GM's message change over time?

Lesson 9:   A virtuous response to a crisis by the organization's leaders may be the most effective in generating support and renewal.

▸ What were the values that were discussed in this case?

Lesson 10:   Leaders have specific communication obligations for managing and learning from crises.

▸ What communication obligations did Wagoner have?

SUMMARY

The GM case study provides valuable lessons for effective crisis communication. First, GM was caught in a complex financial crisis that impacted the organization's ability to secure credit during a serious downturn in the economy. Although GM had been pressed for years to produce more fuel-efficient vehicles, the organization's leadership resisted that change. Ultimately, the financial crisis provided GM the opportunity to make changes to its business practices and its organizational values. Although GM initially responded ineffectively to the crisis, it appears that they are currently on a more solid business trajectory.

REFERENCES

Barbash, T. (2003). *On top of the world: Cantor Fitzgerald, Howard Lutnick, and 9/11: A story of loss and renewal.* New York, NY: Harper Collins.

Centers for Disease Control and Prevention. (2009, May 11). *Salmonellosis.* Retrieved from http://www.cdc.gov/

Centers for Disease Control and Prevention. (2010, May 11). *Multistate outbreak of salmonella typhimurium infections linked to peanut butter, 2008–2009* (Final Update). Retrieved from http://www.cdc.gov/salmonella/typhimurium/update.html

CNN. (2009, February 11). *Peanut company officials spurn Congress' questions.* Retrieved from http://www.cnn.com/2009/POLITICS/02/11/congress.peanut.butter/

Das, J. C. (2008). *Detroit CEOs take road less traveled to Washington.* Retrieved from http://www.reuters.com/article/idUSTRE4B20D720081203

Dunne, H. (2001, September 21). Cantor to give 24pc of profits to families. *The Daily Telegraph,* p. 39.

Hallman, W. K., & Cuite, C. L. (2009). *Food recalls and the American public: Improving communications.* Rutgers, State University of New Jersey, New Brunswick, NJ.

Hartman, B., & Barrett, K. (2009, February 10). Timeline of the salmonella outbreak: Track the chain of events in the recall of more than 1,550 peanut products. *ABCnews.* Retrieved from http://abcnews.go.com/Health/story?id=6837291&page=3#.UZ4c9uvlGi4

Hill, A., Knight, R., & Wiggins, J. (2001, December 22). An American survivor: Man of the year Howard Lutnick: The chairman of the bond broking firm devastated on September 11 is more respected than liked. But now has a higher motive to make money. *The Financial Times,* p. 10.

Ice cream poisoning outbreak in 1994 was largest case on record. (1996, May 16). *The Forum,* p. C1.

Katrina may cost as much as four years of war. (2005). Retrieved from http://www.nbcnews.com/id/9281409/#.Ufl38NKPP5k

King, J. N., & Stoll, J. D. (2009). Government forces out Wagoner at GM. *The Wall Street Journal.* Retrieved from http://online.wsj.com/article/SB123836090755767077.html

Levs, J. (2008). Big three auto CEOs flew private jets to ask for taxpayer money. Retrieved from http://www.cnn.com/2008/US/11/19/autos.ceo.jets/

Millner, A. G. (2011). *Strategic ambiguity and proxy communication in organizational crises: The Peanut Corporation of America case.* Doctoral dissertation. University of Kentucky, Lexington, KY.

Millner, A. G., & Sellnow, T. L. (2013). Silence in the turmoil of crisis: Peanut Corporation of America's response to its sweeping salmonella outbreak. In S. May (Ed.), *Case studies in organizational communication* (2nd ed., pp. 261–270). Thousand Oaks, CA: Sage.

Millner, A. G., Veil, S. R., & Sellnow, T. L. (2011). Proxy communication in crisis response. *Public Relations Review, 37,* 74–76.

Phillips, K. (Reporter). (2009, February 10). CNN newsroom [Television broadcast]. Atlanta, GA: Cable News Network.

Russakoff, D., & Eunjung Cha, A. (2001, September 14). Sketches of the missing: Hardworking early risers. *The Washington Post*, p. 24.

Seeger, M. W., & Ulmer, R. R. (2001). Virtuous responses to organizational crisis: Aaron Feuerstein and Milt Cole. *Journal of Business Ethics, 31*, 369–376.

Seeger, M. W., & Ulmer, R. R. (2002). A post-crisis Discourse of Renewal: The cases of Malden Mills and Cole Hardwoods. *Journal of Applied Communication Research, 30*, 126–142.

Seeger, M. W., Ulmer, R. R., Novak, J. M., & Sellnow, T. L. (2005). Post-crisis discourse and organizational change, failure and renewal. *Journal of Organizational Change Management, 18*, 78–95.

Sellnow, T. L., Sellnow, D. D., Lane, D. R., & Littlefield, R. S. (2012). The value of instructional communication in crisis situations: Restoring order to chaos. *Risk Analysis, 32*(4), 633–643. doi: 10.1111/j.1539–6924.2011.01634.x

Sievers, S., & Yost, D. (1994, October 8). Illness tied to Schwan's. *The Marshall Independent*, p. 1.

Vlasic, B., & Bunkley, N. (2009). Obama is upbeat for G.M.'s future. *The New York Times*, p. A1.

Vlasic, B., & Herszenhorn, D. M. (2008). Auto chiefs fail to get bailout aid. *The New York Times*, p. B1.

Widmer, T. (2005). *Why Katrina is likely to be a disaster for President Bush, too.* Retrieved from http://www.commondreams.org/views05/0901-34.htm

Wilmouth, B. (2005). *NBC's Lisa Meyers reports on Governor Blanco's Katrina mistakes.* Retrieved from http://newsbusters.org/node/2072

Wittenberger, K., & Dohlman, E. (2010, February). *Peanut outlook: Impacts of the 2008–09 food-borne illness outbreak linked to salmonella in peanuts.* Retrieved from http://www.ers.usda.gov/publications/ocs-oil-crops-outlook/ocs10a-01 .aspx#.UoU0enCG2qs

The Opportunities

Learning Through Failure

A capacity crowd composed of tourists, space enthusiasts, students, and the astronauts' family members gathered at NASA's Kennedy Space Center on February 1, 2003, anxious to observe the shuttle *Columbia*'s triumphant return from space. When the shuttle failed to appear, the crowd's emotions moved from confusion to alarm as a loudspeaker announced that there had been a major malfunction. The malfunction was a full-blown crisis. As *Columbia* moved through Earth's atmosphere, the spacecraft shattered, strewing debris for miles near Nacogdoches, Texas.

How could such a disaster have happened?

Seventeen years earlier, the shuttle *Challenger* exploded as it was launched, killing all aboard. After the *Challenger* explosion, the shuttle program was halted as the Reagan administration called for a thorough examination of the NASA program. Dramatic changes in leadership, shuttle structure, and communication procedures were enacted to remedy problems found during the *Challenger* investigation. Yet a review of the *Columbia* disaster reveals that many of the flaws in NASA's organizational culture that led to the *Challenger* disaster reemerged in the *Columbia* crisis. Why, with so much to lose, would an organization fail to learn from one crisis, only to create a similar event a decade and a half later?

Phillip Tompkins (2005) summarizes his extensive study of NASA in his book *Apollo, Challenger, Columbia: The Decline of the Space Program*. Tompkins describes a cautious and responsive organizational culture that had declined as the space shuttle program replaced the Apollo missions. A culture emerged that was less sensitive to safety and much more concerned with bureaucratic procedures and financial matters. Tompkins describes the impact of this changing culture:

> We saw that a culture can divide into two antagonistic cultures, two warring tribes with a cultural fence between them: in this

case the managerial/bureaucratic subculture and the weakened engineering/concertive one. We watched a reversal of status, as the engineers became second-class members, forced to communicate through the formal channels, intimidated by the managers. The informal system of communication could no longer save the formal system. (p. 203)

The bitterest element of the *Columbia* disaster is the fact that the presence of this perilous culture was identified following the *Challenger* tragedy.

In this chapter, we identify several opportunities organizations have to learn from crises. We begin with an exploration of why some organizations fail to learn from them. We continue with a discussion of the process for learning through failure, the possibility for vicarious learning, the necessity of organizational memory, and the need for organizations to unlearn some unproductive habits.

FAILING TO LEARN FROM FAILURE

Simply experiencing a negative event is not sufficient for learning. Think of the stories you may have heard about individuals who have acquired multiple citations and license suspensions for driving while intoxicated. The event alone is not enough to change behavior. Behavior can only change when an individual chooses to learn from an event. This learning requires individuals to change their beliefs and attitudes so that, in turn, their behaviors are altered.

From an organizational perspective, learning can be a complicated process. The acquisition of knowledge and the shifts in behavior must occur at all levels in what can be a highly complex system. Bazerman and Watkins (2004) contend that, when organizations fail to learn from failures, they become vulnerable to predictable surprises. Bazerman and Watkins distinguish *predictable surprises* from *unpredictable surprises*. Predictable surprises occur when an organization's leadership ignores or fails to understand clear evidence that a potentially devastating problem could occur. Unpredictable surprises occur with no clear warning signs.

Bazerman and Watkins (2004) identify four ways in which organizations fail to learn from the failures that occur around them:

1. *Scanning Failures:* failure to pay close attention to potential problems both inside and outside the organization; this failure could be due to arrogance, a lack of resources, or simple inattention

2. *Integration Failures:* failure to understand how pieces of potentially complicated information fit together to provide lessons on how to avoid crises

3. *Incentive Failures:* failure to provide sufficient rewards to people who report problems and take actions to avoid possible crises

4. *Learning Failures:* failure to draw important lessons from crises and preserve their memories in the organization

Organizational leaders who experience one or more of these failures jeopardize the future safety of their organizations.

Mitroff and Anagnos (2001), in their book *Managing Crises Before They Happen: What Every Executive and Manager Needs to Know About Crisis Management*, provide a convincing example of how an organization can fail to learn from a previous crisis. In 1982, Johnson & Johnson responded to a link between Tylenol capsules and several deaths due to cyanide poisoning by pulling the product from the shelves and communicating candidly with the media. Investigators later determined that the product had been tampered with while on a store shelf. During the investigation, both the FBI and the Food and Drug Administration (FDA) advised against pulling the product. Nevertheless, Johnson & Johnson recalled 31 million bottles of Tylenol. Although the short-term losses for Tylenol were staggering, the product reemerged as a top seller. When a second Tylenol poisoning event occurred, Johnson & Johnson's response was equally effective. Its swift and forthright response to the crises established a standard for all organizations facing crises. Mitroff and Anagnos explain, however, that much of Johnson & Johnson's success was based on the fact that, even though the company was not to blame for the crisis, Johnson & Johnson responded without hesitation in the hope that no more consumers would be injured or killed.

Mitroff and Anagnos (2001) assert that, in recent years, Johnson & Johnson has been far less effective in its crisis management. In the past decade, Johnson & Johnson has faced several crises resulting from predictable surprises. The company's products have been linked to overdose problems in children. Tylenol has also been associated with liver damage. In these cases, Mitroff and Anagnos found that Johnson & Johnson's response has been comparatively slow and much less effective. Mitroff and Anagnos explain that "ironically, because J & J did so well in handling its two major crises, it did not learn the proper lessons" (p. 19).

Using Bazerman and Watkins's (2004) foregoing list of failures, we can speculate about Johnson & Johnson's failure to learn. Because the Tylenol poisonings were caused by a criminal, they were unpredictable surprises.

The poisonings offered no incentive for scanning the environment for potential product failures. Second, the criminal cases did not provide an obvious link to other types of failures. Thus, little integration of information was inspired by them. Third, the Tylenol poisonings clearly revealed incentives for responding immediately to a criminal assault on a product. Yet the events gave little incentive to Johnson & Johnson employees for closely monitoring and reporting potential failures related to the daily consumption of its products. Last, Johnson & Johnson experienced a learning failure when it did not draw lessons from the crises that reached beyond the criminal level.

Mitroff and Anagnos (2001) characterize the dwindling effectiveness of Johnson & Johnson in its crisis management as a "failure of success" (p. 20). The company was so successful in its initial Tylenol crises that it failed to respond effectively when faced with a crisis of a different type.

LEARNING THROUGH FAILURE

Most of us can think of a sport, a school subject, or a project of some sort where we learned from our mistakes. Our failures help us better understand what we need to do if we want to improve. We learn from the mistakes or near misses that occur in the world around us. We may not even be aware of a risk until some crisis or near crisis occurs. For example, several teens were recently exploring an unsupervised cave near the Mississippi River in Minneapolis, Minnesota. The cave was a popular summer spot for adolescents in the area. On this occasion, however, something went terribly wrong. As many had done numerous times in the past, four teens entered the cave anticipating a daring adventure. This excursion, however, ended tragically, with three of the teens dying from asphyxiation due to the poor air quality in the cave. The fourth struggled against losing consciousness and eventually crawled from the cave. The story raised community awareness of the cave's danger. Parents in the area, who previously either overlooked or were unaware of the cave, now monitor the progress of authorities as they attempt to seal the cave and to patrol the area. The community learned a painful lesson about such caves. The media carried the story throughout the state and region, thereby spreading the lesson to authorities, parents, and teens who would not have otherwise been aware of the danger.

Organizational learning can function in much the same way. Sitkin (1996) details the way organizations of all kinds may learn through failure, going so far as to argue that failure is an essential part of the learning process. He insists that failures, especially minor ones, should not be overlooked or concealed.

Veil (in press) explains that organizations tend to lock into routines that distort their view of minor failures. As these failures accumulate, crises are much more likely to occur. Veil characterizes this routine view as trained mindlessness—a barrier to recognizing warning signals caused by focusing only on expected outcomes. Veil explains that crises generate recalcitrance to "force us to amend our interpretations" of existing systems and thereby foster learning. Recalcitrance causes a void or a feeling that we "no longer have control over our understanding of the world." Learning actually fills the void created when crises occur. Our understanding must expand through the learning process.

Mittelstaedt (2005) agrees. In his extensive study of organizational crises, Mittelstaedt makes the seemingly paradoxical observation that making mistakes is essential to success. A company that appears to operate free from disruption may simply be operating from an unrealistic and uninformed perspective. Mittelstaedt contends that "learning to identify mistakes in an analytic and timely fashion is often the difference between success and failure" (p. 287).

Sitkin (1996) extends this claim: Too often, he explains, employees and managers are unwilling to admit small failures for fear of reprisal from organizational leadership. The unwillingness to recognize and embrace failure is also a failure to recognize and respond to a potential crisis. The longer a failure is allowed to continue, the more likely it will intensify into a full-blown crisis. Sitkin explains further that, in successful organizations, failure creates a recognition of risk and a motivation for change that otherwise would not exist. He describes this recognition as a "learning readiness" (p. 548) that, without failure, is very difficult to produce in most organizations. Sitkin cautions, however, that not all failures are equally effective in fostering good risk management. He claims that organizations learn best from *intelligent failures*, which have the following five characteristics: They (1) result from thoughtfully planned actions, (2) have uncertain outcomes, (3) are modest in scale, (4) are executed and responded to with alacrity (eagerness), and (5) take place in domains that are familiar enough to permit effective learning.

In summary, organizations learn to recognize risk by accepting and acting on their failures. They learn best when the failures result from competent actions, are not yet crises, and are within the comfort zones of employees who are eager and

> ### OPPORTUNITY 1
>
> Organizations should treat failure as an opportunity to recognize a potential crisis or to prevent a similar crisis in the future.

experienced enough to respond wisely and quickly. Learning from failure leads to Opportunity 1.

VICARIOUS LEARNING

Organizations do not necessarily need to fail themselves in order to learn. Successful organizations engage in *vicarious learning* in order to recognize risk, wherein organizational leaders observe the failures or crises experienced by similar organizations and take action to avoid making the same mistakes. A few examples will emphasize the value of vicarious learning. When a perpetrator mailed a letter claiming that he or she had infected cattle in New Zealand with foot and mouth disease (FMD), the country's agricultural ministry was faced with one of the world's greatest fears. Biological terrorism, or bioterror, on the world's food supply has long been a worrisome prospect for world leaders. New Zealand's government was worried that its worst fears had been realized. If FMD spread, its cattle industry would be decimated. The country responded swiftly to calm its citizens and to avoid losing the confidence of consumers worldwide. Eventually, the letter was proven to be a hoax. The disruption New Zealand faced prompted bioterror experts in other countries, such as the United States, to fortify their plans for managing false claims of terrorist activity. By so doing, many countries learned from New Zealand's successful response.

When college students organized a boycott of all Nike products in response to accusations of worker abuse in its shoe factories in Vietnam, Nike initially failed to react. When the boycott rapidly spread to additional universities and Nike sales figures began to decline, the company responded dramatically. Admitting that he should have responded sooner, Nike's chief operating officer announced that the company was setting a new standard for worker safety and safety inspections in its Asian factories. Nike also raised the minimum working age and provided educational opportunities for workers. To avoid parallel boycotts, companies such as Adidas and Reebok began implementing similar standards.

OPPORTUNITY 2

Organizations can avoid crises by learning from other organizations' failures and crises.

Both the New Zealand and Nike examples offer evidence that organizations can learn and learn well without experiencing a crisis or failure within their corporate boundaries by monitoring other members of their industries. This demonstrates Opportunity 2.

ORGANIZATIONAL MEMORY

Without learning from their own and others' mistakes, organizations stagnate and fail to respond to potential threats in an ever-changing world. Yet, as any student of any subject knows, learning is of little use if the knowledge is not retained. In organizations, this retention of knowledge is referred to as *organizational memory*. From the perspective of crisis communication, organizational memory consists of an accumulation of knowledge based on the observation of successes and failures, both within the company and through vicarious observation. If an organization's members do not remember and act on their knowledge of previous failures, a crisis is much more likely to occur.

A horrific example of a failure in organizational memory occurred at a Union Carbide plant in Bhopal, India, in 1984. Early on a December morning, the plant leaked a deadly cloud of gas that settled over part of the sleeping city of 900,000. Within hours, 2,000 residents were dead, and thousands more were injured.

How could such a crisis occur? Union Carbide was a reputable company. The plant had many safety procedures in place to detect and prevent such leaks. Part of the answer is in a loss of organizational memory. The plant had been slated for closure. Many of the experienced staff had already been transferred to other locations, leaving a minimal crew with little experience. The training program for the workers who remained had been reduced to the minimum. The crisis was eventually traced to staff reductions and oversight failures. Much of the blame for the tragedy rests with a rapid reduction in experienced staff that took with them a large share of the organization's memory.

Bhopal represents one of the most dismal failures in organizational memory to occur in the past century and offers compelling motivation for understanding how to maintain it. In its most general sense, organizational memory consists of the following three stages:

1. *Acquiring knowledge*, as we discussed earlier, is achieved by recognizing failures within the organization and by observing the failures of similar organizations.

2. *Distributing knowledge* is the key to organizational memory. Inevitably, highly experienced employees will leave the organization. Unless these people are given an opportunity to share their knowledge with other employees, the knowledge will leave the organization along with the departing personnel. Thus, the organization is doomed to repeat previous failures.

3. *Acting on knowledge* is essential for organizational memory to serve an organization. If new employees are unwilling to learn from departing ones, the organization's accumulated knowledge is lost. Thus, new employees who want to do things their way could be destined to repeat previous organizational failures.

As the three steps to organizational memory show, employees have many opportunities to disregard hard-earned knowledge.

Organizations can take steps to minimize the likelihood that employees will disregard new knowledge. Novak and Sellnow (2009) offer several suggestions for engaging the workforce in positive change that reduces risk. Access to information is essential. They explain that "information flow and risk discourse occur more readily when employees regularly engage in discourse about operations" (p. 367). This discourse emphasizes the lessons learned onsite or vicariously. Novak and Sellnow explain that when employees "are talking, hearing, and doing training throughout the day and every day, the collective mindfulness of the organizations increases" (p. 367). In this manner, employees are able to consistently retain and act on new information.

Because organizational memory depends on the exchange of information from one person to another, the process will always be imperfect. Rivalry among employees, perceived mistreatment of employees by the organization, or a simple unwillingness by new employees or organizational leaders to learn from their predecessors all disrupt the preservation of organizational memory. Mittelstaedt (2005) offers this blunt assessment: "Not only must we continue to learn, but until we develop 'plug-compatible' brain dumps, each new generation must start learning from scratch but at a higher level" (pp. 120–121). This higher level involves learning and retaining what we can from previous experience while embracing the learning process.

The enormous impact of organizational memory on the crisis prevention process leads us to Opportunity 3.

> ### OPPORTUNITY 3
>
> Organizational training and planning should emphasize the preservation of previous learning in order to make organizational memory a priority.

UNLEARNING

To this point, we have seen the importance of organizational learning and organizational memory. On occasion, however, effective organizational learning depends on an organization's ability to unlearn practices and policies that have become outdated because of environmental changes.

In Chapter 8, we discussed the ruinous flood that occurred along the North Dakota and Minnesota border. For decades prior to the 1997 flood, the communities had focused their flood-fighting energy on the construction of mammoth dikes. Flooding had become a normal occurrence in the expansive valley. The dikes gave residents confidence that, each spring, the waters could be held back from the cities and homes in the region.

After 1997, this flood-fighting philosophy had to be unlearned. The 1997 flood revealed that some neighborhoods were simply too close to the river and at too low an elevation to be protected by dikes. Homeowners who had lived in their houses for 40 or more years were asked to accept government buyouts and move to safer ground. The magnitude of this flood brought the realization that simply adding dikes was a losing proposition. Accordingly, the community leaders were inspired to unlearn their previous dike-building policy for lowland areas. In its place, they adopted a policy that required residents to move to locations where they could be better defended against future floods.

Changes like those adopted after the Red River Valley floods do not come easily to organizations. Employees, management, and other stakeholders become comfortable with the way things are done. This comfort, however, can blind organizations to the urgency of an impending crisis. As Huber (1996) explains, unlearning is much more than simply discarding knowledge. Unlearning occurs when organizations recognize that existing procedures constrain the organization's ability to respond to crises. From this perspective, three results may occur from unlearning:

1. *Expanding Options:* When organizations are unwilling to forgo routine procedures during crisis or potential crisis situations, they lose the capacity to react to unique circumstances. Unlearning enables the organization to expand its options.

2. *Contracting Options:* In some cases, organizations may respond to a crisis with a strategy that has worked well in the past. In the current situation, however, the strategy from the past may actually make matters worse. In such cases, organizations must be willing to reject some strategies in favor of others.

3. *Grafting:* In the previous section, we discussed the need for organizations to hand down existing knowledge to new employees. If the socialization of new employees is so intense that they cannot bring new knowledge to the organization, however, the organization is doing itself a disservice. Although organizational memory is essential, some degree of unlearning in favor of the ideas new employees bring may be helpful in predicting and responding to crises.

Although we may seem to be contradicting ourselves by extolling the benefits of unlearning in organizational crisis communication, we are convinced that unlearning can be a necessary step in the learning process and thus in the crisis management process.

<table>
<tr><td>

OPPORTUNITY 4

Organizations must be willing to unlearn outdated or ineffective procedures if they are to learn better crisis management strategies.

</td></tr>
</table>

Unlearning, then, can be an essential ingredient. Thus, we offer Opportunity 4.

SUMMARY

Conventional wisdom suggests that failures are negative events that should be avoided at all costs. This chapter makes the opposite argument. From the perspective of organizational learning, failing and responding to failure are essential steps in both crisis prevention and crisis management. Effective organizations learn directly from their own failures and vicariously from the failures of similar organizations. The knowledge thus acquired produces organizational memory. If organizations are able to preserve this memory, they have a better repertoire for managing or avoiding crises. Although organizational memory is an essential component of crisis prevention and management, there are times when unlearning is needed. If routine procedures fail, organizations must abandon some strategies and seek out others. One means of developing new strategies is to hire new employees who can bring fresh ideas. If organizations are willing to devote themselves to effective organizational learning, they may experience the following four opportunities:

Opportunity 1: Organizations should treat failure as an opportunity to recognize a potential crisis or to prevent a similar crisis in the future.

Opportunity 2: Organizations can avoid crises by learning from other organizations' failures and crises.

Opportunity 3: Organizational training and planning should emphasize the preservation of previous learning in order to make organizational memory a priority.

Opportunity 4: Organizations must be willing to unlearn outdated or ineffective procedures if they are to learn better crisis management strategies.

REFERENCES

Bazerman, M. H., & Watkins, M. D. (2004). *Predictable surprises: The disasters you should have seen coming and how to prevent them.* Boston, MA: Harvard Business School Press.

Huber, G. P. (1996). Organizational learning: The contributing processes and the literatures. In M. D. Cohen & L. S. Sproull (Eds.), *Organizational learning* (pp. 124–162). Thousand Oaks, CA: Sage.

Mitroff, I. I., & Anagnos, G. (2001). *Managing crises before they happen: What every executive and manager needs to know about crisis management.* New York, NY: AMACOM.

Mittelstaedt, R. E. (2005). *Will your next mistake be fatal? Avoiding the chain of mistakes that can destroy.* Upper Saddle River, NJ: Wharton.

Novak, J. M., & Sellnow, T. L. (2009). Reducing organizational risk through participatory communication. *Journal of Applied Communication Research 37,* 349–373.

Sitkin, S. B. (1996). Learning through failure: The strategy of small losses. In M. D. Cohen & L. S. Sproull (Eds.), *Organizational learning* (pp. 541–578). Thousand Oaks, CA: Sage.

Tompkins, P. K. (2005). *Apollo, Challenger, Columbia: The decline of the space program.* Los Angeles, CA: Roxbury.

Veil, S. R. (in press). Mindful learning in crisis management. *Journal of Business Communication.*

10

Risk Communication

n the United States, genetically altered corn, soybeans, and cotton are grown and consumed broadly. The techniques used in developing these products of modern technology are similar to those used in traditional plant breeding methods. In this case, however, the technology involves actually identifying and transferring selected genes into plants. As a result, some crops are now grown in the United States using considerably less water, pesticides, herbicides, and cultivation than in the past. Despite these advantages, many European countries, such as the United Kingdom and France, reject this technology. They label foods grown from seeds produced through biotechnology "Franken foods" and restrict the importation of many products produced with ingredients from these crops. Policy makers from countries in Southeast Asia have similar reservations to those expressed in Europe. Despite the fact that plant and food scientists in countries such as China, Vietnam, and Indonesia have endorsed biotechnology, the governments of these countries refuse to allow the production of crops using biotechnology. Moreover, many citizens in these countries fear the introduction of products of biotechnology. Although the crops have been consumed in many countries for more than a decade without creating health problems, rumors that these foods cause cancer, autism, or environmental destruction still prevail. The controversy over biotechnology is, to a large extent, a matter of risk communication.

Those who deem biotechnology safe see the technology as a means for addressing a looming risk—a rising world population and a shrinking amount of land available for growing food. For example, the Population Institute (n.d.) projects that the world's population will "increase from 6.8 billion to 8.3 billion" with an increasing demand for meat and dairy products (p. 2). As a result, the institute acknowledges predictions that "by 2030 the world will need to produce around 50 percent more food and energy, together with 30 per cent [sic] more fresh water, whilst mitigating and adapting to climate change" (p. 2). In response to these demands, the

International Food Information Council (2003) explains that "with land availability being constant and the population continuing to grow, food biotechnology offers the potential to produce more food and feed more people using less land than previously possible" (p. 15).

Which side is correct about biotechnology and the world's food supply? Is biotechnology the answer to feeding the world or is it a gateway to disease and environmental destruction? Risk communication is the means by which we answer such questions. Because no crisis has occurred, the debate centers on perceived levels of uncertainty. Neither side on the biotechnology debate can say with certainty that harm is inevitable or that no harm will ever come from these products of modern technology. Those who advocate biotechnology believe sufficient research is available to establish their safety. Those who oppose biotechnology are not yet convinced that sufficient research exists. In this chapter we characterize the nature of risk communication. If we had all the answers regarding biotechnology, risk communication would be unnecessary.

DISTINGUISHING BETWEEN RISK AND CRISIS

In a landmark publication, the National Research Council (NRC) (1989) defines *risk communication* as "an interactive process of exchange of information and opinion among individuals, groups, and institutions" (p. 2). *Interactive* is the key word. The NRC advocates that risk communication be an interactive dialogue among those who are facing risk and those who have some capacity for controlling or reducing that risk. For example, according to this definition, when a factory is built, the organization that built it is responsible for interacting with area residents to help them understand any potential risks that may be caused by the factory and its emissions into the air and water. If an organization simply announces to area residents that its new factory is *safe*, the organization has not met the interactive expectation established by the NRC. Instead, the organization should share the information residents need to determine the risks and economic benefits of the new factory. Through this interaction, residents can better determine whether they (a) perceive a risk or (b) are willing to tolerate the risks because the potential benefits outweigh them.

The interaction process with risk communication differs considerably from crisis communication, yet poor risk communication can, itself, produce crises. For example, when Enron executives misled their employees about the risk of basing their entire pension system on company stock, the result was a crisis for every Enron employee. When the company folded, employees lost everything, while Enron executives pocketed hundreds of millions of dollars.

| Table 10.1 | Distinguishing Risk From Crisis |

Risk	Crisis
Future oriented	Specific incident
Messages of reducing likelihood	Messages of blame and consequences
Based on what is currently known	Based on the known and unknown
Long term	Short term
Technical experts, scientists	Authoritative figures
Personal scope	Community perspective
Mediated communication campaigns	Press conferences, press releases, speeches
Controlled and structured	Spontaneous and reactive

Reynolds and Seeger (2005) offer a clear distinction between risk and crisis communication. Table 10.1 provides a list of eight clear differences between risk and crisis communication. We summarize these distinctions as well:

▶ Risk communication is future oriented, because risk focuses on what may happen. In contrast, crisis, by its nature, is focused on a specific event that is occurring or has already occurred.

▶ Risk communication is designed to avert a crisis, while crisis communication seeks to explain the consequences for a regrettable event.

▶ Risk messages are designed to speculate about what might happen based on current knowledge. Crisis messages typically focus on a known event and speculate about how and why the event happened.

▶ Risk messages are designed for long-term planning. Crisis messages focus on the short term as they seek to address an immediate problem.

▶ Risk messages typically come from technical experts and scientists who use their expertise to foresee potential problems. Once a crisis has occurred, most communication comes from authoritative figures, such as government officials, who are charged with maintaining or reestablishing order.

▶ Risk messages tend to have a personal focus because, as the NRC advocates, they should be interactive so that individuals can decide for themselves whether or not they believe a risk is tolerable. In contrast, crisis messages address the entire community affected by a crisis.

▶ Risk communication has the luxury of time. Full-blown media campaigns, such as appeals for using seat belts, can be designed and implemented over an extended period of time. Crisis messages typically take the form of news conferences, press releases, speeches, and any other available means that can get the information out as quickly as possible.

▶ Risk messages can be carefully crafted and controlled. Crisis messages must be developed spontaneously in reaction to the crisis.

As you can see, risk and crisis communication differ dramatically. They are inextricably linked, however, in that poor risk communication often produces intense crises. Conversely, good risk communication can avert or diminish the impact of a crisis event.

The value of risk communication can clearly be seen in the example provided in the introduction to this chapter. The discussion of biotechnology is firmly rooted in the future. No serious problems have been documented, but there is lingering concern that in the long run biotechnology could produce unforeseen problems. Those on both sides of the issue speculate about future problems. One side anticipates a food shortage without biotechnology. The other side remains concerned that biotechnology could ultimately prove harmful to the food supply. The evidence is highly technical, but both sides eventually seek to persuade consumers to believe their interpretation. As the debate continues, stories about advances in biotechnology and European resistance are often featured in the media. Thus, risk communication offers Opportunity 1.

OPPORTUNITY 1

Effective risk communication can disrupt a crisis and prevent it from reaching its full magnitude.

IDENTIFYING RISK

The first step in eliminating or managing risk is *risk identification*. The process includes recognizing an evolving risk, learning about it, prioritizing it compared with other risks, and changing behavior in order to eliminate or minimize it. In this next section, we describe the role mindfulness plays in the risk identification process.

MINDFULNESS

If we have any hope of avoiding crises by recognizing risk, we must, in Langer's (1989) terms, forgo mindless behavior and embrace mindfulness. *Mindfulness* requires us to constantly adapt our perceptual skills to account for the ever-changing world around us (see Table 10.2). To do so, we must be willing to see new categories of problems and solutions rather than forcing the evidence we observe to fit into the existing categories we have been taught. For example, a 14-year-old girl was killed by a shark in July 2005 while swimming with a friend in the Gulf of Mexico off the Florida Panhandle. Only 3 days later, a 16-year-old boy lost his leg in a shark attack as he stood fishing in waist-deep water at another popular Florida tourist area. The second attack occurred within 80 miles of the first. By standards of the day, neither the girl nor the boy was taking unusual risks. The waters in the area were presumed safe for tourists enjoying Florida's beaches. Because no attacks had been recorded there, the swimmers mindlessly categorized their surroundings as safe. This assumption failed to account for the fact that shark behavior continues to evolve, putting additional tourist areas at higher risks than ever before. Since the attacks, Florida officials have "doubled the staff of sheriff's beach patrol officers" ("Shark attacks," 2005, p. C5).

Mindfulness also requires that risk observers be aware of new information. Think how airport security has changed, for example. Airlines now have more information about each passenger than was ever possible prior to 9/11. The hope is that by acquiring additional information and developing lists of suspicious individuals airlines will be able to identify and detain high-risk passengers. Similarly, the near tragic consequences of diseases, such as severe acute respiratory syndrome (SARS) and avian flu, have resulted in a more mindful approach by WHO. Potentially threatening symptoms are now recorded, shared internationally, and tracked in a more efficient and potentially insightful manner than ever in the history of

Table 10.2   Mindlessness Versus Mindfulness

Mindlessness	Mindfulness
Trapped by categories	Creation of new categories
Automatic behavior	Openness to new information
Acting from a single perspective	Awareness of more than one perspective

modern medicine. This attention to new information is designed to catch a potential epidemic or pandemic in its earliest stages.

Last, mindfulness requires individuals to be aware of more than one perspective. If we insist that our point of view is the only acceptable interpretation of a situation, we have little hope of engaging in effective communication. If we cannot see the concerns and fears of others, we cannot understand their resistance to new ideas. For example, Monsanto developed a genetically modified form of wheat that was not susceptible to herbicides. The result was a form of wheat that could be grown cheaply and more efficiently. When farmers overwhelmingly resisted use of the new product, Monsanto officials were shocked. The company had failed to account for the genuine fear farmers and many consumers have that genetically modified plants could potentially disrupt the ecosystem, rendering entire regions barren. Monsanto may never have seen such fears as legitimate. The company should, however, have seen the potential resistance in the consumers for whom the product was designed. Monsanto simply did not take the farmers' perspective into account.

The notion of mindfulness has appeal for organizations of all types. After all, if organizations can be mindful of risks, they can ultimately avoid crises and save money. This need is particularly great for operations such as nuclear power plants, airlines, and food processing plants, where the potential for crisis is constantly present.

Weick and Sutcliffe (2001) observed five applications of mindfulness in organizations that have managed to maintain impressive records of safety, despite intense potential for crisis. These characteristics include

1. preoccupation with failure,

2. reluctance to simplify interpretations,

3. sensitivity to operations,

4. commitment to resilience, and

5. deference to expertise.

Weick and Sutcliffe (2001) call organizations that maintain these characteristics *high reliability organizations*. These agencies are constantly preoccupied with the possibility that a misstep could lead to crisis. Therefore, they are reluctant to simplify any new evidence that could be a sign of risk. High reliability organizations are sensitive to all operations in all parts of the organization. This sensitivity allows for a mindful approach to training and monitoring. High reliability organizations also commit themselves

<table>
<tr><td>OPPORTUNITY 2</td></tr>
</table>

A mindful outlook is essential to recognizing new risks.

to resilience, which allows them to learn from any failure that they make, no matter how small. We talked about the importance of learning through failure in Chapter 9. Last, high reliability organizations defer decision making to the person with the greatest expertise. Instead of centralizing all decision making with a single individual who cannot possibly understand all the intricacies of every form of operation in an organization, whenever possible, decision making rests with those who know the most about the situation. Naturally, these decisions are made with the rest of the organization in mind. By holding to these standards, high reliability organizations manage risk in a highly mindful manner. This idea is reflected in Opportunity 2.

ANALYZING MULTIPLE AUDIENCES

As we mentioned earlier in this chapter, the NRC endorses a form of risk communication that is interactive in nature. This process functions best as a dialogue or meaningful conversation among all parties who might be affected by a risk. Although the importance and ethical integrity of such a dialogue seems obvious, many cases exist now and have existed in the past where dialogue has been discarded for monologue. In a dialogue, at least two parties discuss an issue and decide what will happen. In a monologue, one party makes a decision and tells the other party or parties what will be done. To better explain this difference, we turn to the dialogue-centered versus technology-centered dichotomy (see Table 10.3).

Table 10.3   Dialogue-Centered Versus Technology-Centered

Dialogue-Centered	Technology-Centered
Democratic, with all sides having a say in the matter	Decision making focused on subject matter experts
Matters of perception addressed as needed	Perceptions dismissed in favor of a series of facts determined by subject matter experts
Assumes subjectivity but works toward objectivity through dialogue and inquiry	Assumes objectivity through science but can be influenced by subjective interests

From a communication perspective, the dialogue-centered and technology-centered philosophies are complete opposites. When the dialogue-centered approach is the primary communication philosophy in a risk situation, the costs and benefits to stakeholders are analyzed in a democratic process: All stakeholders in a risk environment are invited to share their opinions. In the end, a decision is made by the stakeholders that takes into consideration the greatest good for the greatest number. For example, many states have opted to increase the speed limits on public highways. This issue is often put to a vote, either to the general population or by elected representatives. Traffic fatalities and road quality are two of the primary topics that arise in public debate and discussion over the higher limits.

In contrast, if the technology-centered approach is the operative philosophy in a risk communication situation, experts are called on to make recommendations based on their sophisticated knowledge of the subject and situation. These recommendations are then translated into laws and regulations for managing situations. For example, emission standards for factories are seldom open to public debate. Subject matter experts debate the issue, and national standards are set, often changing as one U.S. presidential administration leaves office and another arrives. Few citizens could engage in a coherent and informed discussion of the details about allowable emission levels.

There are advantages and disadvantages to both approaches. The technology-centered advantages are *efficiency* and *complexity*. None of us has the time or desire to study every technical matter that poses some risk to our well-being. We typically trust experts who advise governing officials on matters of public safety. Most of us think very little about the packaged food we eat. We trust that officials from the USDA and FDA have our well-being in mind. We thereby assume that they have established appropriate standards. Not only do we lack the time needed to make such observations, but most of us also lack the expertise. Relatively few citizens have a sophisticated understanding of microbiology. We defer to technical experts in this area to tell us what is and is not safe to eat.

The technology-centered approach loses credibility, however, when the public loses trust in the ability or willingness of technical experts to communicate honestly and without bias. This problem can best be understood by the following equation developed by Peter Sandman (1993, 2000):

$$\text{Risk } f \text{ \{Hazard + Outrage\}}$$

Sandman's equation distinguishes between *hazard*, the scientifically determined risk level, and *outrage*, the public's perceived risk level. Simply put, if the public perceives that something is of high risk, scientific experts will have a very difficult time convincing them otherwise. Conversely, if the public perceives that something is not a high risk, scientific experts will have a very difficult time convincing the public that it is. Leiss (2003) argues that, "the golden rule for risk managers is: always focus on the linked hazard-plus-concern" (p. 369).

Bovine spongiform encephalopathy (BSE), known to the general public as *mad cow disease*, provides a clear example of public outrage outpacing a scientific hazard. You may recall that the discovery of BSE in the United Kingdom resulted in hundreds of thousands of animals being destroyed. In reality, BSE has a very low likelihood of entering the food supply in the United States. The disease has an even lower potential for infecting humans who ingest contaminated meat. Still, there is a possibility, albeit very small, that an infected animal theoretically could reach the food supply and infect consumers. This small risk caused Oprah Winfrey to declare on her program that she would never eat beef again. Public outrage over BSE, not only in the United States but also internationally, devastated Canadian beef producers after several infected cows were discovered in that country. The United States has taken extreme measures to make certain that no cow showing symptoms even remotely similar to BSE can enter the food supply. In June 2005, Agriculture Secretary Mike Johanns announced that a suspicious cow had been identified, destroyed, and tested before it entered the food supply. When the animal tested positive for a strain of BSE, Johanns sought to avoid further intensification of public outrage by making the following statement:

> I am encouraged that our interlocking safeguards are working exactly as intended. . . . This animal was blocked from entering the food supply because of the firewalls we have in place. Americans have every reason to continue to be confident in the safety of our beef. ("U.S. confirms," 2005, p. A4)

In his statements, Johanns recognized that public outrage would not permit him to deemphasize the hazard of BSE. He wisely recognized public concern and emphasized the protective strategies the USDA had developed since the first case of BSE was discovered in the United States 2 years earlier.

The strength of the dialogue-centered philosophy is that, by its nature, it takes into account the public's outrage. Through dialogue, public concerns are heard and considered in the development of risk management practices. This has clearly been the case in dealing with BSE. There are, however, several weaknesses with the dialogue-centered philosophy. These weaknesses are diametrically opposed to the strengths of the technology-centered approach. The dialogue-centered approach functions very slowly, and the opinions shared by the general public are not always based on fact. Thus, if a community functioned solely under the philosophy of the dialogue-centered approach, it could not respond with urgency to a threatening situation. Worse, a totally democratic process could result in an uninformed public actually endorsing very risky behavior.

Rowan (1995) offers a helpful compromise to the tension between the technology-centered and the dialogue-centered approaches. She explains that engaging in the democratic process does not in and of itself mean that we will arrive at the best decision regarding a risk situation. Rowan is concerned about a dialogue process that "tries to outlaw an important communication skill: persuasion" (p. 303). She offers the warning, however, that such persuasion by any party in a risk debate should only occur after a careful examination of the evidence. Unfortunately, persuasive messages are often delivered prematurely by biased individuals and organizations that "should be listening or gathering information rather than attempting to persuade" (p. 303), she explains. Ultimately, Rowan advocates an interactive approach that is "most likely to secure the best possible technical knowledge about hazards and the best possible methods of addressing stakeholders' concerns" (p. 304). This compromise is summarized in Opportunity 3.

> **OPPORTUNITY 3**
>
> Risk communication must account for both hazard and outrage.

CONVERGENCE THEORY AND RISK COMMUNICATION

Palenchar and Heath (2002) explain that the universal objective of risk messages is to promote accurate and ethical decision making about risk issues. Although this objective is straightforward, the complexity of risk issues can cause communicators to lose focus. Many risk issues cause deep divisions among parties. For example, the prevalence of global warming, or the lack thereof, has fostered intense debate due to what Palenchar and Heath call "competing scientific conclusions" (p. 130). Interpretations of global warming evidence range from complete denial of its existence to claims that we have passed the tipping point and that no human effort can reverse the damage to Earth's atmosphere. When such debates about risk issues occur among experts, they "are apt to heighten public uncertainty about what the facts really are, increase doubts about whether the hazards are really understood, and decrease the credibility of official spokespersons" (Kasperson et al., 2000, p. 242). In such contentious cases, sorting through the available risk messages is both difficult and confusing for the lay public.

Convergence theory offers an explanation of how such public debates over risk issues are received, sorted, and assessed by the lay public (Sellnow, Ulmer, Seeger, & Littlefield, 2009). Convergence theory is based on Perelman and Olbrechts-Tyteca's (1969) notion of interacting arguments. They explain that the audience's understanding of a contested risk issue, such as global warming, "shifts each moment as argumentation [public debate] proceeds" (p. 460). In other words, the arguments of opposing parties interact to form a new understanding of the issue.

As arguments interact, both risk communicators and the lay audiences ascertain the strength and weakness of the arguments. Arguments are weak when they have little support and establish a position outside the parameters of competing arguments. Arguments are strong when at least a portion of their reasoning shares a commonality with other reasonable parties involved in the debate (Sellnow et al., 2009). This commonality, as Perelman and Olbrechts-Tyteca (1969) explain, is "almost always recognized" because the "likelihood that several entirely erroneous arguments would reach the same result is very small" (p. 471).

When risk issues are contested in a public setting, Sellnow and colleagues (2009) explain that convergence functions systematically:

> We see convergence as the primary objective in risk communication. The uncertainty in risk situations gives rise to competing claims about the levels of danger and about the appropriate means for responding. Thus, diverse arguments emerge. As the public observes these arguments, it is unlikely to fully accept one line of reasoning and totally reject another. Instead, the public is likely to *make sense* of the issue by observing ways in which the arguments interact. (p. 12)

The convergence Sellnow et al. (2009) describe can be seen through the global warming example introduced above. Figure 10.1 displays several competing positions on the global warming issue. The positions range from the complete extremes that global warming is a myth to the position that global warming is so severe that it cannot be reversed. In this case, the majority of the positions at least acknowledge the existence of global warming. Hence, the varying positions offer strength to the converging position that global warming exists to some degree. Complete denial of global warming is a weak argument in that it does not converge with the other positions (Sellnow et al., 2009). Convergence is represented in the diagram by the points of intersection in the circles. In this example, the likely conclusion is that global warming is a risk, but how to deal with it is still not understood.

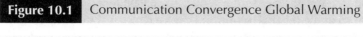

Communication Convergence Global Warming

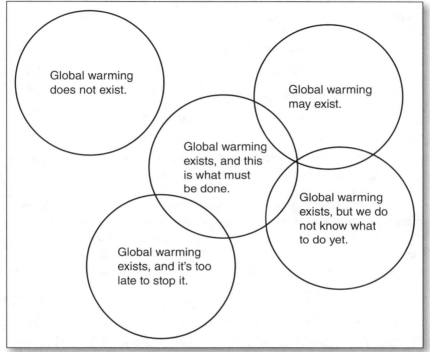

RESPONSIBLE RISK COMMUNICATION

Consideration of the dialogue-centered approach, the technology-centered approach, hazards, and outrage can make crisis communication seem overwhelming. Trying to communicate responsibly in a complex situation may appear to be a daunting task. Having considered this challenge for quite some time, we believe we have arrived at a straightforward and reasonable approach: We introduce significant choice as the foundation for responsible risk communication. We also contrast significant choice with fantasy messages that are designed to mislead the public.

SIGNIFICANT CHOICE

Nilsen (1974) is credited with developing the concept of *significant choice* within the context of communication studies. Nilsen explains that a good share of human dignity resides in the capacity to make rational decisions. As risk communicators, we often seek to influence those decisions. If we provide unclear or biased information to stakeholders, we can corrupt the decision-making process. Significant choice represents the ideal circumstances for free and informed decision making. Nilsen asserts that stakeholders engage in significant choice when the following five standards are met:

1. Stakeholders are free from physical or mental coercion.

2. The choice is made based on all the information that is available.

3. All reasonable alternatives are included in the discussion.

4. Both short-term and long-term consequences are disclosed and discussed.

5. Both senders and receivers of messages are open about the personal motives they have that may influence their decision making.

These five standards provide an initial framework for avoiding bias and manipulation in risk communication. When applied effectively, according to Nilsen, significant choice creates a marketplace of ideas where various viewpoints can be heard and understood for what they are. Hearing these viewpoints, stakeholders can make objective decisions that they believe to be in their best interests.

While emphasizing the five standards for open communication, Nilsen (1974) cautions against several forms of communication that could diminish the opportunity for significant choice. Nilsen labels these forms of problematic communication "misinformation" (p. 71). Misinformation includes the following characteristics:

▸ Incomplete information

▸ Biased information

▸ Statistical units that may be inadequately defined or incomplete

▸ Vague or ambiguous terminology in which listeners find erroneous meanings

▸ Implied relationships between the issue under discussion and other issues when in fact no relationship exists (for example, guilt by association)

▸ A false sense of urgency or false sense of importance

▸ Highly emotionalized language, which may distort meaning (pp. 71–72)

For significant choice to occur, then, communicators must meet the five standards discussed earlier and avoid the seven forms of misinformation.

As risk communicators, we should strive to meet these standards and avoid these pitfalls. As receivers of risk communication, we should demand that speakers hold to these standards and object if we feel they are engaging in misinformation. Above all, risk communication functions best when risk communicators serve as "honest brokers" of information for their stakeholders (Horlick-Jones, Sime, & Pidgeon, 2003).

FANTASY MESSAGES

The greatest threat to significant choice is our vulnerability to messages that tell us what we *want* to hear even when the messages sound too good to be true. Despite familiarity with the age-old adage, "Anything that sounds too good to be true probably is," many of us on occasion fall victim to what Perrow (1999) calls *fantasy messages*. Perrow explains that fantasy messages tell the public what it wants to believe by producing exaggerated crisis management and risk assessment plans that create a fantasy of safety. Perrow argues, for example, that Exxon used their crisis plans as fantasy documents rather than blueprints for action to avoid discussing the real risk of oil transportation in Alaska. Perrow explains that either intentionally or unintentionally, the biases of risk communicators can overwhelm them, leading to deceptive communication that boldly overstates the merits of one position while dismissing all others.

Fantasy messages are an ever-present part of our lives. Advertisers tell us their products will change our lives in ways that sound too good to be true. In early adolescence, we come to realize that such messages cannot be taken seriously. As consumers of risk communication messages, we must be equally vigilant. If a risk communicator discusses only one side of an issue, we should demand to hear the other sides as well. If a risk communicator oversimplifies an issue or uses language and terminology we cannot hope to decipher, we should demand that the message be provided in a clear and appropriate manner. The concept of significant choice offers a time-tested set of standards to which all risk communication should be held. Thus, we offer Opportunity 4.

> ### OPPORTUNITY 4
>
> To ensure social responsibility, all risk communication should be held to the standard of significant choice.

SUMMARY

Every crisis event, no matter how baffling, has some degree of warning before it occurs. This warning is risk. Risk may be readily apparent, as in the shocking maneuvers of athletes in events such as the X Games or the death-defying antics of motorcycle jumpers. Most often, however, risk is subtle. If we are to identify, learn from, and communicate responsibly about risk, we would be wise to keep the following opportunities in mind:

Most important, effective risk communication allows for interaction among all stakeholders in any risk situation. To maximize this interaction, risk communicators should be conscious of the various needs of diverse stakeholders.

Opportunity 1: Effective risk communication can disrupt a crisis and prevent it from reaching its full magnitude.

Opportunity 2: A mindful outlook is essential to recognizing new risks.

Opportunity 3: Risk communication must account for both hazard and outrage.

Opportunity 4: To ensure social responsibility, all risk communication should be held to the standard of significant choice.

REFERENCES

Horlick-Jones, T., Sime, J., & Pidgeon, N. F. (2003). The social dynamics of risk perception; implications for risk communication research and practice. In N. F. Pidgeon, R. K. Kasperson, & P. Slovic (Eds.), *The social amplification of risk* (pp. 262–285). Cambridge, UK: Cambridge University Press.

International Food Information Council. (2003). Food biotechnology: A communications guide to improving understanding. Retrieved from http://www.foodinsight.org/Content/5438/Biotech%20Guide.pdf

Kasperson, R. E., Ortwin, R., Slovic, P., Brown, H. S., Emel, J., Goble, R. . . . Ratlick, S. (2000). The social amplification of risk: A conceptual framework. In P. Slovic (Ed.), *The perception of risk* (pp. 232–245). London, UK: Earthscan Publications Ltd.

Langer, E. J. (1989). *Mindfulness.* Cambridge, MA: Perseus.

Leiss, W. (2003). Searching for the public policy relevance of the risk amplification framework. In N. Pidgeon, R. E. Kasperson, & P. Slovic (Eds.), *The social amplification of risk* (pp. 355–373). Cambridge, UK: Cambridge University Press.

National Research Council. (1989). *Improving risk communication.* Washington, DC: National Academy Press.

Nilsen, T. R. (1974). *Ethics of speech communication* (2nd ed.). Indianapolis, IN: Bobbs-Merrill.

Palenchar, M. J., & Heath, R. L. (2002). Another part of the risk communication model: Analysis of communication processes and message content. *Journal of Public Relations Research, 14*(2), 127–158.

Perelman, C., & Olbrechts-Tyteca, L. (1969). *The new rhetoric: A treatise on argumentation.* London, UK: University of Notre Dame Press.

Perrow, C. (1999). *Normal accidents* (2nd ed.). New York, NY: Basic Books.

Population Institute. (n.d.). 2030: The "Perfect Storm" scenario. Retrieved from http://www.populationinstitute.org/external/files/reports/The_Perfect_Storm_ Scenario_for_2030.pdf

Reynolds, B., & Seeger, M. W. (2005). Crisis and emergency risk communication as an integrative framework. *Journal of Health Communication, 10,* 43–55.

Rowan, K. E. (1995). What risk communicators need to know: An agenda for research. In B. R. Burleson (Ed.), *Communication yearbook* (Vol. 18, pp. 300–319). Thousand Oaks, CA: Sage.

Sandman, P. (1993). *Responding to community outrage: Strategies for effective risk communication.* Fairfax, VA: American Industrial Hygiene Association.

Sandman, P. (2000). Open communication. In E. Mather, P. Stewart, & T. Ten Eyck (Eds.), *Risk communication in food safety: Motivating and building trust.* East Lansing: Michigan State University, National Food Safety and Toxicology Center.

Sellnow, T. L., Ulmer, R. R., Seeger, M. W., & Littlefield, R. S. (2009). *Effective risk communication: A message-centered approach.* New York, NY: Springer Science+Business Media, LLC.

Shark attacks 2nd teen: 16-year-old expected to recover after leg amputation. (2005, July 28). *The Forum,* p. C5.

U.S. confirms 2nd mad cow: Brain disease found in "downer." (2005, July 25). *The Forum,* p. A4.

Weick, K. E., & Sutcliffe, K. M. (2001). *Managing the unexpected: Assuring high performance in an age of complexity.* San Francisco, CA: Jossey-Bass.

11

Responding to the Ethical Demands of Crisis

onfronted with the accusations of lying to the public, investors, and his own employees about the status of his company, Enron CEO Kenneth Lay denied he had done anything wrong. He claimed that his subordinates had misled him and that he was not responsible for Enron's illegal and deceptive business practices. It was later revealed that Enron executives had manipulated stock prices, created electricity shortages so that they could charge higher rates, and bribed officials.

As we saw in Chapter 6, the collapse of Enron resulted in hundreds of employees losing their jobs and wiped out the retirement savings of many more. Kenneth Lay, like many other CEOs involved in financial crisis, used the *hear no evil, see no evil* defense to claim that he did not know what was going on in his own company.

In April of 2013, an 11-story building in Bangladesh housing five garment factories collapsed killing over 1,000 workers and injuring 2,500 more. The factories produced low-cost garments for well-known retailers including Benneton, The Gap, and Children's Palace. The owner of the building had been informed of serious cracks in the walls and the floors and had told workers to ignore them. Initially, politicians claimed that the building collapse was not significant. Protests by garment workers and international outrage prompted several arrests including the building owner.

Garment industry working conditions in developing countries have been severely criticized for their conduct, including hiring of underage workers, paying very low wages, and creating unsafe working conditions. The retailers rely on very cheap labor in developing countries to produce high-profit products for sale in Europe and the United States. Critics charge they exploit workers and put them at risk to protect profits.

The crises at Enron, Bangladesh, and the Catholic Church sex scandal, illustrate the role of ethics in organizational crisis: Many crises are created by unethical and even illegal conduct on the organization's part. Illegal and deceptive business practices, unsafe working conditions, insider trading, knowingly selling defective products, misleading marketing claims, sexual harassment, bribery, and kickbacks, among many other unethical business practices, have led to crises.

In addition, almost all crises, even if they were not caused by unethical conduct, have ethical implications. The 1989 Exxon *Valdez* oil spill, for example, raised questions about blame and responsibility, about environmental exploitation, and about the rights of native people. The 2011 Fukushima Daiichi nuclear disaster in Japan raised questions about the safe use of nuclear energy and the right of access to information about radiation exposure

In this chapter, we define ethics and values and describe some of the key ethical issues and values that arise during a crisis. It is important to recognize that ethics are always part of any crisis situation and failure to address ethics can make the crisis much worse. We also describe some of the ways in which values can create opportunities that inform an effective response.

ETHICS

Ethics concern basic judgments of right and wrong, good and bad, and desirable and undesirable. Ethics are the values, standards, principles, or guidelines we use for making these judgments. Ethical issues and questions arise whenever a situation or a decision has the potential to affect another person. A situation where someone is discriminated against is unethical because of the impact on that person. Lying is unethical because it denies the person being lied to accurate information. Everyone, however, occasionally uses small so-called white lies to help manage their lives (Bok, 1979). There is some disagreement about whether these white lies are unethical because they generally do no harm. As the potential impact on others becomes greater, issues take on more ethical significance. During a crisis, the potential to harm others is often quite large, and therefore, the ethical implications are very great (Simola, 2003; Wilkins, 2010).

Ethical judgments are based on specific values that we have learned and internalized. We all make many ethical judgments every day. We may see a politician trying to spin a particular issue in a way that we judge as misleading and deceptive. We may make purchasing decisions about a produce based on how we judge the behavior of the company. In evaluating or judging behaviors as *wrong* or *unethical*, we are applying some set of standards or values regarding what we think is appropriate behavior. We may believe, for example, that politicians should not lie or distort the truth, that lying is wrong. We may believe that companies should respect the environment and that they should act responsibly in dealing with potentially toxic materials.

Many people reacted negatively to the sexual abuse scandals in the Catholic Church. The behaviors of the priests involved were judged as fundamentally unethical and immoral because they were entirely inconsistent with the values and norms of the church. Basic values about appropriate sexual behavior (priests take vows of celibacy) and protecting children were violated. In addition, many observers believed that the church responded unethically by refusing to accept responsibility and by trying to hide the facts of these cases. The British Petroleum oil spill in the Gulf of Mexico in 2010 created significant harm to the environment, to the fishing and tourism industries, and to many communities. Basic values about respect for the environment were violated because close to 5 million barrels of oil were spilled into the Gulf. Some critics suggested that BP tried to minimize the harm and withhold information about the size of the spill and its impact.

Ethical judgments help inform our behaviors and choices. While no one acts in an ethical manner all the time, most of us at least recognize when we are behaving in ways that might be judged as unethical. In addition, we may choose to avoid interacting with others whom we judge as unethical. A *good* person, for example, is more likely to be believed. This also holds true for our choices about doing business with particular organizations. An organization with a good reputation may have more support from its public and stakeholders than one judged as bad or unethical. Many people stopped giving money to the Catholic Church following the sex scandals. Many people cut up their Exxon credit cards following the *Valdez* oil spill.

These ethical judgments, however, are not easy to make. Some people look to universal ethical standards that can apply in all circumstances and for all people. While universal standards would make ethical judgments much easier, most researchers agree that the specific situation is an important factor in determining how to apply ethics. In addition, ethical standards vary quite widely among cultures, communities, and professional groups. What might be considered an appropriate ethical standard for attorneys might be very different in the case regarding a public relations professional. What is considered ethical conduct in the China might not be considered acceptable in South Africa or Brazil.

In most cases, ethical judgments are more comprehensive when they take into account situational factors, different values, competing loyalties, and complex duties and obligations. These are the conditions faced in most organizations where multiple stakeholders are involved (Christensen & Kohls, 2003).

CORPORATIONS AS MORAL AGENTS

One of the complexities that relates to organizational ethics concerns the question: can an organization act in a moral or immoral way? Philosophers often argue that only humans are moral agents and only they can make moral judgments. Organizations, because they are not humans, cannot be held to human-based ethical standards. Based on this, some have argued that only individual managers can be held morally accountable. When an organization does something wrong, it must be traced back to the individual manager (the moral agent) who made the decision. If a manager can't be found, then it would be inappropriate to hold the organization as a whole accountable because they are not moral agents. Others have suggested that often the individual manager is just a scapegoat for some unethical conduct, and the organization as a whole should be held morally accountable. Organizations, however, often act in collective ways like a moral agent. A third view is that the organization and the managers who make the decisions about organizations should both be held accountable. In this way, society can help ensure that accountability exists and that organizations are forced to act in ethical ways (Seeger & Kuhn, 2011).

In many cases of unethical conduct leading to a crisis, there is a debate about who is responsible and who should be held accountable. This occurs because the causes of crises are often uncertain and unclear, especially at the early stages, and because organizations and individuals want to avoid responsibility. In the case of Enron, which we discussed earlier, the senior managers claimed that they didn't know what was happening and sought to shift blame to one another. While senior managers had obviously acted in unethical ways, the company's entire culture was one that promoted unethical conduct. In the case of Enron, both managers and the entire organization were eventually held accountable. In the case of the BP spill, questions were raised about the company that owned the drilling rig and the contractors who had helped install some of the safety equipment; BP argued that these groups also shared responsibility. The question of moral agency is important because it often determines who will be held responsible for unethical behavior.

VALUES

As noted earlier, ethical judgments are based on values (Beyer & Lutze, 1993). *Values* are the larger positions we have learned and that inform our attitudes, beliefs, and, ultimately, ethical judgments. They are the more specific ought tos, shoulds, ideals, norms, and goals that exist throughout any society, culture, or community. For example, many communication students have learned to value free speech and expression, diversity of opinion, and the free flow of information. The health care profession teaches values of supportiveness, nurturing, and caring for the sick and less fortunate. The Public Relations Society of America (PRSA) suggests the core values of advocacy, honesty, expertise, independence, loyalty, and fairness are instrumental to its profession ("PRSA member statement," 2000). Most schools of business teach their students principles of social responsibility along with the values associated with profits. Of course, values are also taught at home and through religion. Values are thus ubiquitous in our lives.

What is particularly interesting is that not everyone agrees that the same set of values is most important. Some people value personal freedom and personal choice, while others place more importance on religious values and the sanctity of all human life. This value conflict underlies the ongoing abortion debate. In organizations, values concerning profitability and economic gain often conflict with values concerning the well-being of employees or the environment. Values vary widely from individual to individual, context to context, organization to organization, and culture to culture. The fact that not everyone agrees with the same set of values is often described as the *competing value view*. There is almost always a disagreement in any given situation over which values are most important and which values might apply in a situation. Often, before a decision can be made, these values need to be discussed, debated, and sorted out.

In one relevant case, a city in California experienced an earthquake. Residents were afraid to return to their houses because of potential aftershocks and had gathered in city parks. The city had to decide whether or not to set up tents for them. The police chief argued against setting up tents, claiming that he could not ensure security and public order and that people should be encouraged to disperse. The emergency management director argued that tents were necessary to ensure the welfare and psychological well-being of the community. In this case, values related to security were in conflict with those involving public welfare. The mayor, taking into account the situation, decided that the tents would go up.

During the 2009 H1N1 "swine" flu outbreak, many schools and colleges were encouraged to reconsider their attendance policies. Public health officials, who value the well-being of the public, pointed out that having sick students come to class would increase the spread of the disease and make the pandemic much worse. Schools and colleges, however, value learning and education and were reluctant to change their attendance policies. One university tried to balance these competing values with the following message: "Students with flu symptoms will be expected to balance their academic responsibilities with the social responsibility to self-isolate. In return, students should expect their instructors to demonstrate reasonable flexibility in the enforcement of written policies on class attendance and excused absences." In this case, competing values were balanced.

VALUES AND CRISIS

As the preceding examples illustrate, ethical questions are almost always important considerations following a crisis. In addition, crises often create the need to balance competing values. Crises, by definition, have created some harm and have the potential to create even more. Often, a crisis creates victims who are physically, psychologically, and economically vulnerable. Values that are important during times of normalcy and stability may not be as critical during a crisis situation. In many cases, short-term concerns about budgets need to be set aside so that the immediate needs of victims can be addressed.

Three ethical standards often become prominent in crisis situations: responsibility and accountability, access to information, and the ethic of humanistic care.

RESPONSIBILITY AND ACCOUNTABILITY

Following a crisis, there is almost always an effort to sort out what went wrong and why. Part of this process is to determine who might be responsible or culpable. Responsibility is a broad, ethical concept that refers to the fact that individuals and groups have morally based obligations and duties to others and to larger ethical and moral codes, standards, and traditions. In addition, responsibility concerns who or what caused a particular outcome. If someone freely made a choice that led to a particular outcome, then he or she is responsible for that outcome. If I run a stop sign and cause an accident, I am responsible for that accident. I may then be asked to give an account of my actions. If an organization takes some action that causes harm, such as creating a crisis, it too is responsible and will likely be forced to account for its actions. Thus, responsibility and accountability are closely related ethical concepts.

As we described in Chapter 4, many of the approaches associated with postcrisis communication are image restoration strategies designed to respond to the crisis or offer an account or explanation of what happened. Image restoration strategies are also frequently used to limit or contain an organization's responsibility, which might also mean less legal liability. In general, accepting responsibility for actions is considered ethical (Ulmer & Sellnow, 2000). This includes taking action to help victims, providing support and resources, and helping alleviate and contain the harm. Seeking to avoid or deny responsibility would be considered unethical conduct. This includes denying that any harm occurred, shifting blame to others, and refusing to provide assistance to victims on the grounds that it might create legal liability. Following the *Valdez* oil spill, Exxon blamed the captain of the ship for the accident, America's driving habits for the need to transport oil, and the state of Alaska for interfering with the cleanup. This example also illustrates the problem of corporate moral agency we described earlier in this chapter. In addition to the role of responsibility in postcrisis situations, organizations also have ethical responsibilities before a crisis occurs. They are ethically obligated to exercise care in their decisions and operations so that harm does not occur. Machinery should be maintained. Workers should be trained appropriately. Procedures for handling dangerous chemicals need to be established so that no one is harmed. Safety should be taken seriously. Most important, managers have an ethical responsibility to monitor their organizations for warning signs of any impending crisis and must act on those warnings. Opportunity 1, then, involves the role of responsibility in crisis communication. Accepting responsibility is an opportunity for an organization to demonstrate its ethical stance. Organizations that embrace ethics early in a crisis are more likely to be able to move quickly toward renewal than those that get caught up in protracted debates about blame and responsibility.

OPPORTUNITY 1

Organizations are better able to generate productive crisis responses if they are willing to accept responsibility for any actions that may have caused the crisis.

ACCESS TO INFORMATION

As mentioned earlier, fundamental values of communication are free speech and expression and the free flow of information. In general, an ethical obligation exists to provide people with the information necessary for them to make informed choices. This obligation is sometimes referred to as *significant choice*, because it gives people information they need to make significant choices. Organizations dealing with toxic chemicals, for example, have a moral obligation to inform members of the surrounding community of the potential risks so community members can make informed choices about how to respond. Drug companies list the risks of using drugs on their labels. The government often mandates these warnings, and they serve to give consumers information for making informed choices about significant issues.

Any kind of deception is ethically questionable because it restricts the freedom of the person being deceived. Lies place the liar in a powerful position over those being lied to. The person being lied to does not have the information necessary to make an informed choice. As we discussed in Chapter 3, during the Bhopal disaster, where as many as 5,000 people may have died, Union Carbide sought to manage the public concerns associated with its plants by describing the insecticide it produced as benign plant medicines. This subtle description helped reduce the level of public apprehension about the chemical facility, and this meant that residents could not make fully informed choices about the risks. Similarly, as we discussed in Chapter 3, a very effective public relations campaign helped convince the residents of Alaska that oil exploration and shipping was safe and that a major spill was unlikely. The public eventually supported building a terminal in Valdez, Alaska, and allowed shipping oil through Prince William Sound. The fact that people believed that a spill was very unlikely may have contributed to an attitude of complacency and ultimately may have contributed to the Exxon spill and delayed the cleanup.

In some cases, organizations try to avoid providing information because it is too costly and complicated. Food companies, for example, have resisted some efforts to list the country of origin for products. They claim that tracking and reporting this information when foods may include ingredients from dozens of countries would be too hard. Others, however, claim that consumers have a right to know where their food comes from and not having this information makes it hard to support local farmers.

Organizations sometimes withhold information or temporarily postpone its release for a variety of ethically justifiable reasons. In the case of an airline disaster, for example, families of victims are usually notified before passenger lists are released to the press. This action respects the rights of the families. School crisis plans sometimes include provisions to protect the privacy of students.

Organizational crises are public events that create a great deal of close media attention. There is usually much pressure to be open, truthful, and honest. However, organizations often choose to withhold information, try to remain strategically ambiguous, or simply stonewall. These kinds of responses are usually not ethically justifiable and often lead to even more damage to the organization's reputation. The severity of a crisis is

OPPORTUNITY 2

Organizations that are open and honest before and during crises are better prepared to manage and recover from the events.

usually increased by the perception that the organization is dishonest or withholding information (Benoit, 1995). In contrast, the perception that the organization has been open, honest, and forthcoming with all relevant information may reduce the seriousness of a crisis and ultimately help the organization's image. Thus, we offer Opportunity 2.

HUMANISM AND CARE

An ethical standard relevant to many crisis conditions concerns humanistic care. *Humanism* is a philosophical standpoint and value system that emphasizes the uniqueness and inherent worth of human beings. The ethic of care concerns the duty all humans have to others and specifically requires a supportive response to individuals who have suffered some harm and who have some need (Johannesen, 2001; Simola, 2003). In some religious traditions, the ethic of care is portrayed in the parable of the Good Samaritan. In this story a person who has been injured is helped by a stranger. This story teaches the lessons that we all have obligations to help others in times of need, even strangers. This ethical perspective is often particularly important when a crisis or disaster creates victims who have suffered hardship, loss, and physical, economic, and emotional harm.

A humanistic orientation requires that organizations be sensitive to the harm that may be caused by their operations, including what could happen in a crisis. Following the death of an employee due to an organizational accident or workplace violence, many organizations provide financial assistance to the family. Counseling offered to victims, their families, and others affected is often part of a crisis response.

In one case we witnessed, a tragic shooting occurred on a college campus during finals week. Many students were very upset. The college provided psychological counseling to any student who requested it and postponed final exams for any student who felt the need for more time. The college also held memorial services and provided other kinds of support to students, faculty, and staff.

Many relief agencies, including the American Red Cross and various religiously based relief agencies, undertake caring and humanistic responses to large-scale crises. The Red Cross provides medical assistance, food, shelter, counseling, and short-term financial assistance for disaster victims. It defines its mission as the service of humanity by "providing relief to victims of disasters" and helping people "prevent, prepare for and respond to emergencies" ("What is the mission," 2005).

Following 9/11, hundreds of thousands of people from around the world made donations to various funds to help the victims and the families of survivors. Similar responses have occurred for most major disasters. Caring responses to the Indian Ocean tsunami included millions of dollars in private donations. Some $30 million was raised by the One Boston foundation to support the victims of the 2013 Boston Marathon Bombings. Crisis often creates an opportunity for organizations and other groups and agencies to respond in humane and caring ways, to nurture others, and to ethically respond to human suffering. In fact, there is a natural tendency to want to help following a crisis. Seeing media accounts of victims can prompt people to help out following a crisis. From a humanistic perspective, organizations have an ethical duty to avoid harming others. They also have a duty to be supportive of those who are harmed by crises. When an organization acknowledges that following a

> **OPPORTUNITY 3**
>
> Organizations that make humanism and care priorities before crises are better prepared for enacting these values after they have occurred.

crisis one of its first obligations is to help others, it generates good will and bolsters its reputation. This can help the organization move toward renewal. Opportunity 3 suggests that humanism and care are critical following crises.

THE ROLE OF VALUES IN A CRISIS RESPONSE

While crises always create threats and harm, they also create opportunities to clarify values and to demonstrate those values by acting in ethical manners. During a crisis, organizations often struggle to act appropriately. A crisis is an uncertain situation, and organizations sometimes simply don't know what to do. Managers are often confused and even shocked and simply cannot determine what actions to take. In these cases, it is very important to take time and think about the ethical implications. This includes thinking carefully about whom the stakeholders potentially impacted by the crisis are, what their values are, how they might be impacted, and what duties and obligations the organization has to these stakeholders. Stakeholders for a crisis may include customers, suppliers, employees, members of the community, crisis response agencies, and members of the media, among many others. Each of these groups will have its own values, and these values are likely to compete with other values.

One effective approach in a crisis situation where it is not clear how to respond is to consider the organization's own core values (Seeger & Ulmer, 2001). As we discussed in Chapter 7, when faced with the fact that its Tylenol product had been laced with cyanide, for example, Johnson & Johnson turned to its corporate mission statement to determine what to do. The mission statement emphasized the company's duty to its customers, so Johnson

& Johnson withdrew Tylenol from store shelves. The company received a great deal of positive publicity for its actions, which ultimately helped it recover from the crisis. Johnson & Johnson was able to survive this crisis in large part because it followed its core values in determining its response.

Recall the case where Malden Mills suffered a devastating fire at its manufacturing facility in Chapter 4. The company was in complete ruin, and workers faced losing their jobs. CEO Aaron Feuerstein chose to respond to the crisis from a well-established set of values and ethics concerning his duty to workers and to the community (Ulmer, 2001). He announced that workers would continue to be paid and that he would rebuild the company as soon as possible. Feuerstein received a great deal of support and recognition for his actions, and ultimately, he was able to rebuild the company. In fact, the new plant he built was much more efficient than the one that had been destroyed.

The Malden Mills story illustrates that a value-based response to a crisis can actually help a company renew itself. It may find new areas of support and opportunity if it responds ethically to a crisis. As we discussed in Chapter 8, Cantor Fitzgerald was a bond trading company located on the top floor of the World Trade Center. The company and its CEO, Howard Lutnick, were known as cutthroat competitors who did not necessarily let ethics get in the way of profits. The attack on the World Trade Center claimed the lives of 600 CF employees, including Lutnick's brother. Lutnick publicly appealed to people to help him rebuild his company so that he could, in turn, help support the families of those employees who died in the attack (Seeger, Ulmer, Novak, & Sellnow, 2005). Lutnick was publically acknowledging that his most important ethical obligation was to the families of his employees who had lost their lives. CF did survive, and now the company has a renewed set of values and sense of purpose based on the losses of the 9/11 attacks.

Another effective approach to understanding values during a crisis is called *virtue ethics*. This is a traditional approach to ethics that can be traced all the way back to Aristotle. Virtue ethics suggests that people tend to act in predictable ways and follow their established patterns of conduct. Thus, a manager who has developed a habit of being honest in the past tends to be honest in the future. Honesty, in this case, is a virtue of this manager.

Virtuous responses are closely related to the development of a positive reputation and what is sometimes called the reservoir of goodwill. A reservoir of goodwill is a general public perception that the organization has been responsible, trustworthy, ethical, and so on. This public perception may have many benefits. It may create a halo effect that influences how other activities are perceived. It can reduce the impact of a crisis event.

Regarding renewal, a reservoir of goodwill can generate critical public support for an organization attempting to rebuild and recreate itself following a crisis (Jones, Jones, & Little, 2000).

We have found that virtue ethics are one important factor in effective responses to crises. Organizations and senior managers who have established patterns of responsible conduct toward their stakeholders tend to follow those patterns during a crisis. Aaron Feuerstein of Malden Mills and Milt Cole of Cole Hardwood were both managers who had established habits of being virtuous. They were fair to their workers, responsible members of their communities, and honest in their business dealings. When their companies were destroyed, they not only committed to rebuilding, but they also committed to supporting their communities. One additional benefit of virtue ethics is that it helps build a reservoir of goodwill before a crisis that the organization can draw on during a crisis. Both Milt Cole and Aaron Feuerstein had the support of stakeholders because they had established such good relations with stakeholders before a crisis.

To recap, a value-based response to a crisis can bolster an organization's reputation, serve as a rallying point for support, and ultimately lead to renewal. Moreover, during the uncertainty and confusion of a crisis, values and ethics are important landmarks that can help an organization reorient itself and respond in an ethical manner. Two approaches involve the organization's established core values and the habits of virtuous responses established by senior managers. Thus, we offer Opportunity 4.

> **OPPORTUNITY 4**
>
> Organizations have a larger reservoir of goodwill and are better prepared to avoid or manage crises if they have identified, discussed, instituted, and followed core values.

SUMMARY

Ethics and values are always part of a crisis. This includes questions of responsibility and accountability, free flows of information, and a caring, humane response. These and other values and ethics compete with one another and need to be sorted out to determine which values will take precedence. Sadly, values of profitability and self-protection often take priority over everything else. An ethical response to a crisis, however, can help bolster an organization's image and reputation and ultimately help lead an organization toward renewal.

Opportunity 1: Organizations are better able to generate productive crisis responses if they are willing to accept responsibility for any actions they may have taken to cause the crisis.

Opportunity 2: Organizations that are open and honest before and during crises are better prepared to manage and recover from the events.

Opportunity 3: Organizations that make humanism and care priorities before crises are better prepared for enacting these values after they have occurred.

Opportunity 4: Organizations are better prepared to avoid or manage crises if they have identified, discussed, and instituted core values.

REFERENCES

Benoit, W. L. (1995). Sears' repair of its auto service image: Image restoration discourse in the corporate sector. *Communication Studies, 46,* 89–105.

Beyer, J., & Lutze, S. (1993). The ethical nexus: Organizations, values, and decision-making. In C. Conrad (Ed.), *The ethical nexus* (pp. 23–45). Norwood, NJ: Ablex.

Bok, S. (1979). *Lying.* New York, NY: Vintage Books.

Christensen, S. L., & Kohls, J. (2003). Ethical decision making in times of organizational crisis: A framework for analysis. *Business Society, 42*(3), 328–358.

Johannesen, R. L. (2001). *Ethics in human communication* (5th ed.). Prospect Heights, IL: Waveland.

Jones, G. H., Jones, B. H., & Little, P. (2000). Reputation and reservoir: Buffering against loss in times of economic crisis. *Corporate Reputation Review, 3*(1), 21–29.

PRSA member statement of professional values. (2000). Retrieved from http://www .prsa.org

Seeger, M. W., & Kuhn, T. (2011). Communication ethics and organizational contexts: Divergent values and moral puzzles. In G. Cheney, S. May, & D. Munshi (Eds.), *The handbook of communication ethics* (pp. 166–190). New York, NY: Routledge.

Seeger, M. W., & Ulmer, R. R. (2001). Virtuous responses to organizational crisis: Aaron Feuerstein and Milt Cole. *Journal of Business Ethics, 31,* 369–376.

Seeger, M. W., Ulmer, R. R., Novak, J. M., & Sellnow, T. L. (2005). Post-crisis discourse and organizational change, failure and renewal. *Journal of Organizational Change Management, 18,* 78–95.

Simola, S. (2003). Ethics of justice and care in corporate crisis management. *Journal of Business Ethics, 46*(4), 351–361.

Ulmer, R. R. (2001). Effective crisis management through established stakeholder relationships: Malden Mills as a case study. *Management Communication Quarterly, 14,* 590–615.

Ulmer, R. R., & Sellnow, T. L. (2000). Consistent questions of ambiguity in organizational crisis communication: Jack in the Box as a case study. *Journal of Business Ethics, 25,* 143–155.

What is the mission of the American Red Cross? (2005). Retrieved from http://www
.redcross.org/faq/0,1096,0_315_,00.html#383

Wilkins, L. (2010). Mitigation watchdogs: The ethical foundation for a journalist's role. In C. Meyers (Ed.), *Journalism ethics: A philosophical approach* (pp. 311–324). New York, NY: Oxford University Press.

12

Inspiring Renewal Through Effective Crisis Communication

T he focus of this book has been on taking the challenges crises present and, when possible, turning them into opportunities. As we discussed in the first chapter, we see crises as turning points for organizations. Throughout the book, we have provided some evidence that crises can be viewed as they are perceived in Chinese culture, where the symbol for crisis is interpreted as *dangerous opportunity*. We believe that mindfully considering crises as containing the elements of both danger and opportunity is essential to effective crisis communication. In this concluding chapter, we build on the lessons, cases, and opportunities to further discuss the theory of crisis communication called the *Discourse of Renewal*. The Discourse of Renewal describes, explains, and provides a prescriptive approach to communicating during a crisis (Ulmer, 2012). In the remaining chapter, we first discuss some organizations that have emphasized the opportunities associated with crises and created renewal. Second, we delineate a theory of renewal. Third, we consider crisis as an opportunity and renewal as a framework for effective crisis communication. We conclude with some ideas about how the Discourse of Renewal can be used to prepare for responding to crises.

CONSIDERING THE OPPORTUNITIES ASSOCIATED WITH CRISIS

An examination of crises of all types illustrates a preponderance of failures in communication with few examples of successful or effective responses. We contend that many of these failures are related to the threat bias we discussed in the first chapter. After reading this book and the examples provided in the middle section of the book, you should have a good idea of how emphasizing the opportunities over threat to image or reputation can be instrumental in a crisis response. As we discussed earlier in this book, one of the first organizations to take a renewal approach to managing a crisis was Johnson & Johnson following the crisis that involved Tylenol pain reliever. Johnson & Johnson's response to the Tylenol tampering in 1982 is a landmark case of largely effective crisis communication (Benoit & Lindsey, 1987; Benson, 1988; Snyder & Foster, 1983). The company was widely acclaimed in its crisis response for communicating immediately about the crisis, recalling the Tylenol product immediately to protect stakeholders, and for learning from the crisis by developing a new tamper-proof package for their product. Johnson & Johnson actually grew their market share following the crisis and increased its loyalty to its brand. In this case, Johnson & Johnson's crisis triggered an opportunity for the organization to illustrate its value for customer safety and commitment to learn from a crisis. After the tampering, Johnson & Johnson spent little time determining responsibility or protecting its image. After its products were implicated with being tampered with cyanide, Johnson & Johnson immediately sought to make sure that its customers were safe and it could prevent the crisis from happening again.

You have read about several organizations in this book that illustrate the ability to see the opportunities available in a crisis. Organizations like Malden Mills, Cole Hardwood, King Car, Odwalla, Schwan's, Oklahoma City, CF, and GM, along with community-based responses like those in Greensburg, Kansas, and Rudy Giuliani's response to 9/11, exemplify the characteristics of seizing the opportunities inherent in crises. Clearly, there was threat in each of these events, but these organizations also emphasized the opportunities intrinsic to these crises as well. What follows is a discussion of the theory of the Discourse of Renewal.

THEORETICAL COMPONENTS OF THE DISCOURSE OF RENEWAL

We define *renewal* as a fresh sense of purpose and direction an organization or system discovers after it emerges from a crisis (Ulmer, Sellnow, & Seeger, 2009). As we briefly mentioned in Chapter 1, we see four theoretical objectives central to the Discourse of Renewal: organizational learning, ethical communication, a prospective rather than retrospective vision, and sound organizational rhetoric (see Table 12.1). These approaches to crisis communication suggest that organizations need to learn from crises and illustrate learning from stakeholders through their communication. The organization must also communicate ethically in its crisis communication. We provide an in-depth discussion below about what we believe

Table 12.1	Theoretical Elements Related to the Discourse of Renewal

1. Organizational learning
2. Ethical communication
3. Prospective rather than retrospective vision following the crisis
4. Effective organizational rhetoric

constitutes ethical crisis communication and how to evaluate this communication against solid ethical standards. Next, organizations need to be able to resist focusing excessively on their reputations and trying to control interpretations of them. Rather, each should emphasize a prospective vision that moves the organization and its stakeholders forward. Finally, the organization's leadership should exemplify communication that models optimism and commitment to actions that can resolve the crisis. We discuss each of these objectives in more depth below.

ORGANIZATIONAL LEARNING

A central feature in the crisis communication literature is that learning is essential to an effective response (Elliott, Smith, & McGuinness, 2000; Kovoor-Misra & Nathan, 2000; Mittelstaedt, 2005; Nathan, 2000a, 2000b; Roux-Doufort, 2000; Seeger, Sellnow, & Ulmer, 1998; Simon & Pauchant, 2000; Ulmer, Sellnow, & Seeger, 2007). Chapter 9 provides an extensive view of how learning functions as an opportunity during a crisis. In short, crisis creates an opportunity for an organization to confront its problems or deficiencies. Sitkin (1996) argues that failure is an essential part of the learning process for organizations. In this case, an organization should communicate learning in its postcrisis responses as soon as possible. Communication about learning provides organizational stakeholders with confidence that the organization has resolved the crisis.

Simon and Pauchant (2000) describe three types of learning useful for overcoming a crisis. Behavioral learning is the lowest form of learning because changes are not internalized by members of the organization but rather are "maintained by external control, through rules, regulations or technological systems" (p. 7).

Paradigmatic learning involves "both changes due to an external agency and changes enacted by the organization itself" (p. 7). Organizations need to take time to fully integrate learning throughout the organization. This type of learning takes consistent training support from the organization's leadership and members. Systemic learning involves an organization learning in advance of a crisis and preventing it. Organizations seeking renewal are more likely to employ paradigmatic or systemic learning rather than having a regulatory agency enforce behavioral learning on them. Behavioral learning suggests that the organization is experiencing impediments to learning and, as a result, needs external verification that learning is taking place. Organizations seeking to create a renewing crisis response or to avoid some crises altogether should work toward systemic learning.

Elliott et al. (2000) delineated several barriers to organizational learning. They explain that the key barriers include

> rigidity of core beliefs, values and assumptions, ineffective communication and information difficulties, failure to recognize similar or identical situations that happen elsewhere, maladaptation, threat minimization and environmental shifts, cognitive narrowing and event fixation, centrality of expertise, denial and disregard of outsiders, lack of corporate responsibility, and focus upon "single loop" or single cause, learning. (p. 18)

We believe that organizations that emerge from crisis successfully and capitalize on the opportunities of crisis will avoid these barriers and emphasize the importance of what they can learn from the event. It is also important that the organization illustrate to stakeholders how its learning will help ensure that the organization will not experience a similar crisis in the future.

Effective crisis communication messages should include discussions of organizational learning. Several of the case studies in this book emphasize the importance of learning. Odwalla communicated very specific changes about its food processing by creating a flash pasteurization technique that would keep the nutrients in the juice but remove or at least limit the potential for *E. coli* infections. Jack in the Box communicated about changes through its internal communication channels to ensure that messages from state and federal agencies are received and communicated appropriately. King Car clearly communicated its new testing procedures for ensuring the safety of its powdered milk products following the melamine crisis in China. TVA communicated a number of lessons learned in its postcrisis communication to maintain legitimacy following the ash slide near Knoxville. Beyond learning, organizations must also be ethical in their crisis communication.

ETHICAL COMMUNICATION

A second key factor in creating a renewing response is communicating ethically before, during, and after the crisis. As we discussed in Chapter 11, on ethics in crisis communication, we believe that organizations that have not prepared adequately for crisis or are unethical in their business practices are going to have to account for those actions in the wake of a crisis. In fact, unethical actions are often the cause of a crisis. One of the key factors in crisis is that it reveals the ethical values of the organization. If an organization is unethical before the crisis, those values are likely to be identified during the crisis. Crises provide the opportunity to identify failures that have built up over time and have been ignored or gone undetected. Organizations that institute strong, positive value positions with key organizational stakeholders, such as openness, honesty, responsibility, accountability, and trustworthiness, before a crisis happens are best able to create renewal following the crisis. We believe ethical communication involves having strong stakeholder relationships, a provisional response to the crisis, and communication that meets the ethical standard of significant choice. What follows is a description of each of these standards as well as representative examples for each one.

Stakeholder Relationships

Included in ethical communication are the relationships organizations have with their stakeholders. There are few opportunities for the public and stakeholders to view these organizational values prior to crisis. If organizations are going to benefit from a reservoir of goodwill following a crisis, they must invest in true equal partnerships with their stakeholders prior to the crisis. Organizations that want to benefit from renewal focus on developing clear understandings and amicable relationships with their stakeholders. When strong relationships are developed before a crisis, an organization is able to depend on its stakeholders to help it overcome the negative effects of a crisis.

The case study on Malden Mills provides an example of a leader, Aaron Feuerstein, who had developed strong positive relationships with his stakeholders prior to the fire at his textile manufacturing plant. These relationships served as a reservoir of goodwill and support that helped him through the crisis. The Schwan's case provides an example of how the truck drivers' positive relationships with customers played an important role in the company's recovery. Similarly, King Car was also able to build on its strong positive relationships with suppliers to recall a very high percentage of its contaminated product following the melamine crisis. Without these relationships, an important component of each company's crisis response would have been missing. What follows is a discussion of why crisis communication should emphasize positive organizational values to be effective.

Provisional Rather Than Strategic Communication

Renewal and ethics also focus more on provisional or instinctive responses to crisis rather than on strategic communication. Strategic communication can be seen as unethical when it is designed to protect the image of the organization by employing spin to deflect blame from the organization. Renewal is often based on a leader's established ethical character. These leaders often respond in provisional or instinctive ways deriving from long-established patterns of doing business. Typical of the Discourse of Renewal is an immediate and instinctive response based on the positive values and virtues of a leader rather than a strategic response that emphasizes escaping issues of responsibility or blame.

Examples such as Milt Cole's response to the fire at his lumber mill exemplify a provisional response. Milt explained in the case study that he knew immediately that he was going to rebuild the mill. He explained that, the night following the fire, he slept like a baby. Aaron Feuerstein, owner of Malden Mills, responded in a similar manner. Alfred Schwan responded to the salmonella outbreak at Schwan's with a personal value statement that set the tone for the organization's crisis response: "If you were a customer of Schwan's, how would

> **OPPORTUNITY 1**
>
> Organizations that base their crisis communication on strong, positive organizational values are more likely to experience renewal.

you want the company to respond" (D. Jennings, personal communication, January 29, 1996). Clearly, this response was not only consistent with Alfred Schwan's approach to business, but also compatible with his personal values as well. What follows is a discussion of how ethical communication can be determined ethical or unethical.

Significant Choice

As we discussed in our chapter on risk communication, significant choice is an important ethical standard for effectiveness. Nilsen (1974) explains that much of human dignity resides in the capacity to make rational decisions. We advocate the ethic of significant choice as a criterion for ethical crisis communication. In this case, we advocate always communicating the essential information about what is best for the stakeholders while never manipulating information. We use the notion of significant choice as criteria for evaluating the ethicality of postcrisis messages. Nilsen argues for clear and unbiased communication in order for citizens to make rational choices and decisions. Regarding crisis communication, providing unclear or biased information to stakeholders can distort their decision-making process and, as a result, deny them the opportunity to make rational decisions.

The opportunity to make significant choices is crucial to effective crisis communication. Domino's was thrust into a crisis started over social media and over time created significant choice for its stakeholders about the hoax. Cases such as Enron and Katrina restricted significant choice from stakeholders with disastrous results. TVA failed to communicate effectively about the risk of an ash slide prior to the crisis and hence violated the ethic of significant choice in its precrisis communication. Conversely, King Car added to a larger discussion of risk and significant choice by testing their own products for safety and publicly declaring them unsafe in the wake of denials and stonewalling by other companies. Complete and free access of information though communication is essential to effective crisis communication. In addition, this communication should be forward-looking to provide a vision for the future.

> **OPPORTUNITY 2**
>
> Organizations that make significant choice a priority in their crisis communication are more likely to experience renewal.

PROSPECTIVE VERSUS RETROSPECTIVE VISION

A third feature of a renewing response is communication focused on the future rather than the past. Organizations that have created renewing responses to crisis typically are more prospective than retrospective in their crisis communication. These organizations focus on the future, organizational learning, optimism, their core values, and rebuilding rather than on issues of blame or fault. Issues of blame and fault seem to be less important in cases of organizational renewal. Organizations focusing on renewal are typically optimistic and building a vision for the future.

OPTIMISM

The Discourse of Renewal is inherently an optimistic form of communication and focuses on the ability of the organization to reconstitute itself by capitalizing on the opportunities embedded in a crisis. For instance, Meyers and Holusha (1986) explained that "[c]rises present opportunities as well as challenges, opportunities that are not available at any other time"

(p. 45). In their research, they describe seven opportunities associated with crisis: heroes are born, change is accelerated, latent problems are faced, people are changed, new strategies evolve, early warning systems develop, and new competitive edges appear (Meyers & Holusha, 1986). In fact, a number of scholars have suggested more recently that crisis has the potential to create opportunities (Hurst, 1995; Mitroff, 2005; Nathan, 2000b; Witt & Morgan, 2002). With this in mind, similar to Fink (1986), we argue that crisis is a turning point for an organization. The Discourse of Renewal takes into account the potential opportunities associated with crisis and focuses on the organization's fresh sense of purpose and direction after it emerges from a crisis.

Many cases in this book illustrate communication that is optimistic about the future. Milt Cole and Aaron Feuerstein were both optimistic about the futures of their companies and instilled those visions in their stakeholders. Rudy Giuliani was optimistic about New York and the United States following the terrorist attacks on 9/11. The leaders and families of Greensburg, Kansas, were optimistic about their future and the potential opportunity that the tornado provided their town. GM is optimistic about its recovery following the financial disaster. Crisis communication failures like Enron and Hurricane Katrina were much less optimistic and focused more on assigning blame and responsibility for the crisis.

> ### OPPORTUNITY 3
>
> Organizations that focus on moving beyond crises rather than escaping blame are more likely to experience renewal.

EFFECTIVE ORGANIZATIONAL RHETORIC

The Discourse of Renewal is grounded in a larger framework of effective organizational rhetoric (Ulmer, Seeger, & Sellnow, 2007). Cheney and Lair (2005) explain: "Organizational *rhetoric* involves drawing attention to issues and concerns in contemporary organizational life with a focus on issues of persuasion and identification" (p. 75). The Discourse of Renewal involves leaders structuring a particular reality for organizational stakeholders and publics. Managing a crisis most often involves communicating with stakeholders in order to construct and maintain perceptions of reality (Gandy, 1992). Establishing renewal involves leaders motivating stakeholders to stay with an organization through a crisis, as well as rebuilding it better than it was before. We advocate that organizational leaders who hope to inspire others to imitate and embrace their views of crisis as an opportunity to establish themselves as models of optimism and commitment (Ulmer, Seeger, & Sellnow, 2007; Ulmer, Sellnow, & Seeger, 2007;

Ulmer et al., 2009). Perelman and Olbrechts-Tyteca (1969) characterize arguments based on models as follows: "In the realm of conduct, particular behavior may serve, not only to establish or illustrate a general rule, but also to incite to an action inspired by it" (p. 362). Conversely, antimodel arguments involve behaviors that the leader believes should be avoided.

Several cases in this book emphasize leaders inspiring and motivating stakeholders to overcome crises. The Greensburg community developed a vision to be the model of an environmentally sound community following its tornado. King Car developed a vision to be the model of the food industry in Asia by testing its products independently from government tests and disclosing publicly the contamination of its products. Schwan's chose to focus on its customers' needs during its salmonella outbreak and become a model for food recalls and crisis responses. Milt Cole and Aaron Feuerstein both serve as models in their industries of placing importance on employees and the human equation in crisis communication. What follows is a summary of the categories of the Discourse of Renewal and how this theory can be used in crisis communication.

> ### OPPORTUNITY 4
>
> Organizations that distinguish themselves as models for their industries are more likely to experience renewal.

SUMMARY OF THE DISCOURSE OF RENEWAL

The Discourse of Renewal provides a different perspective to crisis communication than is presently examined in the research on Corporate Apologia, Image Repair Theory, or Situational Communication Theories discussed in Chapter 2. Rather than protecting or repairing the image of the organization following a crisis, the Discourse of Renewal emphasizes learning from the crisis, ethical communication, communication that is prospective in nature, and effective organizational rhetoric. The Discourse of Renewal focuses on an optimistic, future-oriented vision of moving beyond the crisis rather than determining legal liability or responsibility for the crisis. What makes these responses so effective is they mobilize the support of stakeholders and give these groups a vision to follow in order to overcome the crisis. Crises that emphasize threat to the image of the organization typically lack these qualities and often have the potential to extend the life cycle of the crisis.

We hope that, after reading this book, you will use this theory to better understand how crisis responses are constructed effectively or ineffectively, to determine whether a crisis response was effective or ineffective, and even to develop crisis responses for your organization or circumstance. Our goal is to have those interested in better understanding crisis responses to use the Discourse of Renewal to evaluate crisis responses based on presence or absence of learning, communication ethics, a prospective vision, and organizational rhetoric. We also see ample opportunity for practitioners to use this theory to develop crisis messages and crisis plans for responding to future potential crises. What follows is a way for practitioners to use the components of the Discourse of Renewal to plan for crises.

THE DISCOURSE OF RENEWAL AND CRISIS PLANNING

Preparing for a crisis is important for any organization or community. The Discourse of Renewal provides an understanding of how organizations and communities can consider developing a crisis plan and, more important, build their crisis communication skills over time. Learning, the first part of the Discourse of Renewal suggests that organizations can learn vicariously from other organizations, or they can learn experientially by going through a crisis itself. Organizations that want to prepare for crises should examine case studies of crises that were managed well as well as ones that failed. This initial form of crisis planning opens discussions about the importance of effective communication understanding and practice during a crisis. It also creates an understanding of the choices that are necessary during a crisis. One choice will be to determine how the organization will define the crisis— as a threat or opportunity. Another choice will be to determine what will be the most important communication choices during a crisis. In this case, will the organization try to protect its image, will it work to communicate openly and honestly, will it focus on making sure stakeholders are safe, or will it focus on determining blame and responsibility? By vicariously discussing case studies and current crises, organizations are better prepared to consider the definitions of crisis, the communication demands associated with the event, and the important questions it will need to answer in its responses.

The second part of any organizations' or communities' crisis response is to determine the values that will guide the response. In this case, determining values such as being open and transparent, or the values the CDC espouse as being first, right, and credible, or a value statement like the one we saw with Schwan's CEO Alfred Schwan during his company's crisis—How would we want our company to respond to this crisis if we were a customer— are essential to an effective crisis response. Organizations should take time to determine the values that will guide their crisis responses and practice through case studies and simulations using those values to respond to a crisis. Without sound values in place, an organization or community is going to struggle in its crisis communication.

Within the content section of ethics, organizations and communities that are preparing for a crisis should work to build strong positive stakeholder relationships, build their capacity to respond to crises with significant choice, and develop a provisional approach over a strategic approach to communication practices. Developing sound ethical practices takes time. Organizations that wish to communicate openly and honestly during a crisis need to practice these skills day to day. As we mentioned in Chapter 1 in the section on crisis misconceptions, crises expose the character of organizations; they do not build character. Organizations must prepare for communicating effectively during a crisis by developing their ethical skills each day.

Organizations and communities must work to develop a prospective vision if they are to meet the standards set out in the Discourse of Renewal. As we mentioned in Chapter 1, another key misconception of effective crisis communication is to focus on the past. We believe that organizations and communities need to practice developing responses to crisis through cases and simulations that build a vision for moving it forward. Since this approach is counterintuitive, it is going to take some time to develop these skills. During practice sessions it will feel natural to focus on who is responsible, who we should blame, and why the crisis is not our fault. However, effective crisis planning involves building the communication skills to develop a vision for moving forward and building consensus with stakeholders to achieve that vision.

The final aspect of crisis planning using the Discourse of Renewal involves organizational rhetoric. In this case, leaders, organizational members, and community members need to build their skills in developing optimism and resilience. Crises are a part of life. Furthermore, as we have extensively discussed in this book, crises actually produce positive results that can improve an organization or community if we allow it. Through effective communication within and outside the organization we can begin to change our mindsets about crises and their impact on our lives. Crisis planning then is about developing new mindsets about crisis, building resilience through effective communication practices within and outside the organization, and establishing a sense of optimism in responding to crisis cases and simulations.

The Discourse of Renewal suggests a process approach to crisis planning. This process approach involves changing mindsets about crises, building communication skills through practice and vicarious learning, establishing the ethical character and communication practices of the organization through discussions and everyday applications, and resisting our misconceptions of crisis through the applications of case studies, simulations, and learning. The goal is to build the skills of organizational members over time so that regardless of the type of crisis the organization experiences its members will be able to adapt and meeting the challenges and opportunities that the crisis presents (Ulmer, in press).

SUMMARY

As we've seen, organizational crises are traumatic events that threaten the existence of organizations, but these events also provide opportunities. When dealing with crises, it is important to recognize an organization has the opportunity for renewal, depending on how it has prepared before the crisis and how it communicates during and following it. For an effective response, organizations would do well to communicate learning, maintain ethical communication, have a prospective vision, and sound organizational communication practices throughout the crisis.

The ultimate goal of this book is to help you view crises differently. We hope you now view crises as not entirely negative events but rather that there is potential for opportunity and renewal inherent to these events. By first examining the lessons of managing uncertainty, effective crisis communication, and leadership, we established some guideposts for better understanding and managing the challenges of crisis communication.

Through the case studies, you should be clear about the impact that your crisis communication choices have on the outcome of a crisis. In addition, through analyzing the cases, you have had some time to develop some of your crisis communication skills. As you see crises develop in the upcoming months and years, we challenge you to continue to apply the lessons discussed in this book to those examples. In this way, you can continue to build your own skills and find ways to see the opportunities inherent to crisis.

Finally, we hope that you will be able to identify the inherent opportunities in crisis through learning from your failures and clarifying your organizational values and risk estimates. Organizations that are going to be successful in managing crisis must be able to communicate effectively before the crisis, see the opportunities inherent in these events, and learn to make the appropriate changes or adjustments so that the event does not happen again. We believe that organizations that follow this advice are likely to emerge from a crisis stronger, more resilient, and with a renewed spirit and purpose.

Opportunity 1: Organizations that base their crisis communication on strong positive organizational values are more likely to experience renewal.

Opportunity 2: Organizations that make significant choice a priority in their crisis communication are more likely to experience renewal.

Opportunity 3: Organizations that focus on moving beyond crises rather than escaping blame are more likely to experience renewal.

Opportunity 4: Organization that distinguish themselves as models of effective communication are more likely to experience renewal.

REFERENCES

Benoit, W. L., & Lindsey, J. J. (1987). Argument strategies: Antidote to Tylenol's poisoned image. *Journal of the American Forensic Association, 23,* 136–146.

Benson, J. A. (1988). Crisis revisited: An analysis of strategies used by Tylenol in the second tampering episode. *Central States Speech Journal, 39,* 49–66.

Cheney, G., & Lair, D. J. (2005). Theorizing about rhetoric and organizations: Classical, interpretive, and critical aspects. In S. May & D. K. Mumby (Eds.), *Engaging organizational theory and research: Multiple perspectives* (pp. 55–84). Thousand Oaks, CA: Sage.

Elliott, D., Smith, D., & McGuinness, M. (2000). Exploring the failure to learn: Crises and the barriers to learning. *Review of Business, 21,* 17–24.

Fink, S. (1986). *Crisis management: Planning for the inevitable.* New York, NY: AMACOM.

Gandy, O. H. (1992). Public relations and public policy: The structuration of dominance in the information age. In E. L. Toth & R. L. Heath (Eds.), *Rhetorical and critical approaches to public relations* (pp. 131–164). Hillsdale, NJ: Lawrence Erlbaum Associates.

Hurst, D. K. (1995). *Crisis and renewal: Meeting the challenge of organizational change.* Boston, MA: Harvard Business School Press.

Kovoor-Misra, S., & Nathan, M. (2000). Timing is everything: The optimal time to learn from crises. *Review of Business, 21,* 31–36.

Meyers, G. C., & Holusha, J. (1986). *When it hits the fan: Managing the nine crises of business.* Boston: Houghton Mifflin.

Mitroff, I. I. (2005). *Why some companies emerge stronger and better from a crisis: 7 essential lessons for surviving disaster.* New York, NY: AMACOM.

Mittelstaedt, R. E. (2005). *Will your next mistake be fatal? Avoiding the chain of mistakes that can destroy.* Upper Saddle River, NJ: Wharton.

Nathan, M. (2000a). From the editor: Crisis learning—Lessons from Sisyphus and others. *Review of Business, 21,* 3–5.

Nathan, M. (2000b). The paradoxical nature of crisis. *Review of Business, 21,* 12–16.

Nilsen, T. R. (1974). *Ethics of speech communication* (2nd ed.). Indianapolis, IN: Bobbs-Merrill.

Perelman, C., & Olbrechts-Tyteca, L. (1969). *The new rhetoric: A treatise on argumentation.* Notre Dame, IN: University of Notre Dame Press.

Roux-Doufort, C. (2000). Why organizations don't learn from crises: The perverse power of normalization. *Review of Business, 21*(21), 25–30.

Seeger, M. W., Sellnow, T. L., & Ulmer, R. R. (1998). Communication, organization, and crisis. In M. E. Roloff (Ed.), *Communication yearbook* (Vol. 21, pp. 231–275). Thousand Oaks, CA: Sage.

Simon, L., & Pauchant, T. C. (2000). Developing the three levels of learning in crisis management: A case study of the Hagersville tire fire. *Review of Business, 21,* 6–11.

Sitkin, S. B. (1996). Learning through failure: The strategy of small losses. In M. D. Cohen & L. S. Sproull (Eds.), *Organizational learning* (pp. 541–578). Thousand Oaks, CA: Sage.

Snyder, L., & Foster, L. G. (1983). An anniversary review and critique: The Tylenol crisis. *Public Relations Review, 9,* 24–34.

Ulmer, R. R. (2012). Increasing the impact of thought leadership in crisis communication. *Management Communication Quarterly, 26*(4), 523–542. doi: 10.1177/0893318912461907

Ulmer, R. R. (in press). International organizational crisis communication: A simple rules approach to managing crisis complexity. In M. Löffelholz, A. Schwarz, & M. W. Seeger (Eds.), *Handbook of international crisis communication research.* Hoboken, NJ: Wiley-Blackwell.

Ulmer, R. R., Seeger, M. W., & Sellnow, T. L. (2007). Post-crisis communication and renewal: Expanding the parameters of post-crisis discourse. *Public Relations Review, 33,* 130–134.

Ulmer, R. R., Sellnow, T. L., & Seeger, M. W. (2007). *Effective crisis communication: Moving from crisis to opportunity.* Thousand Oaks, CA: Sage.

Ulmer, R. R., Sellnow, T. L., & Seeger, M. W. (2009). Post-crisis communication and renewal: Understanding the potential for positive outcomes in crisis communication. In R. L. Heath & D. H. O'Hair (Eds.), *Handbook of risk and crisis communication.* New York, NY: Routledge.

Witt, J. L., & Morgan, G. (2002). *Stronger in broken places: Nine lessons for turning crisis into triumph.* New York, NY: Times Books.

Robert R. Ulmer is Professor and Chair of the Department of Speech Communication at the University of Arkansas at Little Rock. He also holds two secondary appointments, as Professor, in the Departments of Health Policy and Management and Health Behavior and Management in the College of Public Health at the University of Arkansas for Medical Sciences. His teaching, research, and advisory roles focus on producing effective risk and crisis communication through renewal, growth, and transformation.. His current work is funded by the Centers for Disease Control and Prevention and the Environmental Protection Agency. He has worked in an advisory role both nationally and internationally for a wide variety of public and private organizations during risk and crisis events. He has served as an advisor on several oil spills, issues of homeland security and terrorism, financial crises, environmental disasters, food safety crises, and public health crises. He is currently co-director of the Communication Division of the Arkansas Prevention Research Center funded by the Centers for Disease Control and Prevention. The center is designed to address health risks and crises in Arkansas and throughout the United States.

He has published articles in *Management Communication Quarterly*; *Journal of Applied Poultry Research*; *Communication Yearbook*; *Journal of Business Ethics*; *Public Relations Review*; *Journal of Organizational Change Management*; *Journal of Applied Communication Research*; *Handbook of Crisis Communication, Argumentation, and Advocacy*; *Public Relations Review*; *Communication Studies*; *Handbook of Risk and Crisis Communication*; *Encyclopedia of Public Relations*; *Handbook of Crisis Communication*; and *Handbook of Public Relations*.

Timothy L. Sellnow is professor of Communication and Risk Sciences at the University of Kentucky where he is Associate Dean for Graduate Studies in Communication and teaches courses in risk and crisis communication. He is a past winner of the University of Kentucky College of Communication and Information's Faculty Research Excellence Award. Dr. Sellnow's research focuses on bioterrorism, precrisis planning, and communication strategies for crisis management and mitigation. He has conducted funded research for the Department of Homeland Security, the United States

Department of Agriculture, the Centers for Disease Control and Prevention, and the Environmental Protection Agency. He has also served in an advisory role for the National Academy of Sciences, United States Geological Survey, and the World Health Organization. Dr. Sellnow currently serves as theme leader for the risk communication division of the National Center for Food Protection and Defense, a Department of Homeland Security center of excellence.

His work on crisis, risk, and communication has appeared in the *Handbook of Crisis and Risk Communication; International Encyclopedia of Communication; Communication Yearbook; Handbook of Public Relations; Handbook of Applied Communication Research; Public Relations Review; Communication Studies; Journal of Business Ethics; Journal of Business Communication, Argumentation and Advocacy; Critical Studies in Media Communication;* and *Journal of Applied Communication Research, Health Communication, Risk Analysis, and Management Communication Quarterly.* Sellnow is the coauthor of five books on crisis and risk communication and past editor of the *Journal of Applied Communication Research.*

Matthew W. Seeger is Professor and Chair of the Department of Communication at Wayne State University in Detroit, Michigan. Seeger's research interests concern crisis, risk communication, crisis response, agency coordination, health communication, the role of media in crisis, crisis and communication ethics, failure of complex systems, and postcrisis renewal. He has worked closely with the United States CDC on communication and the anthrax attack and on communication and pandemic influenza preparedness. He is an affiliate of the National Center for Food Protection and Defense, where he studies issues of food safety and recalls. He is coprimary investigator on the National Science Foundation Grant, Multi-Agency Jurisdictional Organized Response, a project involving crisis coordination in complex social-technical systems. Seeger also works with the National Center for Border Security and Immigration.

His work on crisis, risk, and communication has appeared in the *Handbook of Crisis and Risk Communication; International Encyclopedia of Communication; Journal of Health Communication Research; Communication Yearbook; Handbook of Public Relations; Handbook of Applied Communication Research; Communication Monographs; Public Relations Review; Communication Studies; Southern Communication Journal; Journal of Business Ethics; Journal of Business Communication; Management Communication Quarterly; Journal of Applied Communication Research;*

and *Journal of Organizational Change Management,* among several others. Seeger is the author or coauthor of five books on crisis and risk communication.

⑤SAGE research**methods**

The essential online tool for researchers from the world's leading methods publisher

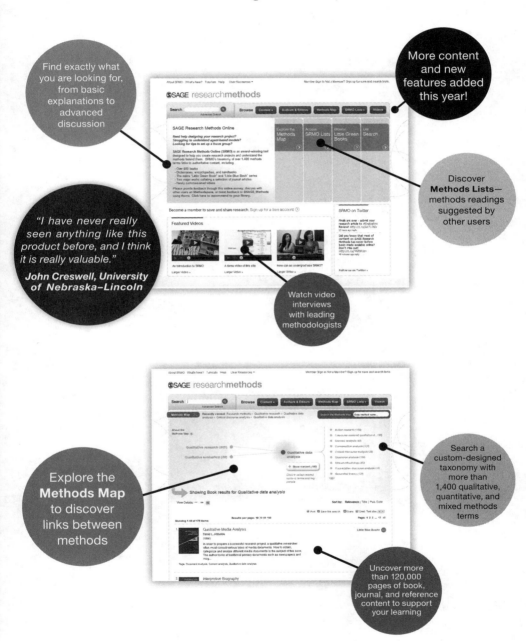

Find exactly what you are looking for, from basic explanations to advanced discussion

More content and new features added this year!

Discover **Methods Lists**— methods readings suggested by other users

"*I have never really seen anything like this product before, and I think it is really valuable.*"

John Creswell, University of Nebraska–Lincoln

Watch video interviews with leading methodologists

Explore the **Methods Map** to discover links between methods

Search a custom-designed taxonomy with more than 1,400 qualitative, quantitative, and mixed methods terms

Uncover more than 120,000 pages of book, journal, and reference content to support your learning

Find out more at
www.sageresearchmethods.com